Neural Geographies

Neural Geographies

Feminism and the Microstructure of Cognition

Elizabeth A. Wilson

Routledge
New York and London

Published in 1998 by
Routledge
29 West 35th Street
New York, NY 10001

Published in Great Britain by
Routledge
11 New Fetter Lane
London EC4P 4EE

Parts of chapter 1 first appeared as "Knowing women: The limits of
feminist psychology," in B. Caine and R. Pringle (eds.), *Transitions:
New Australian feminisms* (Sydney: Allen and Unwin, 1995), pp.
29–41; parts of chapter 2 first appeared as "'Loving the computer':
Cognition, embodiment and the influencing machine," *Theory and
Psychology* 6, 3 (1996), pp. 577–599; parts of chapter 4 first appeared as
"Projects for a Scientific Psychology: Freud, Derrida and Connectionist
Theories of Cognition," *differences: A journal of feminist cultural
studies,* and are reproduced here with permission.

Library of Congress Cataloging-in-Publication Data
Wilson, Elizabeth A. (Elizabeth Ann), 1964–
Neural geographies : feminism and the microstructure of cognition /
Elizabeth A. Wilson
p. cm.
Includes bibliographical references.
ISBN 0-415-91599-6 (hardcover). — ISBN 0-415-91600-3 (pbk).
1. Feminist theory. 2. Feminism—Psychological aspects.
3. Women—Psychology. 4. Cognition and culture. I. Title.
HQ1190.W55   1998
150'.82—dc21   97-28344   CIP
British Cataloging-in-Publication Data forthcoming

contents

~

acknowledgments

~

This book had its beginnings in the Psychology Department at the University of Sydney. The Psychology Department provided me with excellent research resources, even though no one ever seemed quite sure what my research was about, and despite their quiet suspicions that, whatever it was, it was neither properly psychological nor properly theoretical. I was fortunate enough to share my time in the department with a number of dynamic and generous people: Margaret Charles, Helen Loughlin, Doris McIlwain, Kate Stevens, John Sutton, and Shirley Wyver. I am also indebted to the supervisors of my Ph.D. thesis, from which this book has been grafted. Without Terry Threadgold's initial enthusiasm, this project might never have been started; her personal warmth and intellectual generosity enabled the thesis to grow and mutate past its original, limited formulation. I am also grateful to Alison Turtle, whose careful eye kept me engaged with my discipline.

The final preparations of the manuscript were completed at the Centre for Women's Studies at the Australian National University. I am grateful to Rosanne Kennedy and Jill Julius Matthews for providing the support that allowed me to finish this work. Thanks also to Maureen McGrogan and Bill Germano, my editors at Routledge, for their initial support for this book and subsequent patience in waiting for the manuscript.

There have been a number of friends and colleagues who have supported the writing of this project in many different circumstances, and sometimes over many years: Penny Deutscher, Anna Gibbs, Melissa Hardie, Valerie Hazel, Katy Jenkins, Vicki Kirby, Kate Lilley, Cate Oliver, Vicki Sowry, Fiona Symington, and Mary Zournazi. These are relationships that have expanded my horizons and animated the routine of my work.

I am deeply, and happily, indebted to Liz Grosz. She has sustained and diverted me during the long and sometimes difficult period of this book's production. At every moment, and even across great distance, I have been nourished by her insight, generosity, and encouragement.

Throughout the long period that has led to this book, and across the geographical distance that the pursuit of this project has put between me and home, I have been supported unreservedly by my family. To Mary and Denis Howorth, Louise Wilson, Christopher Wilson and Kay McDowall, Barbara Wilson and Michael Lee, and James and Marion Wilson, I owe many thanks.

Elizabeth A. Wilson
Canberra
March 1997

Connectionism, Feminism, Deconstruction

In their introduction to the work of psychologist Silvan Tomkins, Eve Kosofsky Sedgwick and Adam Frank consider the provocation that his work presents to our usual theoretical habits and procedures. "Our" refers here to those of us schooled in certain critical techniques now collected under the dubious rubric of theory, or, more specifically, those of us who might be collected under the even more dubious rubric of applied theory—what Sedgwick and Frank refer to as "the routinizing critical projects of . . . theory after Foucault and Greenblatt, after Freud and Lacan, after Lévi-Strauss, after Derrida, after feminism" (1995, 1). Sedgwick and Frank suggest that the theoretical habits and procedures of such projects—specifically, their compulsive antiessentialism—have become not merely routinized, but naturalized. That is, arguments driven by critiques of essentialism have not only become de rigueur, they have become the foundational supposition of many contemporary critical projects.

Silvan Tomkins's theories of innate affect systems, derived from biological, cybernetic, and neurological tenets now long considered to be dated, are theories that any contemporary critic would intuitively tend to avoid, or censure, or correct—this disciplining compulsion having been naturalized not simply as good critical practice, but as the sine qua non of criticism itself. However, Sedgwick and Frank explain that reading Tomkins involved them in a "peculiar double movement" (1995, 2) that these routinized critical practices are not able to accommodate. That is, their increasing interest in Tomkins's work seemed to accentuate the reasons why that work could—perhaps should—be subjected to the most thorough critical discreditation. Yet their partiality remained. Tomkins captivates Sedgwick and Frank, even though he is a figure whom our/their theoretical habits and procedures would censure instinctively. His theories of innate affect systems are at once compelling and irresistibly easy to discredit, at once captivating and simplistically, scientistically quaint.

We don't have to know much about the particularities of Tomkins's work to identify the circumstances that Sedgwick and Frank describe. These circumstances might be similar to, say, our earliest readings of Freud. How can we respond to this powerful alloy of scientism and interpretation? What sense can be made of a text that so persistently invokes both our keen interest and our keen distrust? And what relation should we recognize between our interest and distrust: interest despite distrust; or because of it? Sedgwick and Frank make this homology between reading Tomkins and reading Freud explicit: Tomkins is "like Freud, a figure through whose work a lot of sharply different, competing, and often conflicting interpretive paths require to be cleared" (1995, 24). I will return to the particularities of reading Freud shortly. The peculiar provocation of the double movement in Tomkins's work is this: how to negotiate between his "formidably rich phenomenology of emotions," on the one hand, and his "highly suspect scientism" (1995, 2), on the other? Sedgwick and Frank suggest that when we read Tomkins we may find that our critical habits draw us into gestures of adjudication—specifically, into gestures that have been formulated through an increasingly commonplace critical choice: *either* How subversive is this theory of affect? *or* To what extent does this theory of affect propagate certain normative, hegemonic, or restrictive expectations? These readings limit our political options to a choice between subversion or hegemony, or, in what amounts to the same thing, that routinized concession "kinda subversive, kinda hegemonic" (1995, 5).

For Sedgwick and Frank, these gestures of adjudication produce impoverished readings—readings that cannot accommodate the nature and productivity of the "peculiar double movement" that the conjunction phenomenology-scientism incites. It is only the least inquisitive reading that is content with a narration of Tomkins's scientism; it is only the most pious reading that seeks a corrective to such perverting and contaminating tendencies; it is only the most banal reading that deduces a benign cohabitation of the phenomenological and the scientific. Against such inclinations, Sedgwick and Frank argue that this nexus—phenomenology-scientism—is not simply accidental, or correctable, or degenerate. Instead it produces a theory of affect that would not otherwise be available. That is, there is a contingent relation between the difficulties of this conjunction and what is generated by this conjunction. To separate affect from these biological, cybernetic, and neurological tenets is to miss this point, and to destroy the tension, and thus the vigor, of Tomkins's theories under the imperative of a sanitizing, compulsive critical practice.

If one of the things that theory claims to know today is that it is distance from biology or science that allows the possibility of difference and change (i.e., the possibility of politics), then Sedgwick and Frank put such confidence into doubt. They dispute the naturalized critical tendency that would force an orderly distinction between Tomkins's innate affect systems and his rich phenomenology. Once mobilized, such a distinction can only serve a number of suspect critical ends: to ascertain the extent to which phenomenology can be *rescued from* scientism, or the extent to which phenomenology has emerged *despite* scientism, or the extent to which phenomenology has been *compromised* by its juxtaposition with science. Betraying a zealous but disavowed moralism against the miscegenation between science and its others, readings such as these tend to deliver tired rearticulations of antiessentialist, antibiological, antiscientific axioms, and thus promote a kind of interpretive eugenics that breeds out the bastard children of any liaison with biological or scientific systems.

An argument will be made in chapters 4 and 5 that such sanitizing maneuvers have already been exercised on the body of Freud's work. Adjudications over the quality and intensity of Freud's own scientism, essentialism, and biologism are as frequent as they are naturalized. The utility of Freud to many theoretical-critical projects seems to depend on the ease and clarity with which certain concepts (e.g., castration, *Trieb*, ego, femininity) can be disassociated from the biological or scientific foundation that Freud ascribes to them. The seamless incorporation of these debiologized or descientized Freudian elements *as* theory indicates the indispensability of a disjunction between science and interpretation to the infrastructure of our present reading habits and procedures. It is this orderly incorporation of Freud qua theory and contra science that has been the means by which any useful interrogation of the "peculiar double movement" in his work has been foreclosed. We cannot be surprised, then, at the increasing tedium and routine of many critical projects "after Freud." These maneuvers with Freudian theory are indicative of a more widespread imperative to force a disjunction (or enforce a hierarchy) between science and criticism, between biology and politics—the end effect of which has been to cripple our critical abilities and thereby blunt the cogency, force, and political efficacy of the readings that we produce.

Tomkins, on the other hand, has yet to be so sanitized. Sedgwick and Frank's introduction lingers on the pleasure and productivity to be had in this moment before the establishment of certain contemporary demands: the conjoint moment of structuralism and cybernetic theory before the installation of theories as Theory, and before the ascendancy of contemporary cognitive models of affect. Sedgwick and Frank argue that it is in this moment that there is the most to be gained for a theory of affect, and for our current reading habits and procedures. It is through these unlikely conjunctions of theory-biology, affect-cognition, neurology-psychoanalysis that Sedgwick and Frank are able to denaturalize our current theoretical and empirical intuitions, and so render problematic that which both theory and psychology claim to know today. Sedgwick and Frank's partiality to Tomkins cannot be reduced, then, to mere critical perversity (the embrace of the patently disreputable). Rather, the peculiar double movement they describe functions critically: not only to disclose the strength and subtlety of Tomkins's work, but also to disclose the increasingly restrictive parameters of our own critical methodologies. The relevance of Sedgwick and Frank's comments to this introduction is primarily methodological: Sedgwick and Frank provide a reading of traditional (i.e., disciplinary) psychological texts (a rarity in "our" critical domain), and they use such a reading to reorient our natural political tendencies. More specifically, they recognize that a competent execution of the first task *requires* a competent execution of the second task. The dexterity of their introduction is exemplified by their success in rendering the presumptions of our critical reading habits and procedures visible without obscuring the value of such interventions in general, and in promoting the fruits of Tomkins's empiricism without falling into a naive celebration of the scientific.

This book pursues a political and methodological agenda broadly similar to that prefaced by Sedgwick and Frank. Situated at the nexus—at once unlikely and overdetermined—of cognitive psychology, deconstruction, psychoanalysis and feminism, this book takes recent developments in connectionist theory as the means by which a number of questions can be asked not only about cognition, the brain, and psychology, but also about the politics of feminist-critical interventions in contemporary scientific psychology. What will be at stake is not simply a critique of contemporary cognitive theory, but the nature—the presumptions and aspirations—of such critiques in general.

~

What is connectionism? Connectionism is the name given to a group of relatively new theories and models of cognitive function. These are sometimes referred to as neural networks or parallel distributed processing (PDP) models. While connectionist theories and models are in use in many fields outside psychology (e.g., computer science, engineering, physics, mathematics, anthropology, linguistics), where their relation to cognition is of little or no relevance, it has been psychological theory and interests that have been at the heart of the new connectionist revival (Rumelhart, McClelland, and the PDP Research Group 1986). I am interested in connectionism only as it is mobilized as a theory of psychology or cognition. What interests me is not the computational, industrial, biomedical, or technical utility of networks in general, but what connectionism offers to a rethinking and reinstantiation of cognition. Connectionist models and theories differ significantly from the models and theories hitherto used in cognitive psychology. Where conventional models take cognition to be the manipulation of symbols in accordance with preexisting computational rules, connectionist models figure cognitive processing as the spread of activation across a network of interconnected, neuron-like units (a more detailed account of a connectionist network is supplied in chapter 4). It is the connections between these units, rather than the units per se, that take on the pivotal role in the functioning of the network. Thus, *connectionism*.

The idea of connectionism or associationism is not new: it can be traced back to Aristotle, and it was given due consideration by a variety of nineteenth-century philosophers, specifically Hartley and J. S. Mill, and by William James (Valentine 1989). However, the particularities of this most recent manifestation of connectionism—what some call neoconnectionism—are indebted primarily to the ascendancy of twentieth-century cognitive science. While connectionism is often introduced and promoted as a very recent innovation, and specifically as that which surpasses or replaces traditional symbolic models, connectionism and traditional symbolic models of artificial intelligence (AI) share the same postwar history—the heady days of cybernetics-structuralism in which Sedgwick and Frank locate the work of Silvan Tomkins. Both AI and connectionism are indebted to McCulloch and Pitts's (1988 [1943]) amalgamation of the neuron and bivalent logic; to the Turing and von Neumann machines; and to Hebb's (1959) hypothesis that learning alters synaptic connections. In the 1950s and 1960s connectionist models and symbolic models shared equally in the spoils of the newly emerging cognitive science. The bifurcation of connectionist and AI models that now structures cognitive research and theory was not evident at this time.

In 1969 this happy coexistence was shattered by Minsky and Papert's revelation that the exemplary network models of that time (perceptrons) were empirically and theoretically untenable. Their devastating critique of these early networks effectively put an end to research in connectionist and parallel models for the next decade and a half, and AI models claimed center stage (and the bulk of the research funding) in cognitive research until the mid-1980s. It was in this period that our notions of cognition and computation became synonymous with the processing exemplified in AI models. That today the idea of cognition is so narrowly defined may be due less to the essentially restrictive foundations of computationalism than to the institutional-theoretical narrowing that has allowed only one mode of computationalism to flower. It may not be problems with computationalism per se that underlie the widespread dissatisfaction with the definition of cognition in contemporary scientific psychology. This dissatisfaction may be more rightly attributed to the reduction or foreclosure of the vicissitudes of computational theory in general.

Despite these early setbacks, a number of researchers remained interested in parallel processing models, and by the early 1980s work was being published that suggested that connectionist or associative models were being revisited (Hinton and Anderson 1989). Connectionist modeling emerged full force in 1986 with the publication of Rumelhart, McClelland and the PDP Research Group's instantly classic two-volume guidebook (the first printing of these two volumes, still widely referred to as "the bible of PDP," were sold out prior to publication). Since then connectionist theory and research has expanded at an exponential rate, and some of its advocates breathlessly claim that a paradigm shift within cognitive science is now under way (Allman 1989; Bechtel and Abrahamsen 1991; Miers 1992). The theoretical-institutional relation between traditional AI and connectionist models has been tense since Minsky and Papert successfully scuttled the early connectionist research project. Today, Minsky and Papert are sometimes blamed for the costly disruption of a highly productive research project. On the other hand, defenders of traditional AI claim that connectionist networks fail to deliver either empirically or theoretically on their promised paradigm shift. A good deal of the theoretical literature in cognitive science and cognitive psychology continues to participate in this tension.

What is it about connectionist models that has incited this partitioning in cognitive theory and research in psychology? The cognitive models that dominated psychology in the 1960s, 1970s, and the first half of the 1980s were almost entirely of the symbolic type (drawn from an amalgamation of the traditions of formal logic, cybernetic theory, and Chomskian linguistics). In such models, cognition is taken to be isomorphic with the sentential and propositional operations of standard computational programming. Specifically, cognition is a formal logic system wherein cognitive symbols are manipulated and transformed according to stored universal rules. Simply put, cognition, under this regime, is the processing of information (see chapter 3). Memory encoding, for example, was initially modeled as the transfer of perceptual information through a series of stores (sensory register, short-term store, and long-term store) until it either decays or is placed in a designated cognitive location. Memory retrieval was the systematic search for these encoded cognitive traces, and their subsequent recovery from specific memory locations (Shiffrin and Atkinson 1969). While this kind of modeling produced interesting simulations of, and hypotheses about, cognitive function, nonetheless the limitations of such modeling became increasingly difficult to ignore. The working hypothesis that cognition is isomorphic with von Neumann computation was severely tested by the accumulation of empirical data and theoretical arguments in both psychology and cognitive science. With the demonstration of fundamental differences in the cognitive capacities of humans and von Neumann machines (especially with respect to speed, constraint flexibility, and the fundamentally different nature of crucial systems like memory), the marriage of psychology and traditional cognitive theory became increasingly difficult to justify. The inability of computational cognitive models to simulate the most basic aspects of human psychology (e.g., error) suggested to many critics that these models were of little or no value to psychological theory.

The specifics of connectionist architecture and function addressed many of these problems. The most arresting aspect of neural networks has been their capacity to simulate human cognition more convincingly and more accurately than traditional symbolic models. While most connectionist research in psychology has remained focused on the traditional interests of the "old" cognitive psychology—pattern recognition, language development, memory, and perception—the performance of these new modeling systems has been quite different from the performance of traditional cognitive models. Escaping the inflexible constraints of formal symbolic models, these networks are able to mimic the peculiarities of human psychology in ways that render them instantly and intuitively appealing. A quick example here will illustrate some of the power of these models, and we will return to a more detailed examination of these capacities in chapters 4 and 5. Hinton and Shallice (1991) trained a neural network to assign accurately written words to various semantic categories. Put more technically, it is the mapping of an orthographic domain onto a semantic one; put more optimistically, it is reading. Containing 136 units arranged in a standard three-layer configuration with around 3,300 connections, this network was able to recognize and categorize words without the help of stored semantic rules or stored representations of words. The task was performed entirely on the basis of the flow of activation through the network and the subsequent changes in the weight of connections between units. These units and connections are cognitively empty: They do not individually represent either orthographic or semantic information. There is no unit for the word *peach*, for example, or for the semantic category "food." Instead information (orthographic-semantic associations) is distributed across the network—it is "stored" not in designated locations, but in the differences between connection weights (see Plaut and Shallice 1994 for an extended discussion of this work).

Hinton and Shallice's goal was to inquire into the mechanisms of acquired dyslexia (i.e., dyslexia acquired through known and discrete neurological damage), and to use this information to inquire into reading processes in general. Specifically, they argue that any cognitively accurate model of reading must respond to damage in a way similar to that of brain-damaged patients. Patients with acquired dyslexia exhibit a number of regular but seemingly arbitrary symptoms that a cognitive theory of reading needs to be able to explain. For example, certain kinds of patients with acquired dyslexia are able to read a word aloud only once they have understood what it means (and so they are unable to read nonsense words). Reading errors in these patients (e.g., saying "apricot" in response to the word *peach*) tend to be systematic, although they appear to be cognitively arbitrary.

Having successfully trained their network to "read," Hinton and Shallice proceeded to "lesion" regions of the network (i.e., certain units were disconnected from the network). Once lesioned, the network's reading performance was similar to that shown by patients with acquired dyslexia—specifically, the network exhibited the same kind of semantic errors. Moreover, lesions at different levels of the network produced differing and systematic deficits in reading performance that mimicked the performance for certain types of patients with acquired dyslexia. Hinton and Shallice conclude:

> Overall, a similarity exists, in the present domain, between the effects of lesions in a connectionist model and in certain types of neurological patients. Because the relevant phenomena are counterintuitive, this similarity strengthens the plausibility that the connectionist approach is capturing a key aspect of human cognitive processing. (1991, 91)

Leaving aside any concerns about the psychopathology of dyslexia, about what constitutes reading in Hinton and Shallice's model, and about the feasibility of mimicry as a foundation for cognition explanation, my only concern at this moment is to demonstrate the difference between a model such as this and a traditional information-processing model. Any lesion to a traditional information-processing model results in system failure: If any part of the structure of a traditional AI model is removed, then the model itself will cease to function. Such models are said to be brittle, for small alterations to the structure or function of the model will leave the model crippled. Brittleness is not a feature of human cognitive systems; they are remarkably resilient to all manner of lesions and alterations. When they are damaged, they tend to decay gracefully rather then crash. Hinton and

Shallice's connectionist model more ably reproduces the organic and psychic nature of human cognitive systems: Not only is it resilient to lesions (removal of large numbers of processing units does not crash the network), but the kinds of performance deficit that the network exhibits are systematic and meaningful. It has been this kind of performance in connectionist models that has captivated many cognitive researchers. By refiguring the structure and function of computation and cognition (rather than merely amending existing systems), connectionist models extend the horizons of empirical and theoretical research in cognitive psychology. While they are clearly not representative of a paradigm shift in the strict Kuhnian sense, connectionist models nevertheless reorient our approaches to, and expectations of, cognitive theory.

The appeal and success of connectionist models can be attributed in no small part to the influence of neuroscience. The impressive empirical results in models such as Hinton and Shallice's are the direct consequence of the refiguring of the cognitive architecture, and this refiguring is neurologically inspired (even if it is not neurologically accurate). Neurological plausibility has been a major component in the marketing of connectionism. Neuroscience has lent an air of contemporaneity to connectionist computation (hybridity being the identifying mark of science at this *fin de siècle*), and its organic realism provides a rejoinder to the artificiality of conventional computational theory. Over and again it is neurology that is the yardstick of connectionism's credibility and potential:

> The network was trained using the iterative version of the backpropogation training procedure explained in Rumelhart et al. (1986). We do not believe that a literal implementation of this procedure is a good model for learning in the brain. (Hinton and Shallice 1991, 80)

> The main point, therefore, is that model nets may be a valuable source of ideas relevant to real neural nets. By analyzing the features of the trained-up net, one can make predictions concerning the actual nervous system, which can then be tested neurobiologically. (Churchland and Sejnowski 1992, 134)

> Connectionist units and neurons are both elementary process-

ing units that combine inputs from some units and send out-
puts to yet other units. In both connectionist networks and nervous systems it is the pattern of connectivity that seems to
be the principal determinant of behavior. These and other similarities lend plausibility to the assumption that whatever processing can be done in connectionist architectures could be
performed in the nervous system. (Bechtel and Abrahamsen
1991, 280)

Opinions vary as to the veracity or relevance of connectionism's
neuroplausibility. Some researchers claim a direct neurophysiological correlation between their models and the human brain; some are
more interested in simulating psychological processes, irrespective
of their biological accuracy; others claim that connectionist models
represent a level of cognitive explanation somewhere between the
neurological and the psychological. Whether one argues for the neuroplausibility of networks or not, neurology nonetheless remains the
touchstone for connectionism's intelligibility. Consequently, neurology will be a crucial part of the analysis this book delivers.

With the exception of a few scattered papers (Canfield 1993; Cilliers 1990; Globus 1995; Miers 1992, 1993), the theoretical commentary on connectionism does not come from "our" critical domain. It
has been Anglo-American analytic philosophy, specifically philosophy of mind, that has dominated the theoretical discussion about
connectionism (e.g., Bechtel 1987; P. S. Churchland 1986; P. M.
Churchland 1990, 1995; Ramsey, Stich, and Rumelhart 1991; Stich
1996). For many of these commentators, the influence of neuroscience in cognitive theory has been an opportunity for advancing a
psychological reductionism or eliminativism. Paul M. Churchland
(1990), for example, argues that the computational neuroscience
promised by connectionism will eventually displace or eliminate
psychological theory. Most of the commentary on neurology and
connectionism, emerging as it does from the analytical debates on
mind and materialism, presumes that if we embrace neurology, we
will be led inevitably to an antipsychological biologism. Opinions
vary as to whether such a reductionism is desirable, but there is very
little dispute that such a reduction inevitably follows once neurolo-

gy has been incorporated into psychological theory. The reductionist and antireductionist squabbles that structure this commentary are, in the end, arguments for and against neurology.

Neurological explanation and reductionism are conflated not only in traditional philosophy of mind, but also in our own critical domain. There has been a persistent deflection of neurological explanations of psychological or behavioral attributes on the grounds that such explanations are a priori reductionist and apolitical. Neurological explanation is not simply antipsychological; it is reductively asocial and acultural. For example, while neurological theories of homosexuality are deemed inadequate primarily for methodological reasons (e.g., Fausto-Sterling 1992; Rose 1996), such critiques seem to be premised on an unarticulated but nonetheless strongly held conviction that neurology itself is regressive and politically dangerous. Such is the strength of the association of neurology with reductionism, and reductionism with the politically regressive, that it is widely presumed (but seldom argued) that neurological explanations of homosexuality must *necessarily* lead to reductive, homophobic ends.

My ambitions for reading neurology are different. Avoiding the correspondingly banal position that neurological theories of psychological or behavioral tendencies are liberatory, I will argue that the neurological facets of connectionism are indispensable to rethinking cognition, psyche, and biology. If neurology has been one of the vicissitudes that has been foreclosed in traditional psychological and computational theory, then its reinjection into that field, while risking a generalized reductionism, also promises to refigure and rejuvenate cognition. Rather than reducing the possibilities of thinking cognition and psyche, neurology may give access to an internal movement in cognition that has hitherto been foreclosed by traditional cognitivism. I will pursue the possibilities of this neurological interjection in the uncanny convergence around the question of neurology and psyche in Freud's *Project for a scientific psychology*, Derrida's reading of that project, and connectionist theory. Specifically, there is a formulation of neurology latent in all three projects that exceeds scientific and critical expectations of biological presence, political stasis, and psychical locationism.

Connectionism, then, becomes the opportunity not merely to rethink cognition, but also to rethink our reflexive critical recoil from neurological theories of the psyche. Rather than being the object or endpoint of analysis, or even the solution to the problems I raise, connectionism serves as the means through which I can gain leverage on both scientific cognitive theory and our own critical habits and procedures. Connectionist models will not be presented as the exemplars of a new, revolutionary moment in cognitive science (as occurs in P. S. Churchland 1986, for example). Neither will they serve as the scientific instantiation of certain postmodern tendencies (as occurs in Canfield 1993 and Globus 1992). There is no attempt to solidify or fix the conjunction of connectionism-feminism-deconstruction beyond this specific critical project. There is no new (feminist-deconstructive) theory of cognition, there is no attempt to correct or improve current cognitive theory, and there is no attempt to authorize recent theoretical maneuvers via scientific homology. Having no interest in either censoring or applauding connectionism, the ambitions of this book lie in a different direction. Can we think the subtlety of neurology and cognition on their own terms? Can we read the internal machinations of traditional empiricism in ways that do not return us to the routinized accusations of essentialism, reductionism, and political stasis? Specifically, does connectionism offer a political reading of psyche, cognition, and biology not despite its neurocomputational inclinations, but *because of them?*

~

Can we remain comfortable with an insistence that there is nothing natural about women? Or more precisely, can we still be sure of just what it is that an affirmative answer to this question defends or denies? (Kirby 1991, 90–91)

Feminism has been as deeply implicated in routinized antiessentialism as any of our critical procedures. Even though questions of "the body" have become increasingly fashionable in all manner of feminist projects (surely "the body" has become, in a very short space of time, one of our most routinized theoretical gestures), the schedule of feminism's antibiologism has been little altered. In most of these projects on "the body," the body in question is pursued in its socially, culturally, experientially, or psychically constituted forms, but rarely in its physiologically, biochemically, or microbiologically constituted form, the idea of *biological* construction having been rendered either unintelligible or naive. Despite an avowed interest in the body, there is a persistent distaste for biological detail. The body is read as a social, cultural, experiential, or psychical object that touches on the biological realm only lightly, discreetly, hygienically. The body at the center of these projects is curiously abiological—its social, cultural, experiential, or psychical construction having been posited *against* or *beyond* any putative biological claims.

This aversion from the biological particularity of the body cannot be attributed simply to the disciplinary-institutional order that has restricted most feminist work to nonscientific domains (although this is part of the problem). More broadly, it testifies to a widespread political presumption that when we speak of "the body" we do not mean "this (biological) body." This presumption has been exemplified in Vicki Kirby's telling anecdote about the speaker at a feminist conference who explains and defends Irigaray's notion of the morphological body through the exasperated gesture of pinching herself and declaring, "Well, I certainly don't mean *this* body" (Kirby 1991, 91). "This body," presumably, is the crudely nonmorphological (i.e., biological) body. The injunction against biology has remained intact for this speaker despite Irigaray's explicit pursuit of the body. What presumptions are already in operation for this disjunction between "the body" and "this body" to be so self-evident? It must be axiomatic for this speaker, before she even opens Irigaray, that when we feminists, we theoretically schooled critics, speak of "the body," we mean something other than "this (biological) body." The biological body is coded in these routinized projects as the untheorized body, the mechanical, tangible, artless body. In an accomplished gesture of disavowal, "the body" has become the means through which "this (biological) body" is once again expelled, trivialized, or neutralized.

A large part of the difficulty in generating politically engaging feminist critiques of the biological and behavioral sciences must be attributed to feminism's own naturalized antiessentialism. After all, how can a critical habit nurtured on antibiologism produce anything but the most cursory and negating critique of biology? For example, Ruth Bleier (1984) and Lesley Rogers (1988)—both neurophysiologists—respond to the reductionism of contemporary neurological research on sexual difference by gesturing to the outside of neurology (usually figured as culture or the environment). It is culture or the environment that delivers difference and malleability to otherwise barren neurological matter. If the brains of men and women are different, they argue, it is because of postnatal, environmental influence. The political self-evidence of this gesture to neurology's outside is legitimated by feminism's naturalized antiessentialism (here specifically, antineurologism); but this antiessentialism is also the means through which such political interventions inevitably disappoint. This gesture to a nonneurological culture or environment not only misrepresents the complex relation between neurology and its outside, but also, by locating malleability, politics, and difference only in the domain of culture or environment, it abandons neurology to the very biologism it claims to be contesting. Bleier and Rogers do not offer a feminist critique of the neuron, of the cellular architecture of the brain, or of the chemical transformations at the synaptic membranes. While Bleier includes a few introductory pages on the physiology of the brain, this information is presented as a series of facts that stand before or outside of the political issues at stake. If the conjunction feminism-neurophysiology appears to be unlikely, unstable, or unproductive, this may have more to do with conventionalized feminist politics than with the nature of neurology itself.

Critiques of neurological reduction such as Bleier's and Rogers's are authorized not only by feminism's antiessentialism, but also by a persistent hostility toward any systematic examination of the theoretical and political foundations of their own feminist presumptions. For most feminist critics in the sciences, the force of the conjunction feminism-science operates in only one direction: feminism critiquing science. In a reversal of fortune, science becomes the object of feminism's masterful interrogations. Moreover, the ground from which such feminist critiques emerge is taken to be self-evident: the explicitness of a feminist signature guaranteeing the political and epistemological ambitions of such interventions. That the sciences (here neurology) could generate politically useful perspectives for feminism (as distinct from politically useful data) is unthinkable for both Bleier and Rogers. They are unable to think scientific politics outside the routinized critical expectation that the sciences are either objective sites of truth or oppressive forces of social control (or some schizoid combination of both). Specifically, they are unable to envisage the possibility that neurology may already enact and disseminate the malleability, politics, and difference that they ascribe only to nonneurological forces.

One of the central considerations of this book is that feminist criticism in the sciences, as elsewhere, is irreducibly political—not simply because it contests the presumptions of the sciences, but also because it raises difficult political and conceptual issues about the nature of feminist intervention in general. It is not a return to biological determinism, but rather an expectation that feminism should ask questions about its own political tendencies that prompts Kirby to put her rhetorical question, "Can we remain comfortable with the insistence that there is nothing natural about women?" If the critique of biological determinism is now somewhat routine, indeed somewhat obligatory for feminism, Kirby wants to ask what feminist-political orthodoxies are supported by such critiques. The issue for Kirby is less an inventory of what problems reside in natural or biological theories of women that would make these theories the target of feminist criticism, but what presumptions reside in feminist politics that make such inventories and their correlative recoil from the natural self-evident and politically uncontentious. Moreover, once established, what kind of narrowing or censoring of feminist-political projects do these presumptions enact? What kinds of feminist projects remain unthinkable and unable to be enacted because of these presumptive foreclosures?

What makes Kirby's position all the more interesting is that, contra Bleier and Rogers and the speaker at the feminist conference, she considers that it is the biological details of "this body" that may provide feminism with its most cogent analytical tools. It is through an interrogation of the "peristaltic movements of the viscera, the mitosis of cells, the electrical activity that plays across a synapse, the itinerary of a virus" (Kirby 1991, 97) that feminism, in our current context, may gain its most effective political purchase on biology. There are (at least) two important gestures being made here. In the first instance, there is a resistance to the routinization of theories of the body that has been only marginally less phobic of encounters with biological matter than the most orthodox antibiologism. Secondly, the naming of viscera, cells, synapses, and viruses as the matter of feminist criticism opens such criticism up to the challenge of theorizing feminism in the absence of any explicit reference to women or sexual difference.

Both of these gestures will be important to the refiguring of the politics of feminist psychology that occupies chapter 1. It is perhaps not surprising that feminist psychology has concerned itself with theories of psychology at the expense of theories of the body. While there have been occasional critiques that engage feminist psychology with the body (e.g., Ussher 1989), by and large these are structured according to the equation *psychology + body*. It has been a politics of correction or inclusion that motivate such projects rather than a rethinking of the terms of this relation. That is, these projects have been content to restore to psychology what it has excluded, or to broaden psychological theories to include hitherto neglected data, but they have been less inclined to think psychology *as* body, or body *as* psychology (as, say, Elizabeth Grosz [1994b] has done from a philosophical perspective). Theories of gender are central to this problem. If gender is the exemplary feminist psychological concept, then the distinction between psyche and body that gender usually entails will likely be axiomatic to most feminist criticism in psychology. A crucial part of rethinking the politics of feminist psychology will be rethinking the utility of gender, especially as it is formulated against biological sex.

This interrogation of gender touches on another, closely related issue: the centrality of theories of women to feminist psychology. While most feminist psychologists have taken psychological knowledges about women to be their self-evident point of entry into psychology, I will argue that feminist criticism in psychology need to be premised on something other than the question "What is (the psyche of) woman?" My argument throughout will be that feminism needs to engage with scientific authority not simply at those sites where it takes women as its objects, but also in the neutral zones, in those places where feminism appears to have no place and no political purchase.

These sites of "neutrality" present, perhaps, the most pressing concern for current feminist interventions into scientific psychology. If it has been in the interests of scientific and phallocentric authority to divide its knowledges between those about women and those about the world (i.e., between sexed knowledges and neutral knowledges), then it is crucial that we investigate the effects of that division. To what extent does the division of knowledges about women from more general knowledges ordain the constitution of those general knowledges as neutral rather than sexed? Moreover, what kind of sexed position is being hidden beneath the designation "neutral"? If feminist psychology focuses only on those knowledges about women, does it unwittingly legitimate this division and its effects? Scientific phallocentricity does not just reside in the sites occupied by women; indeed, with the ever-increasing efficacy of feminist critiques of scientific knowledges about women, the sciences seems to be reinvesting their authority in sites of neutrality (e.g., in the neuron, in sexually undifferentiated chemicals, in the sequencing of DNA). What is required most urgently from feminist criticism in the sciences is a clear demonstration that such neutral sites are no less implicated in the deployment of patriarchal presumption than are those sites marked as sexed. In psychology, then, we need to be able to ask feminist questions not only about women, but also about cognition, learning, the brain, statistics, the rat, the perceptual system.

More specifically, the ambition of this book is to ascertain what can be gleaned from the domain of cognitive psychology and connectionism that is of use to feminist politics. Rather than examining the empirical adequacy of the research in sex differences in cognitive abilities (e.g., Maccoby and Jacklin 1974), I will be concerned with the nature of cognition itself: How does such a seemingly benign and indispensable notion (cognition) act in the service of phallocentric authority? This question needs to be addressed before any systematic examination of experimentation into cognition and sex differences can be broached. While computational theories of cognition will be shown to be implicated in a series of presumptions about the body and about sexual difference, this is not the only analytical goal this book will pursue. The refiguration of cognitive architecture that connectionism enacts—while saying nothing explicitly about women or sexual difference—will provide a rethinking of psychical location, neurological matter, and cognitive process that is indispensable to contemporary feminist criticism in psychology.

If feminist psychology is to rethink the nature of its interventions, then it also needs to reorient its theoretical commitments. While Sedgwick and Frank lament the routinization of our critical habits and procedures, the theoretical material that these routinized projects vandalize has yet to be deployed in feminist psychology at all. The theories of subjectivity, critiques of gender, analyses of power, accounts of the body or theories of texuality that have been in wide circulation in other domains have been all but ignored by both mainstream psychological theory and feminist psychology. With very few exceptions (e.g., Henriques et al. 1984), the theoretical orientations of feminist psychology have been allied with the mainstream empiricist tradition and/or liberal humanism (and the politics of equality that that has inspired). Interestingly, this has not been true of critical work in psychology in general, where there are an increasing number of nonfeminist papers drawing (with varying degrees of success) on what might be called "poststructuralist," "postmodern," or "deconstructive" theories. The particular reorientations that I will pursue in this book are inspired by psychoanalysis and deconstruction. While both of these orientations are widely caricatured as being hostile to feminist politics, I will argue that they have generated a set of perspectives, *unavailable anywhere else*, that enable us not only to identify the vicissitudes of patriarchal authority in specific scientific sites, but also to enact effective political responses to that authority.

~

You criticize the existing order of things: what do you propose to put in its place? (Bennington 1993, 264)

One of Nancy Hartsock's (1990) primary concerns about the value of "postmodern theories" to contemporary politics (and feminism in particular) is that they offer nothing in the way of a positive project. More concerned with negative criticism of Enlightenment or modernist projects than with constructive strategies for change, these critical theories are deemed dangerously apolitical. Such charges of political lethargy are commonly directed not just at "postmodern theory" in general, but at deconstruction in particular. Where postmodernism is characterized as wantonly pluralistic or nihilistic, deconstruction is often marked as a negating, destructive philosophical turn. Set up in opposition to construction, deconstruction is readily misconstrued as destruction. Committed to the overthrow of reason, truth, and intelligibility, this caricatured deconstruction is variously described by its detractors as deeply conservative or wildly anarchistic (see, for example, Rosenau 1992). In either case, it is deconstruction's calculated refusal to produce a circumscribed project or clear political platform that confounds and vexes its critics.

There are many vicissitudes of these antideconstruction misreadings: deconstruction simply reverses binaries, privileging the secondary term; deconstruction reinstalls the binaries it criticizes; deconstruction destroys binary structures; deconstruction makes knowledges impossible; deconstruction is rhetorical free play; deconstruction marks the end of politics. These concerns—often owing more to a popularized understanding of deconstruction than to a close reading of any particular deconstructive texts—have become the commonsense political responses to the complexities of deconstructive procedure. However, as Geoffrey Bennington (1993) reminds us, they are classical political concerns that are exceeded by deconstruction. Putting aside those criticisms that would be discredited by even the most cursory examination of Derrida's own work (e.g., that deconstruction simply reverses binary structures), the anxiety that deconstruction is synonymous with destruction, that it cannot provide anything in place of what it criticizes, persists in a variety of commentaries on deconstruction. This anxiety is one that deconstruction would like to turn back on itself. What notion of politics inheres in these demands for positive projects? More specifically, what type of politics is adjudicating over what may count as a positive project? If deconstruction is more complex than these political anxieties are able to allow, that is, if deconstruction is itself already concerned with the epistemological and political presumptions that not only allow such anxieties but authorize them as common sense, then we can say that deconstruction exceeds such classical concerns.

What this means is that rather than negating, excluding, or preventing classical political and epistemological projects, deconstruction is engaged in an examination of the conditions that make such projects possible and the implications and effects of their operations. As Spivak (1993a) notes, the issue is not that deconstruction cannot found a political program while other modes of analysis can, but rather that deconstruction can articulate the problematic foundations of our currently founded political programs. In so positioning deconstruction, Spivak does not want us to presume that its analytic examinations operate from the outside of our political projects, in a simplistically parasitic or supplementary fashion. In the first instance, the notion of an unadulterated outside will have to be subjected to rigorous scrutiny. Moreover, this "parasitism" of deconstruction is enabling rather than leeching. The irreducible double binds that have been deconstruction's persistent concern (what Spivak calls the negotiation with structures of violence) are at the "origin" of every political practice. While a political project (in the classical sense) cannot occupy itself entirely with these deconstructive concerns, nonetheless any political project or system of analysis that shuns or forgets the effects of these double binds risks falling into political or analytical stasis. Feminism's complicity with patriarchy, for example, is the structure of violence that is the "origin" of feminist politics in general. An examination of this "origin" is neither a disinterested pursuit nor a leeching one; on the contrary, it is the hard, political work of feminism itself. Without such (self-) scrutiny, that is without an examination of how this violent origin enables feminism in general, feminism may be tempted to declare itself a sanitized and sanitizing political practice (the routinizing effects of which have already been addressed by Sedgwick and Frank).

I understand Spivak's use of "political" to not exclude the empirical. Nonetheless, what use deconstruction may be to empirical projects is not yet certain. Moreover, under the pressure of the routinized antiempiricist presumptions of our critical habits and procedures, it is even less certain what use empirical projects may be to deconstruction. We can know in the first instance that the projects that might emerge from deconstructive examinations of the biological or behavioral sciences are not what the sciences have come to expect from criticism: Deconstruction does not produce new, improved theories from its labors. Deconstruction cannot found a new scientific practice. On the other hand, we cannot presume that the value of deconstruction to criticism in the biological and behavioral sciences is that it brings critical sophistication to a politically naive or politically recalcitrant domain. When carefully deployed the conjunction deconstruction-empiricism will arrest both the progressivist presumptions of much empirical work and the antiempiricist presumptions of our own critical habits. If deconstruction is not an analysis from the outside, if it is not a nonempirical endeavor that is brought to bear on empiricism from elsewhere (philosophy? literature?)—that is, if deconstruction and empiricism already cohabit or are mutually implicating and enforcing—then we will need to map this relation with great care.

There has been very little use of (an explicitly defined) deconstruction within scientific psychology. In those few readings that have emerged, the relation between deconstruction and scientific psychology has been mapped in a familiar and orthodox manner. Specifically, these readings tend to treat deconstruction as a generalized methodology that can be used to adjudicate over empirical progress in the psychological domain. As such, deconstruction becomes another device in a very conventional narrative about scientific progress and authority. For Kurtzman, the ambitions of scientific psychology are the eventual liberation from "illegitimately restrictive metaphysical assumptions" (1987, 33). While cognitivism claims to have escaped the metaphysical restraints of behaviorism, Kurtzman counterclaims that theories of computational structure and process (exemplified in the cybernetic machine) implicate contemporary scientific psychology in a series of "illegitimate" metaphysical assumptions. Deconstruction is the methodological apparatus that will release psychology from these restrictions:

> The metaphysical assumptions that persist within the cognitivist approach can be revealed and overcome by application of concepts of "deconstruction." . . . [In this paper] the fundamental principles of the cognitivist approach are submitted to a deconstructionist analysis and some preliminary notions for a post-cognitivist "deconstructionist psychology," free of metaphysical structures are sketched. (Kurtzman 1987, 33)

Kurtzman's "deconstructionist" methodology is a qualifier or corrective to cognitive psychology. If the cybernetic machine holds psychology within illegitimate (i.e., metaphysical) limits, then deconstruction will "reveal and overcome" these limitations.

Let me respond bluntly: This claim that deconstruction positions itself against metaphysics is *incorrect*. A more careful inquiry into any of Derrida's texts would demonstrate the great care he takes to formulate deconstruction as something other than the argumentative antithesis of a pathologized metaphysics. As Spivak patiently reminds us, "Deconstruction is not an exposure of error, nor a tabulation of error; logocentrism is not a pathology, nor is the metaphysical closure a prison to overthrow by violent means" (Spivak 1993a, 130). It is an interrogation of the enabling limits of metaphysics, not their eradication, that is deconstruction's goal. For Derrida, it is never a matter of progress by ridding ourselves of certain methodological or epistemological concepts that are deemed metaphysical in favor of some allegedly nonmetaphysical concepts (in the first instance, the notion of a concept itself is indebted to the metaphysical distinction between the intelligible and the sensible). Where Kurtzman, for example, claims that deconstruction can be used to *negate* the metaphysical concept "structure" in cognitive psychology, Derrida is more circumspect. In speaking of "structure" in semiotic theory, he offers the following account of how deconstruction operates with such a concept:

The case of the concept of *structure* . . . is certainly more ambiguous. Everything depends upon how one sets it to work. Like the concept of the sign—and therefore of semiology—it can simultaneously confirm and shake logocentric and ethnocentric assuredness. It is not a question of junking these concepts, nor do we have the means to do so. Doubtless it is more necessary, from within semiology, to transform concepts, to displace them, to turn them against their presuppositions, to reinscribe them in other chains, and little by little to modify the terrain of our work and thereby produce new configurations. (Derrida 1981, 24)

Derrida's (historical and textual) relation to structure is intimate and complex, and certainly not reducible to an antistructural position, as Kurtzman's progressivist notions would hope (see chapter 2). Spivak (1974) notes, for example, that it was through a close and careful negotiation with Saussure's structural formulation of the sign, rather than its negation, that Derrida's crucial deconstruction of semiology became possible. Any attempt to mobilize deconstruction in a generalized fashion against "structure" will simply and uncritically reinstall that project back inside the very tradition that it is assumedly attempting to contest.

This figuration of deconstruction as a generalized methodology in opposition to metaphysics is not Kurtzman's alone. Globus (1992) repeats the same prescription in a paper on Derrida and connectionism. Globus's ambition is to formulate a direct mapping of deconstructive concepts onto recent developments in connectionist psychology. Specifically, he hypothesizes an isomorphism between certain deconstructive concepts (e.g., *différance*) and certain structural characteristics of connectionist networks. Simply put, the connectionist network is the scientific instantiation of *différance*. Where Kurtzman was concerned with the metaphysical constraints of cognitivism, Globus's bugbear is the "metaphysically conceived brain" (1992, 183). Where Kurtzman pursues a "post-cognitivist deconstructionist psychology," Globus envisages "brain deconstruction." Specifically, Globus uses the conjunction of Derrida and connectionism to hypothesize a "deconstructed brain" that would liberate us from the "metaphysical brain " (1992, 193) of traditional computational theory. Putting aside the concern that there is no brain, as such, in traditional computational theory (the absence of neurology being traditional computationalism's founding gesture), Globus's expectation that deconstruction could generate or even reflect a "better" brain owes less to deconstruction than it does to Globus's own unreflexive fantasies of scientific progress.

This application of a generalized deconstructive methodology to cognitivism and connectionism bears the marks not only of fantasies of scientific progress and authority, but also of the routinized applied theoretical projects "after Derrida" that Sedgwick and Frank deplore. So ubiquitous have critiques of binarized structure become, the specificity of the deconstructive procedure with binarized structures has been lost. For example, the hinge (*la brisure*) has become exemplary of deconstruction's "method." In Derrida's work these hinge terms go by many names: trace, gram, supplement, *différance*, dissemination, hymen, etc. These hinge terms do not provide a solution to the binary; they do not pursue synthesis. Instead they serve to inflame that binary. They undo the self-evident character of the binary division by manifesting the point at which such a division becomes unworkable or incoherent. Rather than negating the binary, moving outside it, destroying, trivializing, or neutralizing it, the hinge term seeks to expose and internally displace its operations. Specific to particular texts (and this cannot be repeated often enough), these hinge terms *have no value as generalized methodological tools*. Deconstruction, then, is a close and particular procedure; it is never interested in generalized methodologies. It is the interrogation of specific concepts/texts and their enabling effects, rather than a generalized critique of binaries, that is deconstruction's concern.

Given that deconstruction is not a generalized methodology, that it cannot be applied, like a structuralist framework, within any domain, and moreover that it requires a consistent misreading to mobilize deconstruction in this manner, we might be led to ask what ambitions underlie the union of deconstruction and scientific psychology in Kurtzman's and Globus's projects. Might we not suspect that traditional notions of scientific progress are being reauthorized and disseminated by this particular conjunction of contemporary science and contemporary philosophy? It appears that both Kurtzman and Globus utilize deconstruction as a generalized meth-odology for the most orthodox of purposes: the proclamation of a new direction or tradition in scientific psychology (see Parker and Shotter 1990 for a similar kind of ambition with respect to social psychology). That is, this generalized deconstruction simply serves to verify the notion that cognitive (or postcognitivist) psychology is the newest and most complete development in scientific psychology. All this despite Derrida's (1981) repeated insistence that deconstruction eschews the possibility of definite breaks or revolutions in the structure of knowledge and that deconstruction has little to do with conventional notions of scientific or epistemological progress. The end effect of these unions between deconstruction and psychology (even if it is not Kurtzman's and Globus's said intention) is to add a certain radical shine to psychology's empirical projects without in any way contesting the integrity of the psychological domain in general.

If the uses of deconstruction must be something other than a programmatic or generalized methodology, then to what types of projects and effects does a deconstructive analysis commit itself? There are three broad implications of deconstruction that I wish to introduce here (although these are not exhaustive of deconstruction's political effects): negotiating the necessary and the impossible; the problem of solutions; and acknowledging complicity. Presented here only briefly, these implications will expand and proliferate in the following chapters.

1. Our relation to any metaphysical concept is complex: Neither able to rid ourselves of it (as it enables our very critique) nor able to accommodate its violences, we are forced into an endless negotiation with its constitutive and its constraining effects. The double gesture of deconstruction could be understood as the conjunction of the necessary and the impossible. That is, metaphysical concepts are simultaneously necessary to the operations of language and knowledges, yet their very structure, their exclusions and violences, render them impossible and unsustainable modes of

operation. Deconstructive analysis operates at this difficult nexus. The detail and complexity of deconstructive texts is an effect of negotiating with necessary but impossible concepts. Kirby (1991) has demonstrated both the difficulty and the finesse of such a negotiation. Her examination of the question of essentialism in feminism elucidates the irreducible nature of such "metaphysical" concepts. While feminism seems to be grounded in an antiessentialist philosophy, Kirby makes it clear that we are not able easily to avoid essentialism's ruses, and moreover we may find that the domain of antiessentialism is equally problematic in that it seems to rely on a covert and indispensable essentialism as its excluded other. Kirby recognizes that we are caught in an impasse where we can no more say no to essentialism than we can say yes; yet at the same time she stresses that we can no more remain paralyzed at this impasse than we can return to the original pro- or antiessentialist positions. It is at this seemingly impossible point that Kirby suggests there is the most to be won for feminist uses of essentialism. It is only through this difficult recognition of our (necessary but impossible) relation to essentialism that any feminist profit can be made from it.

2. If deconstructive interventions cannot be characterized as either constructive or destructive, then we must expect that the political goals of such interventions will differ significantly from more classical projects. Specifically, deconstruction is wary of the desire in such classical projects to produce an empirical or theoretical solution, to articulate a final synthesis or definitive conclusion to a particular problematic. The search for solutions manifests politically as the demand for positive projects, clear programs, and blueprints for future work. Instead, deconstruction might be more concerned with the structure of solutions themselves. If metaphysical projects are driven by a nostalgia for the origin as a lost presence, then might we not understand the notion of a solution as simply an inversion of this desire? It is not solutions that deconstruction seeks, but openings: "We insist on strategy without finality, on a ruse which does not aim at a determinate goal" (Bennington 1993, 264). Knowledge under decon-

struction becomes a perversion: It has no natural aim/solution, and it is always already dislodged from its source/origin. It is the very notion of a final resting point in knowledges that deconstruction disputes. If the goal of classical projects in the sciences and humanities alike has been to halt the proliferation of knowledges, to bring an end to writing, history, politics, and experimentation, then it is deconstruction's place to investigate this goal and expose its effects.

3. Deconstruction is always a politics that takes effect from *within* (Derrida 1974): Deconstruction has effect by inhabiting the structures it contests. This means, of course, that deconstruction and its practitioners are always internal to and complicit with the structures they examine. Deconstruction is, above all, a *faithful* intervention, and it cannot be effective except by risking the effects of such a faithful and parasitic relation (Spivak 1990). A deconstructive reading of cognitive psychology places itself internally to that domain, and it is reliant on that domain for its coherence and efficacy. We are never given the luxury of simply refusing a territory (e.g., behaviorism) or accepting a territory (e.g., cognitivism). Instead, we are forced to negotiate perpetually a position with respect to these different fields of operation. Contrary to popular representation, the position of the deconstructionist is not a position of high theoretical purity; it is not a position above or outside a whole number of problematic entanglements. These acknowledgments of complicity present an important challenge to the political premises of a feminism that claims it can operate outside the influence of those phallocentric fields it contests.

This book is not a deconstructive project in the strict sense. Instead, I utilize the politics that emerge from Derrida's work and the work of some of his better commentators (here, Bennington, Kirby, Spivak) in order to gain some perspective on both cognitive psychology and the critical procedures that might be mobilized with it.

These broad political implications of deconstruction, sketched only briefly here, promise to reorient and enliven our critical interventions into scientific knowledges. To preface and condense an argument that will emerge more slowly in the coming chapters: The conjunction deconstruction-cognition will effect a twist in the conventional critical grasp of scientific psychology. Recognizing our debt to, but intolerance of, the operations of cognitivism, this analysis draws on the double gesture at the core of deconstructive procedure: "Double gesture again: we recognize a primordial indebtedness toward a tradition that the point is not however to preserve or celebrate as such" (Bennington 1993, 263). This twist will move concurrently in another direction: toward a critique of our own naturalized critical habits and procedures. The conjunction deconstruction–cognition will demand a reconsideration of the relation of empiricism to our critical habits, allowing us to think through the logic of empiricism/theory that structures not only science but criticism in general. Sedgwick and Frank have already prefaced the urgency of this rethinking by contemplating the peculiar double movement in Silvan Tomkins's remarkable work that our contemporary scientific and critical habits are not able to accommodate.

It is this rethinking of cognition and criticism that will be extracted from the conjunction connectionism–feminism–deconstruction. It is this that is offered not in *place* of what I criticize, but *through* what I criticize.

~

The Natural Habits of Feminist Psychology

One always inhabits, and all the more when one does not suspect it.
(Derrida 1974, 24)

Feminism's critical relation to psychology seems to be already decided by the stability and intelligibility of the name *feminist psychology*, and by the many monographs, journals, conferences, and teaching courses enacted under that name. Hinting at a critical but orderly amalgamation of feminism into the psychological domain, the name *feminist psychology* supposes that feminist criticism can be readily located with respect to psychology. On the one hand, this critical relation is structurally homologous to other feminist occupations (feminist history, feminist anthropology, feminist sociology . . .), and on the other, it invokes psychology's own internal territories (cognitive psychology, perceptual psychology, social psychology . . .). So even if we know very little about psychology per se, we would not be surprised to learn that this feminist psychology concerns itself with structures of inequity in theories of social, cognitive, or developmental psychology; with how the psychology of women has been misrepresented or marginalized in the mainstream psychological tradition; with the revalorization of questions of gender and sexuality in psychological theory; and with the transformation of empirical methodologies to accommodate feminism's own research priorities. As such, this feminist psychology occupies a certain, clearly recognizable, institutionally locatable, critical position with respect to the discipline.

To say that feminism inhabits psychology, then, seems simply to be reiterating what the name *feminist psychology* already declares. Nonetheless, it is the nature of this critical habitation that I will interrogate here: In what manner and how effectively does feminism inhabit psychology? The concern at the heart of this book is that feminist criticism in psychology has engaged in only certain kinds of projects, that it has been effective in only certain kinds of domains, that it has inhabited in a certain restricted and restricting manner. Specifically, feminist psychology has been too concerned with constructing a "new theory of woman" within the confines of already established disciplinary parameters (what are women's and girls' intellectual, developmental, and social capacities, *really*?). Such projects have been facilitated and authorized by a feminist politics that is limited in two crucial ways: first, it concerns itself only with those areas of psychology that bear directly on the category "women"; second, it can articulate itself only through an analysis of gender. The traditional projects of feminist psychology have left those areas of the discipline that appear to cover a more neutral or sexually indifferent terrain (perception, cognition, neurology) outside feminist critical consideration. As a consequence of these traditional affiliations, feminist psychology has become too readily locatable within the general epistemological, political, and economic frameworks that order psychological knowledges. It has become too static and predictable in terms of its critical relation to psychology.

If feminism's critical relation to disciplinary psychology has become conventionalized, how can this relation be more effectively enacted? What would be the critical manner of different kinds of feminist psychology projects? Since its inception, feminist psychology has been occupied with the question of its critical placement: Should it be located inside or outside the empirical and theoretical frameworks of the discipline? Opinions have differed as to whether feminist psychology is a subfield within an already extensive set of psychological schools, or whether is it a critical endeavor more properly situated beyond psychology's disciplinary parameters:

> Feminist psychology can advance qualified psychological findings that recognize commonalities and differences across groups of women, incorporate an understanding of structural and economic influences on women's psychologies, produce complex, non-victim-blaming analyses of women's conditions, and distinguish between ideologies and realities for distinct groups of women across different settings and in varied power relationships. (Fine 1985, 180)

> Feminist psychology should be a liminal place. (Marecek 1989, 375)

Concerns such as these betray a generalized anxiety about political location: The viability of feminist criticism is presumed to be dependent on securing a clear epistemological and political position in relation to the discipline. Moreover, feminist criticism is supposed to occupy a terrain that is politically distinct from the discipline with which it engages. The intelligibility and security of a distinction between a feminist psychology and a nonfeminist one is deemed imperative to the efficacy of feminist criticism in psychology. Under the weight of these anxieties, the key political task for feminist psychology has been the resolution of the paradox that demands that it be both faithful to and critical of its master discipline. On the one hand, any project operating under the name *feminist psychology* must (by definition) align itself with psychology, yet on the other hand, such a project must also protect itself against too close an alignment with the presumptions of disciplinary psychology if its critical interventions are to be effective. Feminist psychology is required to be both inside and outside the embrace of psychology. This situation is most often read not as the enabling force of feminist psychology itself, but as a paradox to be resolved: "Too often our dual loyalties [to feminism and to psychology] seem to tug us in opposing directions. But our location also places us in a position to work toward rapprochement" (Marecek 1989, 375). Consequently, feminist projects in/of psychology have tended to pursue a politics that argues for or against particular critical positionings, and for or against the possibility of a harmonious relation between psychology and feminism, but which rarely brings the nature of habitation (or location) itself into question.

This difficulty with critical location and habitation is nowhere better demonstrated than in the work of Naomi Weisstein. Recently the subject of an extended reappraisal in a leading international journal of feminist psychology (Kitzinger, 1993), the work of Weisstein has been figured as seminal to the emergence of feminist psychology in the United States in the early 1970s. Weisstein's (1971) polemical paper "Psychology constructs the female; or, the fantasy life of the male psychologist (with some attention to the fantasies of his friends, the male biologist and the male anthropologist)" has been singled out in this regard. I will return to this paper later on. What is interesting for my purposes here is that in the six commentaries on this paper collected in this reappraisal—commentaries that talk expansively about Weisstein's career in and influence on feminist psychology—there is barely a mention of Weisstein's "other" psychological research, in neuropsychology and cognitive psychology (e.g., Weisstein 1970; Wong and Weisstein 1982). Unger remarks briefly on how Weisstein's neuropsychological and cognitive work might contribute to the possibility of "subjective construction . . . at a very basic physiological level" (1993, 213), but this is never properly pursued by either Unger or the other commentators. Weisstein, in a response to her commentators, figures herself as a "neuroscientist" of thirty years' standing (1993, 242), but she makes no explicit connection between the content of her neurological research and her feminist critiques of psychology. All those involved in this reappraisal seem to agree—without discussion or explanation—that this neurological and cognitive research "would appear to have nothing to do with sex or gender" (Unger 1993, 213), and is thus outside the interests of feminist psychology. (This pattern of exclusion and self-representation is evident in a recent reader for a "new" psychology of gender: Gergen and Davis 1997.)

This marginalization of neuropsychology and cognitive psychology in feminist psychology's self-representation demonstrates the naturalization of a certain kind of politics of critical habitation. The feminism of Weisstein and her commentators occupies the domain of psychology in the most orthodox of ways, and this produces two troubling effects that I will discuss in this chapter. First, Weisstein et al. have deemed the domain of feminist psychology to be defined, and exhausted, by questions of "sex or gender." Like the constitution of all proper domains, this maneuver violently and habitually excludes certain questions, objects, and analytical processes from (feminist) consideration. Second, by dividing psychological knowledges into those of concern to feminism and those that have "nothing to do with sex or gender," feminist psychology becomes party to one of scientific psychology's most orthodox procedures—the distinction between sexed and unsexed (or neutral) knowledges. Curiously, the promise of (sexual) neutrality or indifference—instantiated here as neurology or cognition—is pursued by feminist and nonfeminist psychology alike. Feminist psychology is not merely narrowed by these exclusionary and proprietorial practices; more insidiously, the *naturalization* of these practices has become the very means by which feminist psychology installs itself right back inside the very heart of traditional scientific and psychological presumption.

The issue of feminism's critical relation to, location in, and contamination by psychology has been resolved by Weisstein and her commentators by enforcing a distinction between feminism and psychology. What is unargued but nonetheless crucial to these commentaries is that feminism has no purchase in certain areas of disciplinary psychology: Even now, after thirty years as a neuroscientist, it remains unthinkable for Weisstein that there may be feminist questions in psychology about "very basic physiological processes." This figuration of a nonfeminist psychological domain is not simply incidental to the critical politics that Weisstein et al. pursue. Rather, it is this figuration that allows the reciprocal construction of a nonpsychological feminist domain from which unimpeachable feminist criticism may be launched. That is, only when feminism and psychology can be separated, only when each forms a containable, locatable, and discrete identity, is (this kind of) feminist criticism possible. Consequently, the conjunction feminism-psychology works not as criticism, but as the maintenance and reduplication of the epistemological and political privileges of each domain. The feminist psychology of Weisstein and her commentators demands a coherent psychology in order for its own coherence and political privilege to be maintained. For this reason the ground of psychology itself is rarely in question: These feminist projects are circumscribed and animated by an unacknowledged but powerful allegiance to psychological authority.

My concern with feminist psychology, however, is not simply that it inhabits, or is located in, or borrows from, or is restricted by problematic epistemological and political frameworks—as though it would be best if it were not. For Derrida, the question of criticism can never be a question of whether or not one inhabits the domain that one criticizes, whether or not one is contaminated by the logic and violences one wishes to contest. One always inhabits, excludes, violates; contamination is the condition of criticism in general. Deconstruction's concern has been to examine the nature and consequences of this critical habitation and contamination. So the question of feminism's critical relation to psychology might be more appropriately phrased this way: If one must inhabit, how can one inhabit *well*?

The critical morphology that guides my assessment of feminist psychology is this: To inhabit well means to be undecidable with regard to one's critical location, or, more specifically, to put the idea of location itself into doubt. Deconstruction suggests that the habitat or locality of criticism is displaced; neither simply inside or outside a territory, criticism is required to inhabit even as it presses urgently for a breach in the configuration of that territory. Criticism, via deconstruction, is the paradox of a faithful transgression. What deconstruction offers feminist psychology is the means for managing and exploiting this critical paradox. Derrida's lesson for us is not simply that feminism inhabits psychology, but that any gesture to deny such habitation, or to enact that habitation as consciously chosen or benevolently enacted or fully controlled, is a habitation of the most conventional kind. For feminism to inhabit psychology well, it must first of all recognize and examine the constraints of its own necessary critical habitations. Not reducible to conscious self-scrutiny or conscious self-correction, this task of examining the nature of one's critical location is a hard and complex negotiation with complicity and with the structures of violence that enable feminist psychology in general. This interrogation of the relation between feminism and psychology is indispensable for the analysis that this book pursues; the value of connectionist psychology for feminism, and the value of feminism for connectionist psychology, will become intelligible only once the politics of these critical locations and habitations have been explored.

~ Institutionalization and Its Risks

> As feminists within psychology, we share major dissatisfactions with our discipline's failure to engage with the lives of the majority of women, and the distortion and damage often produced when it does engage. We are committed to changing this and to developing a psychology which properly represents women's concerns in all their diversity. (Wilkinson 1991, 5)

While there has always been feminist research and criticism in psychology (Lewin 1984; Russo and Denmark 1987), the emergence of feminist psychology as an acknowledged and identifiable area of research is a fairly recent event. We could locate this emergence somewhere between Weisstein's (1971) polemical, SCUM-esque attack on psychology and Mednick and Weissman's (1975) more restrained survey of feminism and psychology for the institutionally respectable *Annual Review of Psychology*. Weisstein's text is not as clever, biting, or savagely written as the SCUM Manifesto, (Solanas 1967) but it does share a similar revolutionary, antiestablishment tone that contrasts strongly with the more institutionalized position of Mednick and Weissman's review:

> It then goes without saying that present psychology is less than worthless in contributing to a vision which could truly liberate—men as well as women. . . . The central argument of my paper, then, is this. Psychology has nothing to say about what women are really like, what they need and what they want, essentially because psychology does not know. (Weisstein 1971, 1)

This selective review on the psychology of women has, as we predicted at the outset, raised many questions. It is perhaps banal, but nevertheless necessary, to stress that there are unresolved conceptual and methodological issues within each area which will have to be raised again and reevaluated as the field develops. (Mednick and Weissman 1975, 13)

Somewhere between Weisstein's independently published broadsheet and Mednick and Weissman's review for a major psychological journal there was a shift in the way feminist criticism interacted with psychology. No longer a voice from the margins, feminist psychology had become an identifiable, locatable research domain with its own set of conceptual and methodological parameters. No longer content to simply criticize the masculinism lying at the core of many scientific psychological projects, feminist psychologists embarked on a series of their own avowedly political projects in social, clinical, developmental, and cognitive psychology. Their goal: to win back the truth about women from mainstream psychology—in Weisstein's words, to establish *what women are really like*.

There were a number of important institutional changes in the mid-1970s. Division 35 (Psychology of Women) of the American Psychological Association (APA) was established in 1975, and already there was a substantial amount of research claiming the name *feminist psychology*. For example, Bem's highly influential work on androgyny was presented at an APA conference in 1975, Parlee (1975) and Vaughter (1976) wrote reviews of the psychology of women for the prestigious feminist journal *Signs*, and Maccoby and Jacklin's landmark text on psychological sex differences had been published in 1974. The journals *Sex Roles* and *Psychology of Women Quarterly* (the publication of Division 35 of the APA) began publishing in 1975 and 1976, respectively. At the same time, similar progress was made in both Canada (Pyke and Stark-Adamec 1981) and Britain (Parlee 1991).

These institutional reforms clearly signaled the entrance of feminism into psychology as a coherent and identifiable force. Nonetheless, as these feminist psychology projects have become more established, and as the whole idea of feminist psychology becomes respectable, the risks that such reforms produce are becoming more obvious. Any type of critical endeavor always risks being co-opted by what it contests, but such co-option increasingly threatens to paralyze the critical strategies mobilized by feminist psychology.

This issue of co-option and an appropriate political response to it are the subject of Derrida's (1987) seminar discussion on the status of women's studies in North American universities. While this discussion draws on broader problems of interdisciplinarity, institutions, and feminist theory, there are a number of issues raised here that may guide our understanding of feminist psychology. In this seminar it is argued that the university as it now stands is indebted to a nineteenth-century model of the institution (the beehive), wherein each discipline and the knowledges it produces are discrete and containable within clearly administered boundaries. It is argued that women's studies, while producing a number of crucial feminist projects, has done little to challenge substantially the traditional structure of the university and its concomitant modes of knowledge production. Moreover, this co-opted position is judged to be an *irreducible* effect of establishing a women's studies domain.

Of particular interest for Derrida and the seminar participants is the issue of the Law. If the Law is the means through which the institution of the university is established, maintained, and rendered coherent, and if the institution in turn promulgates this Law, then those who become the guardians of the institution also become guardians of the Law. As women's studies becomes more institutionally legitimate, the practitioners of women's studies likewise become more legitimated within the institution. This means that women's studies eventually and unavoidably finds that it too "constitutes, constructs, and produces guardians of the Law" (Derrida 1987, 190). Where women's studies does not put the institutional and epistemological structure of the university into question, it too becomes the guardian of another cell in the university beehive:

> One can only wonder: what are the risks and the stakes of the institution of women's studies? Do the women who manage these programs, do they not become, in turn, the guardians of the Law, and do they not risk constructing an institution simi-

lar to the institution against which they are fighting? In other words . . . what is the difference, if there is one, between a university institution of research and teaching called "women's studies" and any other institution of learning or teaching around it in the university or in society as a whole? It is certain . . . that women's studies has a great future. Nevertheless, if this future is of the same type as that of all other departments, of all other university institutions, is this not a sign of failure of the principles of women's studies? (Derrida 1987, 190)

There is, then, an irreducible political paradox at the core of women's studies: The mark of its success (legitimation) is the very mark of its failure (co-option inside the structure it contests). The more it proves its own necessity and legitimacy, the more it covers over its original critique of legitimation, institutionalization, and power. Women's studies is caught in a constitutive paradox: One can no more withdraw from the fight for legitimacy and institutionalization than proceed with it. Women's studies is a necessary but impossible political project.

This argument attunes us to the political difficulties and risks that any women's studies program must negotiate. Specifically, it warns us that there is no institutionalized space that is not problematically indebted to the Law, and that there needs to be another political gesture besides simply and only claiming an institutionalized feminist location. Such an acknowledgment is particularly pertinent to feminist psychology: If feminist psychology seeks only to establish itself as another cell in the psychological beehive, it will fail to address, and remain uncritically dutiful to, many of the dominant theoretical and empirical assumptions in the discipline. To the extent that feminist psychology is unaware of the ways in which it does this, its co-option and neutralization will become all the more likely. Nonetheless, the imperative "Do not become guardians of the Law!" is not the most appropriate response to this dilemma. By definition, a location outside psychology is unable to engage with the discipline at all. Rather, we need to learn how to negotiate carefully with the Law. What this negotiation will inevitably disclose is that the difference between feminist psychology and psychology proper, between criticism and the Law, between a location inside and a location outside psychology is unclear and cannot be determined or secured in advance.

While the positive projects of feminist psychology are a necessary condition for the rewriting of psychology's institutions and knowledges, on their own they are an insufficient condition for bringing this about. Something else, some other type of political gesture, is also necessary. The very ground that renders both psychology and feminist psychology coherent must also, ceaselessly, be contested. Herein lies the greatest political and epistemological difficulty for any feminist intervention into psychology: How can one negotiate between the necessity of the traditional projects in feminist psychology (e.g., equitable clinical practice, nonsexist theories of cognitive performance, IQ, development, etc.) and a more critical or deconstructive project that seeks to render the ground of such projects deeply problematic? While the former project is perhaps more politically secure, it will find itself unable to launch a more thoroughgoing critique of psychology in general. The latter project, while able to offer just such a thoroughgoing critique, risks being dangerously reactive, and it is unable to offer a grounded political program. I will discuss this more closely in chapter 2 as the negotiation between empiricism and theory in psychology; here I want only to introduce the idea that this risk that deconstructive projects entail, the risk that we may render the very ground of the conjunction feminism-psychology incoherent, is a risk that is increasingly worth taking. More specifically, we must be ever vigilant about what is at stake politically (what investments in the Law are being mobilized) when we find that criticism of the ground of feminism is being foreclosed. As Kirby (1993) argues, there is a more dangerous gesture in operation in those attempts to prevent a dialogue between feminism and deconstruction than there is in deconstruction itself. What cost is extracted by the vicious anti-intellectualism of Weisstein's recent response to the role of "postmodernist poststructuralist counter-Enlightenment feminism" in psychology?

Of course, there is paralysis: once knowledge is reduced to insurmountable personal subjectivity, there is no place to go;

we are in a swamp of self-referential passivity. Poststructuralist feminism is a high cult of retreat. Sometimes I think that, when the fashion passes, we will find many bodies, drowned in their own wordy words, like the Druids in the bogs. Meanwhile, the patriarchy continues to prosper. (Weisstein 1993, 243–44)

~

It would be inaccurate to imply that feminist psychology is unaware of these problems of co-option and domestication. Such concerns have been expressed right from the very beginning (Parlee 1975), and they remain pertinent to current debates (Parlee 1991). In general, however, co-option is not seen to be a problem foundational to the structure of feminist psychology. Rather, the most common political response to questions of co-option and domestication has been to advocate conscious self-scrutiny. Feminist psychologists are counseled to remain ever vigilant against the insinuation of "traditional/masculinist" methodologies and perspectives into their own projects. Fine, for example, provides a list of methodological strategies to "enhance contextual validity" (1985, 178) in feminist psychology projects, and thus ensure that such studies are more representative of the "real world" and more equitable to the women they study than are the empirical projects of the mainstream discipline. Such strategies include checking the face validity of projects, accessing cross-disciplinary research, avoiding the tendency to psychologize socially produced problems, and focusing on diversity among women. Without wanting to negate the essential work of refining and improving the methodologies of feminist psychology, I want to insist that such methodological concerns do little to contest the already established consensus about what feminist psychology should study and what its methodologies and political goals should be. What is less often up for discussion is the very ground that supports such methodological corrections: What are the unsaid or nonnegotiable grounds of feminist psychology? In what ways do these grounds allow the co-option of feminist psychology's political effectiveness?

There is one particular problem in the grounding of feminist psychology that concerns me here: the utility of the category "women." By taking the category "women" as the final referent for their projects, feminist psychology not only narrows the scope and effectiveness of its interventions into psychology, but it also unwittingly provides the means for its own co-option and domestication. To argue this more carefully, I need, first of all, to explain the institutional grounds from which feminist psychology emerged.

The field of feminist psychology is indebted, historically and politically, to the previously established field of the psychology of women, which had operated for most of this century as a kind of prefeminist women's studies. Up until the influx of women into academic psychology and the concomitant institutional changes of the early 1970s, the research area known as the "psychology of women" was governed by research agendas designed to provide data for a number of socially sanctioned stereotypes about women and their place. Women's inherent masochism, their natural mothering instincts, their inferior motor and cognitive skills, and sex differences in brain weight, emotionality, and IQ were typical sites of concern in the field (Shields 1975).

For Parlee, this psychology of women was a "conceptual monstrosity" born out of the belief that we need a "special set of laws and theories to account for the behavior and experiences of females" (1975, 120). Such a special set of laws contravenes the dominant feminist ethos of equality and perverts the pursuit of a scientific study of *human* behavior. For these reasons, Parlee advised against adopting the name *psychology of women* for the newly emerging field of feminist study in psychology. Instead, she offered Nancy Henley's three-part typology as a means for guiding feminist research: psychology of women, psychology against women, psychology for women. It is the last of these that Parlee promoted as the most appropriate rubric for feminist research in psychology. Nonetheless, Parlee's recommendations were not adopted. The name *psychology of women* persisted, and within a few years it had become synonymous with *feminist psychology*. The psychology of women, liberated from its masculinist past, was now the domain of feminist inquiry. Parlee herself later documents this transition:

> The "psychology of women" here refers to psychological research and theory that is *for* women. . . . Sexist research on women is of course still being done, but its creators do not identify themselves as being in the field of the psychology of women. Feminist psychologists' power to define and name their own field has evidently prevailed. (Parlee 1979, 121)

Nonetheless, contrary to Parlee's suggestion, feminist psychologists had not defined and named "their own field." Rather, feminist psychology had hijacked a field that already existed. Hijacking per se is not in question here as a political strategy; rather, my concern is that this co-option of another field was conducted so uncritically. In capturing the field of the "psychology of women," not only did feminist psychologists inherit the content of the field (women), but they also inherited the presumptions, limitations, and boundaries that made that field coherent. The boundaries of the field "psychology of women" were already firmly established, and in general these foundations were unchallenged by the new feminist psychology. As we have already seen with Weisstein, what is inside (women) and what is outside (neurology, cognition) the domain of feminist psychology is widely considered to be uncontroversial and self-evident.

Judith Butler (1990) has been particularly concerned with interrogating the place that the category "women" takes within feminist politics. She argues that feminism has assumed a category, "women," that precedes and initiates feminist knowledges, and which guides feminism's practice of political representation. The problem for Butler is that it is unclear, in the light of recent feminist and poststructuralist critiques of identity, exactly what or who would be represented in this category "women." More specifically, it seems that the category "women" is made coherent through a number of exclusionary practices that undermine its stated intention to represent equitably.

Drawing on Foucault's notion of juridical power, Butler (1990) contends that representational systems "*produce* the subjects they subsequently come to represent" (1990, 2). The very notion of feminism as a representative politics draws on this wider juridical power, which means that feminism, too, constitutes the subjects it claims to be representing. Moreover, the category "women" can be constituted only through a series of exclusionary practices, practices that are subsequently repressed and naturalized by feminist practice itself under the imperative of representing diversity. Butler argues that feminism needs to be attuned to the dual discursive function of power as both productive and juridical; feminism must recognize that it both produces its subject and then renders that production invisible. This dual operation serves as the means of installing women as the legitimate, self-evident, and necessary object of its knowledges:

> It is not enough to inquire how women might become more fully represented in language and politics. Feminist critique ought also to understand how the category "women," the subject of feminism, is produced and restrained by the very structures of power through which emancipation is sought. (Butler 1990, 2)

If there is no subject before feminism, awaiting representation, if feminism produces such a subject and subsequently renders it natural, then the political effects of such discursive operations need to be investigated. For Butler, perhaps the most important of these effects is the guarantee of a sure and solid political base for feminist practice. The mobilization of "women" as the subject of feminism assumes a common identity among women that can be clearly and unproblematically elucidated and which forms the basis for feminism's representational claims. Ironically, however, it is this very attempt to guarantee a sure and stable base to feminist politics that has been the means for a much wider destabilization of, and dissatisfaction with, those politics. The presumed universality and unity of the category "women" has inevitably provoked "multiple refusals" of its authority (Butler 1990, 4). Such refusals have labored to reveal the coercive, regulatory, and exclusionary practices that have enabled and promulgated the category "women" as the foundation of feminist politics. More broadly, such labors have shown the limits of a representational identity politics for feminism. Butler warns us: "The suggestion that feminism can seek wider representation for a subject that it itself constructs has the ironic consequence that feminist goals risk failure by refusing to take account of the constitutive powers of their own representational claims" (Butler 1990, 4). This means that even recent feminist claims to acknowledge diversity within the women they represent (e.g., Wilkinson 1991) have not found their way out of Butler's political conundrum. Unless there is a recognition that even this diversified category of women is still produced by feminism, a production that still necessarily requires exclusions, coercions, and regulatory foreclosures, feminism's politics will again fall back into a precritical notion of representation, and will once again unwittingly repeat and promulgate these exclusions, coercions, and foreclosures as self-evident and uncontroversial.

It is perhaps the idea that feminism can ever fully extract itself from systems of exclusionary, coercive, and violent representation that needs to be examined (and I will comment on this further in a moment). The import of Butler's critique is that it contests the necessity of building feminist politics and knowledges on the singular ground of the stable identity of "women." If there is an inherent instability in the category "women," as Butler (1990) suggests, then a more heterogeneous approach to knowledges and politics must be demanded from feminism. Rather than being a focus of concern for Butler (or a problem to be resolved), the instability of the category "women" is the means for opening up new and more effective epistemological and political possibilities for feminism.

Through Butler we gain a critical perspective on the limits of a feminist psychology constituted through a discourse on women. The notion that women or female subjectivity is the natural or only object for a feminist psychology is a discursive construction of feminist psychology itself. At this historical moment, this particular construction of feminist psychology's object may be more constraining than enabling. The more feminist psychology pursues the question of women, the more it will find itself unwittingly caught back in the very epistemological structures that it needs to contest. While Butler remains committed to a feminist politics in which women remain a crucial (even if not a foundational) component, this book will take a different trajectory. It will outline and demonstrate the possibility of a feminist psychology where questions about women are explicitly deferred. Taking the risk of charges of elitism and indifference to the conditions of "real women," this analysis seeks to open up other kinds of feminist spaces in psychology. The ambitions of this book are to demonstrate the excesses of, and disruptions within, the phallogocentrism of cognitive psychology. Consequently, questions of how female psychology or the psychology of women could be articulated within the logic of cognitive psychology are deferred.

~

It is not simply the choice of a particular object of study that constrains feminist psychology; it is also the epistemological structure within which that object is placed that narrows feminist psychology's critical scope. By pursuing the woman question so enthusiastically, feminist psychology finds itself no less implicated in a series of problematic and powerful epistemological presumptions than the conventional psychology of women and the mainstream discipline that it wishes to contest: "Where feminism remains committed to the project of *knowing women*, of making women the objects of knowledge, *without in turn submitting the position of knower or subject of knowledge to a reorganization*, it remains as problematic as the knowledges it attempts to supplement or replace" (Grosz 1993, 207). The presumption to know what women are really like rests on a three-pointed foundation: that feminist psychologists can act as pure, rational, and conscious knowers outside the systems they contest; that their object (female psychology) is a stable, containable, and quantifiable entity; and that there is a benignly descriptive, rather than constitutive, relation between the subject and the object of knowledge. Even when put to "good feminist ends" or when enacted in modified form, such a paradigm reproduces and reinstalls the epistemological structure of subject/object, knower/known that lies at the heart of mainstream psychology. Such a reproduction is all the more insidious in the case of feminist psychology, as its interventions are so often premised on its ability to contest the ruses of patriarchal knowledge systems.

Perhaps the central organizing political and epistemological presumption in feminist psychology is that it can know women outside the systems of violence and falsity that mark traditional knowledges about female psychology. Feminist psychology takes its modes of knowledge production to be largely uncompromised by the injustices and injuries of the mainstream discipline. Up to a certain point, this can be granted: The positivist projects of feminist psychology have made important and necessary correctives to the psychology of women. But if we examine this desire to know a little more closely, we can see that it is always and necessarily caught in a notion of violence that is the same as the violations of psychology in general. Vicki Kirby (1993) gives a careful and astute reading of this desire to know in feminist anthropology. Feminist anthropologists have carefully documented the violences inflicted on the anthropological other in traditional ethnographic discourses. However, feminist anthropology has been seduced by the security of a well-intentioned feminist politics into believing that it can know the anthropological other outside the discursive injuries of traditional anthropology. Kirby cites one of Donna Haraway's interventions into such debates as being exemplary in this regard. Haraway has recognized, first of all, that the oppositional logic of anthropological discourse serves to obliterate the specificity of the other (it can know the other only by reducing that other to a version of itself), and that this obliteration is constitutive of ethnographic practice. Yet Haraway then proceeds to claim that a sufficiently self-aware feminist practice can avoid such violent obliteration, that a careful feminist ethnographic practice can allow the radical difference of the voice of the other to be heard.

How, Kirby asks, are we to differentiate this feminist discourse—without violence, without distortion or "othering"—from the traditional discourses of an objective ethnography that likewise claims to present an authentic, undistorted other? What is it that secures the first gesture of benevolent objectivity, but not the second? If knowing is always an act of incorporation and digestion, then the knowledges of feminist psychology and anthropology will always, necessarily, manufacture and then claim merely to represent the specificity and difference of that other. The sense of crisis for Kirby is not that feminists should not be doing this (as Haraway suggests), but rather that *they cannot do anything other than this*—every intervention must operate through the process of "othering." To insist that we can know what women are really like represses, rather than avoids, this othering in our practice. The (often violent) resistance to an interrogation of the effects of such discursive operations (as in Weisstein, above) betrays feminism's own desire to maintain a knowing and authoritative position, a desire to be "a sovereign subject caught in the embrace of an auto-affection that could thereby presume to know itself, account for itself, and be trusted to do the right thing" (Kirby 1993, 30).

For Kirby, however, recourse to good and honest intentions will not maintain a safe distinction between feminism and violence. Against these dreams of benevolent nonviolence, Kirby calls for— and demonstrates—the difficult, detailed, and confronting assessment of our own complicity with that which we contest. No idle play with "wordy words," this kind of assessment has become one of feminism's most urgent tasks. As Butler claims, a feminism that refuses to "engage—take stock of, become transformed by—the exclusions which put it into play" is a feminism that has lost its critical and political efficacy (1993, 29).

~ The Nature of Gender and the Politics of Biology

The restrictive boundaries and practices of feminist psychology are not simply the effect of problematic epistemological and institutional relations to its "outside," to mainstream psychology. Feminist psychology is also constrained by its own internal configurations, that is, by the kinds of feminist theory and politics it chooses to enact. Feminist psychology's pursuit of knowledges about women is not simply enabled by the empiricist and positivist commitments of mainstream psychology; it is also enabled by a number of key feminist political presumptions—specifically, a series of liberal, humanist presumptions that privilege a politics of equality over a politics of difference, and consciousness over corporeality.

The theoretical kingpin in this feminist tradition is the notion of gender. Within feminist psychology, the notion of gender has become indispensable to critical practice. It has become difficult to imagine the possibility of feminist psychology at all without the notion of gender. Or rather, a feminist psychology that did not rely on the articulation of gender would operate through a radically different understanding of what feminism has to contribute to the psychological domain. In the second half of the chapter, I will explore the ubiquity and viability of gender as an explanatory and analytical tool in feminist psychology. If the sex/gender distinction is problematically informed by the mind/body distinction, then what is the efficacy of the notion of gender for analyses of sex, biology, cognition, and neurology? Put another way, what limits does the notion of gender place on the scope and nature of feminist projects in psychology? I am less concerned with engaging in the sex/gender debate per se than I am in how gender—whether analytically naturalized or explicitly contested—unproductively limits the kinds of projects possible in feminist psychology. That is, I wish to pursue the exclusionary practices gender entails—even in its sophisticated reformulations—in order to ascertain what is at stake in its widespread mobilization, and what might be opened up by its analytic deferral.

~

The origin of contemporary feminist uses of the term *gender* is often attributed to Robert Stoller's psychoanalytic theories of transsexuality (Chanter 1995; Gatens 1983) or to psychoanalysis in general (Butler 1990). For psychoanalysis and feminism alike, the notion of gender owes its epistemological and political purchase to its opposition to, or distance from, sex. For Stoller, the notion of gender allowed him to conceive of a psychological component to sexuality that may exist independently of one's biological sex—thus the nonpathological articulation of the experience of being a woman in a man's body, or a man in a woman's body. The appeal of such a notion was immediately apparent to many feminist theorists, for it allowed the origin of certain psychological capacities and behavioral patterns differentially attributed to women and men to be severed from any fixed biological foundation. If the domain of biology and the notion of an essentialized sex had been used against women, then the notion of a socialized and psychologized gender unfettered by sex promised to radically reorient our understanding of the differences between the sexes.

Gatens's early critique of the sex/gender distinction is directed at both Stoller and those feminists for whom gender has become "a central explanatory and organizing category of their accounts of the social and familial and/or discursive construction of subjectivity" (Gatens 1983, 144). The most pressing implication of Gatens's critique is that the notion of gender is *irreducibly* caught in an oppositional and exclusionary relation to sex. By definition, gender is assumed to have political effect only to the extent that it is distanced from, or other than, sex (as I will argue shortly, this is the case even when gender has undergone radical reformulation). In feminist psychology this has meant that sex and gender have frequently congealed into discrete, self-contained categories: "By sex, I will be referring to the biologically based categories of male and female. In the use of gender, I refer to the psychological features frequently associated with these biological states" (Deaux 1985, 51).

Taking the nature of sex to be self-evident and given, theories of gender define gender as separate and supplemental to sex. Gender (femininity and masculinity) is the effect of the social, cultural, or psychological inscription of a subject whose biological sex (female and male) is already given. Simply put, gender is oppositional to sex in the same way that mind is oppositional to body. Rather than effecting a critique, then, gender operates in much the same way as those other terms traditionally privileged by patriarchal knowledges of subjectivity: *mind, consciousness, rationality.* This affinity with mind as noncorporeal consciousness is the central difficulty that this project will have with the notion of gender. If cognition in contemporary psychological theory is constitutively caught in the thinking of neurology—that is, if psychology is being thought through its relation to matter—then the analytic use to this project of a notion of gender premised on the exclusion of the biological will be limited. Specifically, the notion of an antibiological gender will too readily reduce an analysis of the matter of cognition to the exclusion or trivialization of neurology.

This placement, delimitation, or exclusion of biological matter haunts all conventional theories of gender. In assuming sex to be a bedrock of unchanging and unchangeable biology upon which gender is inscribed or to which gender is added, conventional theories of gender exclude the body from questions of culturation that the notion of gender alone is thought to entail. In these theories of gendered construction, the body is as the biological and medical sciences have described it: Determined by a genetic blueprint, the nature of matter remains constant, knowable, and prior to the forces of construction. While there may be various social practices or discourses that understand or represent or engage with the body in restricted and hierarchical ways, the body itself remains outside the field of constructive influence. This analysis may seem to be at odds with the widespread feminist folklore about the "social construction" of biological and medical knowledges; moreover, hasn't "the body" been one of feminism's most consistently analyzed topics? If we take the body not simply as a singular, total unit of human form, but as biological matter in general, my argument may become more legible. Take, for example, the extensive feminist writing (particularly in psychology) on the body and eating disorders. While many feminists have argued that women may diet and starve themselves according to "gendered" regimes of health and beauty (e.g., Bordo 1993; Lawrence 1995; Orbach 1986), these analyses consider the cellular processes of digestion, the biochemistry of muscle action, and the secretion of digestive glands to be the domain of factual and empirical verification. Despite the plethora of work on the gendered nature of eating and on representations of the gendered eating body, there is surprisingly little feminist criticism on the nature of the stomach, the bowels, or the internal cavity of the mouth. Only a certain understanding of the body has currency for these feminist analyses, an understanding that seems to exclude what I have called in the introduction "this (biological) body."

These exclusions of the biological in theories of gender are not solely the effect of the nonscientific disciplinary affiliations of academic feminist research in general. No mere disciplinary oversight, these exclusionary moments are what render theories of gender intelligible in our current political context. Even feminists trained as scientists, researching as scientists, or researching science produce the same kinds of analytical presumptions about gender. Nelly Oudshoorn (1994), for example, has written a comprehensive historical account of sex hormones that repeats all the conventional presumptions of gender analysis. This is all the more surprising since Oudshoorn begins with a critique of the limitations that theories of gender have placed on feminist critiques in the sciences:

> My argument is that the sex-gender distinction did not chal-
> lenge the notion of a natural body. Although the concept of
> gender was developed to contest the naturalization of feminin-
> ity, the opposite has happened. Feminist theorists of socializa-
> tion did not question the biological sex of those subjects that
> became socialized as woman; they took the sex and the body
> for granted as unchanging biological realities that needed no
> further explanation. (1994, 2–3)

Despite this suspicion that biology has been misdiagnosed in feminist criticism, Oudshoorn does not subject the biological objects of her analysis—sex hormones—to critical inquiry at all. While Oudshoorn writes extensively about how "the concept of sex hor-mones" and "the concept of the hormonal body" have been manu-factured (i.e., gendered) through certain culturally sanctioned ideas about sex differences, everywhere else she takes the molecular and metabolic nature of sex hormones to be uncontentiously prior to these debates. Once again, this (biological) body seems to be inartic-ulable within feminist criticism. In what turns out to be a surprising-ly conventional history of modern scientific discourse and debate about sex hormones, sex hormones themselves are outside the ter-rain in which such analyses are enacted. For example, Oudshoorn shows us the molecular structure of estrogen in order to demonstrate how disputes over the alleged sexual specificity and duality of so-called male and female hormones were settled. The molecular illus-tration shows us that "male" and "female" sex hormones—rather than being dualistically conceived opposites—are *in fact* "closely related chemical compounds differing in just one hydroxyl group" (1994, 29). In ways that seriously limit the scope of her analysis, Oudshoorn offers the chemical structure of sex hormones as the (nondiscursive, nonconstructed) adjudicator of the accuracy of vari-ous social and cultural constructions of hormones.

There is a point to be made (and Butler 1993 had made it convinc-ingly) that such exclusionary practices constitute hormones as originary, real biological matter. That is, this gesture of exclusion is the discursive maneuver that manufactures biology as natural and beyond the effects of culture. While hormonal structure appears to exist prior to various debates about its nature, this is in fact a discursive effect of these debates. The naturalization of this gesture is that against which a political intervention needs to act. What Butler's analysis would offer here is a way of disclosing the naturalness of hormonal structure (and the naturalness of biology more generally) as a discursive ruse. I will return to Butler's analysis shortly; in the meantime, I have a slightly different argument to make here about these exclusionary practices and their relation to theories of gender. While Butler's analysis discloses the constitutive effects of these exclusionary gestures on biology (i.e., such exclusions render biology natural), I want to inquire into the effects of these exclusionary gestures on theories of gender. Are these theories of gender rendered coherent *because of* their distance from biology? That is, is the constitution of biology as natural and distant the very means by which theories of gender are initiated, and through which their political efficacy is maintained? Does not every theory of gender—necessarily, as its first presumption—mark a distance from biology, a distance that may later be folded back within gender's analytic terrain but which in the first instance remains unargued, self-evident, foundational? The recuperation of sex within a theory of gender involves a disavowal or a misrecognition: The exclusion of sex was gender's own critical ruse. If this is the case, thinking biology productively within the circumscription of theories of gender—theories for which biology is always already a conventionalized sham—becomes extraordinarily difficult. And this difficulty need not automatically be attributed to the allegedly mysterious nature of biology itself; it is rather a difficulty produced by feminist theories of gender. Even if we encapsulate biology or "sex" within the discursive field of a generalized gender (as Butler urges us to do), we have not yet produced the means by which the positive and productive vicissitudes of biology can be thought. On the contrary, this encapsulation renders such a rethinking greatly compromised, if not impossible.

Because gender is premised on the expulsion of biology, and because gender has indeed become feminism's "central explanatory and organizing category" (Gatens, 144), the possibility of thinking biology as other than an excluded, distant, and foundational ruse has been foreclosed in the majority of feminist projects. Feminist critiques of the stomach or hormonal structure are not merely unlikely in this critical environment; they have been rendered unthinkable. It is no longer simply the case that feminist politics must advance a notion of gender against the insidiousness of biological determinism, *for isn't this biological threat already one of gender's own constitutive effects?* Despite its widespread mobilization as such, gender is not simply the secondary, cultural inscription of an originary sex. Gender has now also become the privileged and dominating analytical term of a new distinction: the gender/sex distinction, wherein biology becomes the excluded, unthought, simple ground from which feminist analysis is fashioned. It is my contention that with the solidification of this new analytic regime, feminist appropriations of gender reached their critical limits.

~

Sandra Bem's (1987 [1976]) seminal text on the psychological study of androgyny demonstrates the privileging of this analytic regime of gender in feminist psychology. Highly influential for a number of years after its publication, Bem's account of androgyny is exemplary of the uses and effects of theories of gender in feminist psychology. While the notion of androgyny has largely fallen into disrepute in both feminist psychology and in feminist discourse more widely, the issues that her paper on androgyny raises about gender and its relation to biology remain salient to the current practices (empirical and theoretical) of feminist psychology.

Bem's work on androgyny was prompted by the prevalence of rigid and stereotypical sex roles for both men and women. Bem, along with many other feminist psychologists at the time (e.g., Chesler 1972; Miller 1976), considered such roles to be psychologically damaging:

> Masculinity and femininity may each become negative and even destructive when they are represented in extreme and unadulterated form. . . . For fully effective and healthy human

functioning, both masculinity and femininity must each be tempered by the other, and the two must be integrated into a more balanced, a more fully human, a truly androgynous personality. An androgynous personality would thus represent the very best of what masculinity and femininity have each come to represent, and the more negative exaggerations of masculinity and femininity would tend to be canceled out. (Bem 1987, 209)

Such concern with the effects of sex role stereotypes has been one of feminist psychology's most useful interventions. Nonetheless, it is only via a negation of the role of the body in the constitution of femininity and masculinity that Bem's personality eugenics are possible. It is only if gender is a secondary inscription on a sex-neutral surface that the logic of androgyny can be upheld. Theories of androgyny, as exemplifications of the psychologism and antibiologism of theories of gender, ensure that the body is always (and necessarily) attributed a benign and cursory role in the constitution of personality. For Bem, the role of the body in the psychological domain can be circumscribed by one's ability "to look into the mirror and to be perfectly comfortable with the body that one sees there" (1987, 223)—as if both the looking and the mirror do not already presuppose a libidinal and cultural investment in bodies that is the founding moment of the psychological domain (Lacan 1977) and its endless reinscription (Irigaray 1985a).

Bem instantiates this psychologized androgyny through a series of empirical tests. First, subjects were asked to complete a sex role inventory that ascertained the degree of their sex role affiliation (masculine, feminine, or androgynous) on the basis of their self-identification with a series of adjectives that had been judged "masculine" (e.g., aggressive, ambitious, analytical), "feminine" (e.g., cheerful, childlike, compassionate), or "neutral" (e.g., secretive, sincere, solemn). Second, subjects were required to complete a laboratory-based task: playing with a kitten, playing with a baby, taking part in a social conformity experiment, or taking part in a listening/empathy task. Bem's hypotheses were concerned with how well measures of sex role affiliation would correlate with willingness to undertake, and competency in, such tasks. It seems to go without saying in all these various empirical tests and hypotheses that a psychological measure of androgyny—even if it includes behavioral ·tasks—does not require measurement of the body. Indeed, the very notion of such bodily measurement would seem to be exactly what the notion of androgyny is moving against: the malleability and "health" of androgyny would be severely compromised by the interjection of biological attributes. In such a schema, biology can figure only as politically, ontologically, and epistemologically immaterial. In deeming the psyche to be the only, or the most cogent, site for feminist intervention, Bem's theory of androgyny repeats a division of psyche and biology that has been axiomatic to traditional psychological theory. As such, Bem's account of androgyny is less a critique of the presumptions of mainstream psychology than it is their further exemplification.

This division between body and psyche has been problematically constitutive of all feminist psychological knowledges that rely on an articulation of gender. Because conventional theories of gender enforce a distinction between gender and sex, and champion the effects of the first over the effects of the second in the psychological realm, feminist psychology has found itself not merely disinterested but de-skilled in approaching questions of the body and biology in general. Jane Ussher's (1989) investigation of the psychology of the female body is a case in point. Potentially an opportunity for an interesting examination of the relation of psyche, body, and sexual difference in psychological knowledges, Ussher's book disappoints. This is primarily because the female body that Ussher attempts to rescue from the distortions of biological determinism is completely circumscribed by questions of reproduction. The only specificity that the female body has for Ussher lies in its reproductive capacities—the female body is reductively equated with a reproductive body. By contemplating the female body only within the cycle of menarche to menopause, Ussher perpetuates the very biological determinism she claims to be contesting. Even if we were to accept the notion of a single, exemplary female body, is it not also the case that the sexual specificity of such a body extends to the skin, the internal organs, the nervous system, bone structure, biochemistry, et cetera? Why are the psychological concomitants of the body confined to the processes of reproduction at the expense of digestion, excretion, circulation, and so on? And even then, isn't this very division between a body and its secondary psychological effects already assuming too much? Ussher manufactures a feminist psychology wherein the eating body, the sweating body, and the physiologically active body are incarcerated within the domain of a supposedly neutral human biology and are thus outside the purview of feminist criticism. Like Bem's account of androgyny, Ussher's analysis is less a critique of psychology than it is a (feminist) defense of psychology's foundational presumptions.

Bem's anticorporeal project is an impossible one, as is the feminist psychology it has institutionalized. While Bem wishes to focus exclusively on gender and psychology, she is forced, at the end of her paper, to address the question that nags throughout: How is this androgynous gender to mesh with biology and sexual difference? It is here that the coherence of her paper dissolves. Her argument slips into confusion, not accidentally but necessarily, at precisely that point in the paper where sex resists its exclusion and the opposition between sex and gender becomes impossible to maintain:

> For even if people were all to become psychologically androgynous, the world would continue to exist of two sexes, male and female would continue to be one of the first and most basic dichotomies that young children would learn, and no one would grow up ignorant of or even indifferent to his or her gender. After all, even if one is psychologically androgynous, one's gender continues to have certain profound physical implications. (Bem 1987, 222)

The same set of problems with respect to the place of biology can be found in Bem's more recent work. Bem's (1993) critique of biological essentialism—perhaps typically—leaves until the very end the question of whether there are fixed biological differences between the sexes that are not amenable to social construction, whether there may be anatomy or physiology beyond the reaches of gender. In response to this question, Bem declares herself to be "agnostic" (1993, 37). In a curious admission for a critic who champions the gendered nature of difference, Bem suggests that maybe it *is* hormonal differences that explain aggressive behavior in men, maternal behavior in women, and differential mathematical ability between females and males. This claim of agnosticism is somewhat disingenuous, for while she claims a studied ignorance with respect to biological matters beyond gender, Bem is in fact *mute* with respect to such matters. That is, she is unable to articulate this kind of biological matter because of gender's exclusionary regime. Her allegiance to theories of gender—even when bent directly to questions of biological determinism, or perhaps precisely because of such bending—has left Bem unable to think the body except as the passive, sinister threat to psychological integrity. But hasn't this been patriarchy's most consistent, and restrictive, formulation of biology and its relation to the psychological? And hasn't this formulation in turn been found to replicate a treacherous set of judgments about the masculinization of the mind and the feminization of the body?

~

More recent uses of the sex/gender distinction, particularly those written under the auspices of poststructuralist and queer theory, cannot be said to mobilize sex and gender at the same level of simplicity that characterizes feminist psychology texts. The difference between sex and gender is now considered to be much more complicated than the notion of cultural inscription on a fixed biological body. Butler's work (1990, 1993) is perhaps exemplary of this recent approach to gender theory:

> And there will be no way to understand "gender" as a cultural construct which is imposed upon the surface of matter, understood either as "the body" or its given sex. Rather, once "sex" itself is understood in its normativity, the materiality of the body will not be thinkable apart from the materialization of that regulatory norm. "Sex" is, thus, not simply what one has, or a static description of what one is: it will be one of the norms

by which the "one" becomes viable at all, that which qualifies the body for life within the domain of cultural intelligibility. (Butler 1993, 2)

Butler's deconstruction of the sex/gender distinction sees her displace sex inside gender. Rather than being the secondary mode of inscription on a given sex, gender—understood as a generalized discursive matrix—becomes the means by which sex is produced. Drawing on Foucault's critique of sex and sexuality, Butler takes sex to be given not by biology but by historically contingent discursive operations. The notion that sex constitutes the ground before discourse, that it is the origin of subjectivity, is itself a discursive construction:

Are the ostensibly natural facts of sex discursively produced by various scientific discourses in the service of other political and social interests? If the immutable character of sex is contested, perhaps this construct called "sex" is as culturally constructed as gender; indeed, perhaps it was always already gender, with the consequence that the distinction between sex and gender turns out to be no distinction at all. (Butler 1990, 7)

Butler's main contention here is that the distinction between sex and gender is itself a discursive construction in the service of political and social interests other than feminist ones. For this reason, feminism must remain suspicious of this distinction; specifically, feminism should not repeat the discursive sleight of hand that produces sex as the origin to a secondary gender.

Butler introduces her own sleight of hand to counteract this discursive regime. She argues that gender can no longer be taken simply as the cultural inscription of sex—it "must also designate the very apparatus of production whereby the sexes themselves are established" (1990, 7). That is, gender as a discursive system becomes the ground on which both essentialized sex and inscriptive gender are rendered coherent. More specifically, it is the heterosexual imperative immanent in this broad matrix of gender that congeals the binary nature of sex and gender as they are commonly understood. Butler formulates two notions of gender in a way that mirrors Derrida's mobilization of writing: first, a specific and narrow understanding of gender as the secondary inscription of an originary sex; second, a more generalized notion of gender as the discursive apparatus by which both sex and gender, in the narrow sense, are brought into play. The challenge Butler has presented to both feminist and queer theorists is to formulate this generalized matrix of gender in a way that discloses the power relations that produce the effect of a prediscursive sex and a natural heterosexuality and that conceal the very operation of this discursive production.

In a detailed deconstructive reading of the relation of sex and gender, Butler (1990) has displaced sex from its origin by situating it inside the discursive operations of a generalized gender. Gender becomes that which precedes and exceeds any formulation of sex. However, I remain uneasy about how politically effective such a displacement has been. Butler seeks to trouble the discursive logic that allows "various scientific discourses" to produce sex as originary and natural. But isn't this maneuver also what motivates Butler's own critique and motivates theories of gender in general? That is, isn't the first presumption that initiates any theory of gender, the unargued ground on which any such theory is built, that sex or biology automatically solicit critique? Notwithstanding the considerable and important differences between a position like Bem's and a position like Butler's, what appears to be common to all theories of gender is the presumption that there is a certain critical supplement that sex or biology requires in order for them to be politically admissible, that biology requires modification and supplementation to be analytically viable. This modifying imperative is figured typographically by Butler (1993) in her persistent articulation of sex as "sex": the ubiquitous quotation marks recording the *necessity* of a critical intervention into biological material. The difference between sex and "sex" marks, for Butler, the transition in biological matter from political bankruptcy to political solvency.

I have argued above that this first premise of gender theory (i.e., that sex and biology naturally incite the need for critical supplementation) is already an *effect* of gender theory. That is, the political presumption that sex naturally provokes criticism is spawned by gender's own antibiological intuitions; in the end, theories of gender are not able to escape their historical origins in the rhetoric of antibiological social constructionism. Put another way, gender infantilizes and pathologizes sex, not accidentally, but as its foundational political presumption; this foundational gesture is an irreducible and naturalized effect of gender theory, even in its sophisticated reformulations. In Butler, this constitutive pathologization of the biological has been enacted before the formulation of a generalized gender has even begun, and this pathologization is what initiates and renders intelligible the deconstruction that Butler executes. Effective as Butler's notion of gender as generalized writing is, it is nonetheless founded on an antibiological moment that will always limit the critical efficacy of gender trouble. In chapter 4, I will make a similar argument (although one disconnected from specific questions of gender theory) with respect to Derrida's (1978a) reading of Freud. Founded on an unargued but constitutive antineurologism, Derrida's reading of the early neurological work of Freud deflects the political contributions of biological matter (here neurology) to a thinking of psyche, memory, and writing.

The first premise of this book is that if our critical habits and procedures can be redirected so that biology and neurology are not the natural enemies of politics—that is, if we defer gender theory from the start—then we will find a greater critical productivity in biology than theories of gender would lead us to believe. My point is not that biology requires no critique, not that it is given, self-obvious material, but rather that in the regime of gender theory biology can only ever figure as poisonously foundational, originary, and normative. Consequently, the critical habits assembled in this regime are limited to supposing that any critique of the foundational, the originary, or the normative comes from a place other than biology, and should be mobilized against the biological. With the increasing critical routine of gender theory, denaturalization becomes antinaturalism. A refiguring of this gender regime is necessary if this book is to approach the materiality of cognition via the neuron without reducing or pathologizing such neuronal effects. It is my contention that theories of gender—even when subject to radical reformulation— cannot generate, accommodate, or sustain feminist questions about the nexus cognition-neurology without presuming or enacting a dismissal of neurology.

~

Recognizing the irreducibility of gender as antibiologism, Grosz has argued that any notion of sex or biology as a cultural/social/discursive (i.e., gendered) expression is unnecessary because "sex is itself always/already an expression" (1994a, 139). Grosz claims that trouble can be made not through gender but through a rearticulation of the sexed body itself:

> Isn't it even more threatening to show, not that gender can be at variance with sex . . . but that there is an instability at the very heart of sex and bodies, that the body is what it is capable of doing, and what anybody is capable of doing is well beyond the tolerance of any given culture? (Grosz 1994a, 140)

Which is not to say that sex or biology are self-present or self-referential, but rather to claim that the gesture to a nonbiological outside (figured as culture, the social, or discourse) is a political flaw from which theories of gender can never recover. Grosz implies that any critique of the biological that locates the vicissitudes and thus the political efficacy of biology in the hands of another, outside force not only assumes that biological matter is inert but also reduces and simplifies the complexity of the relation between biology and its outside. I will return to this point shortly.

If the difficulties of gender are such that it is deferred as an analytical tool, the challenge for feminism becomes how to think the body and the psyche without falling back into biologically essentialist presumptions. How can we engage with the vicissitudes of neurological matter, for example, without in some way reinstalling the idea of direct access to biology-as-truth?

While the abandonment of gender may seem to lead to the abandonment of feminism, I would argue that the options for feminist psychology exceed a choice between gender and biological determinism. This excess goes under the name of *morphology* in the writing of Luce Irigaray (1977, 1985a, 1985b). Irigaray's notion of morphology is normally glossed as "imaginary anatomy" (Chanter 1995;

Whitford 1991). That is, it is the body as it is lived and as it lives a specific set of biocultural and biopsychical parameters. These explications of morphology have required a careful articulation of its relation to anatomy. On the one hand, morphology cannot be understood as simply the social representation of the body or the psychic internalization of the body (body image), as both these designations are predicated on an anatomical body that is outside such representations or internalizations and which acts as their referent; morphology then becomes reducible to gender as inscription. On the other hand, morphology is not anatomy in the narrow sense of a foundational substrate. Chanter and Whitford advise that where Irigaray refers to the differential nature of female and male morphology, this is best understood not as originary fixed anatomy or as a secondary or gendered production, but as a particular biocultural instantiation of the body. The use of morphology to this project is that, unlike gender, morphology implies no distinction from, or opposition to, sex, although it does imply a critique of sex as given or natural. Moreover, morphology has the idea of "this (biological) body" already written within it. As such, morphology may be more useful to feminist psychology than either anatomy or gender, as it incorporates those aspects of the body that anatomy and gender can only incompletely grasp.

Kirby (1991) has suggested a reading of morphology that encapsulates the more general sense of biological matter that analyses of the body modeled from theories of gender have usually ignored. If one of the difficulties of thinking morphology has been the conventionalized difference between gender and anatomy (i.e., the difference between representations of "the body" and "this (biological) body,") then Kirby addresses this difficulty by placing "this (biological) body" at the very center of morphology's intelligibility. For Kirby, "this (biological) body" is not something that might eventually be incorporated into a general theory of morphology, as though it were always somehow peripheral to that theory; rather, it is the "origin" from which all morphological accounts emerge:

> Biology's scriptures cannot be left out of this account [of morphology]. Biology is volatile; a mutable intertexture—a discur-

sive effect. It is the stuff than informs our interventions. And such is the implication of biology that Irigaray's "*poétique du corps*" might also be thought as biology rewriting itself. (Kirby 1991, 98)

Like Grosz's claim that sex is "always/already an expression," this idea of morphology as "biology rewriting itself" is exactly what theories of gender are unable to broach. Nowhere articulated in theories of gender is the possibility that biology is always already rewriting itself according to a morphological complexity of difference. Theories of gender always take biological writing to be the writing of a self-presence: a vulgar writing, or a discursive ruse, that requires the deconstructive subtlety of gender. One of the most important implications of Kirby's claim that biology is rewriting itself is that the relation of any biological space, structure, or element to its outside (and thus the nature of biology itself) is figured as one of considerable complexity. Biology's outside is already within, its interiority already scattered. Consequently, the separation of biology from culture that theories of gender require as their first premise is no longer operative. Those "outside" effects (which we may wish to call cultural, but which, by virtue of their intimate relation to biology, we can no longer call nonbiological) hold no determining force over biological matter—if by "determining force" we mean the effect of a fully present inscriptive power on inert and submissive matter. The nature of biology can be "cultural" only where we understand any cultural effects to be always/already biological. Likewise, biology itself, as a bundle of facilitating traces, can never emerge as a full presence, as originary matter. The Saussurian and Derridean orientations of both Grosz and Kirby, uncompromised by the imperative of gender theory, have produced readings of biological matter wherein biology is thought as excess to the limits of presence, location, and stasis that theories of biological determinism and theories of gender alike have ascribed to it:

Morphology then is not anatomy, or indeed biology, although it must nevertheless include them. We might think of morphology as . . . an immanence, a semiological complicity or binding together of traces. And the complexity of this weaving is such that the referent never coincides with itself. (Kirby 1991, 99)

It is not adequate to simply dismiss the category of nature outright, to completely retranscribe it without residue into the cultural: this in itself is the monist, or logocentric, gesture par excellence. . . . Nature may be understood not as an origin or as an invariable template but as materiality in its most general sense, as destination (with all the impossibilities, since Derrida, that this term implies). (Grosz 1994b, 21)

If cognition and neurology have been illegible to feminist psychology (as we saw with Weisstein), this may be attributed less to the nature of cognition and neurology than to the nature of feminist psychology. This limitation in the scope of feminist psychology's projects has become critical. In recent years there have been an increasing number of researchers claiming to have found the origin of sexual difference, sexual preference, psychological pathology, and all manner of behavioral and cultural differences in locatable biological entities: in the brain, in DNA, in biochemistry. The typical response from feminist psychology has been to demonstrate how such claims are a social construction, an ideological fabrication, or a discursive ruse. In all such accounts, the nature of biological matter (the neuron, the gene, the chemical) remains enigmatic. As a result, feminist critiques in psychology have been unable to engage effectively with the very matter at the core of contemporary theories of cognition. They have pointed to sexist descriptions of brain function (Shields 1975) or to sexist research on sex differences in cognitive capacities (Maccoby and Jacklin 1974), but they have been unable to address the very status of the brain and cognition. Such projects have been confined to negotiation over empirical procedure and the interpretation of neurological or cognitive data (Bleier 1984; Fausto-Sterling 1992), at the expense of a wider analysis of the ontological status of neurocognitive matter itself. The possibilities entailed in thinking biology as writing (rather than as the excluded other of a gender analysis) will allow such matters to become legible to feminist psychology and will lead us from the narrow projects on gender into a wider field of possible feminist psychologies.

~ Conclusion

I have argued here that the limits of feminist psychology are set by both its inattentive complicity with the mainstream discipline and its adherence to particular, restrictive feminist tenets. By authorizing a certain kind of feminist intervention that takes women as its proper and only concern, and that mobilizes theories of gender as its central critical device, feminist psychology has foreclosed other sorts of projects that could operate under its name. It is my contention that feminist interventions into those areas of psychology that have previously been figured as outside the scope of feminist inquiry (e.g., neuropsychology and cognitive psychology) will enable feminist psychology to rethink the nature of feminist psychological knowledges, and to rethink the politics of feminist intervention in general. This process of rethinking holds out the promise of a revitalized and astute feminist practice inside psychology.

~

chapter two

The Origins of Scientific Psychology

The question of psychology's status as a scientific domain is one that simply will not go away. Despite more than a hundred years of established laboratory experimentation, despite the development of many unambiguously scientific paradigms (behaviorism, cognitive psychology, neuropsychology, perceptual psychology), despite the institutional demand for empirical procedure, the question *How scientific is psychology, really?* remains curiously unresolved. It is supposedly the historical choice of science over philosophy that marks the birth of modern psychology (Boring 1957); yet this modern-day psychology finds itself unable to affirm this choice and secure its position as a science (Koch and Leary 1992). Never quite scientific enough, yet clearly too scientific for some, psychology finds itself caught in a dilemma of identity that has been variously described as inhibiting, paralyzing, or self-destructive.

In this chapter, the nature of psychology's identity as scientific will be examined. How is a scientific identity procured for psychology? What exclusions and fixations are necessary for the maintenance of such an identity? My initial concern will be to argue that psychology is enabled rather than damaged by this "crisis" in its scientific identity. While the most common responses to psychology's uncertain scientific status have been either to move psychology out of the domain of science altogether (e.g., Robinson 1992) or to insist on an ever more rigorous and thorough application of scientific principles (e.g., Giorgi 1992), I will maintain that it is the very negotiation between the scientific and the nonscientific that produces an identifiable psychological domain. This means that psychology's location with respect to both science and interpretation remains undecidable. This undecidability is not a secondary or exterior effect, which is brought to bear on an already existing psychological domain; it is not a condition against which an already formed psychology could struggle. Rather, this undecidability is the condition that establishes psychology as such. Consequently, the pertinent questions about the identity of psychology as scientific may be less questions of whether one is *for* or *against* a scientific psychology, or whether we are able to adjudicate over how scientific psychology could become, than questions of how the equivocation over scientificity constitutes and propels psychological research in general.

These questions about psychology's scientific status are particularly important for an analysis of cognitive psychology. It is with reference to computation and neurology that cognitive psychology in general, and connectionism in particular, has endeavored to give a scientific explanation of the psychological. Cognitive psychology is commonly taken to be the most recent manifestation of psychology's struggle to assert a scientific identity over a philosophical, interpretive, or speculative one (e.g., Kurtzman 1987). Neurology and cognition, then, do not only offer a material grounding for psychological phenomena; they also offer an epistemological foundation from which a stable scientific identity can be forged. Neurology and cognition hold the promise of resolving the undecidability of psychology's identity: to secure it as scientific once and for all. One of the goals of this book is to demonstrate that neurology and cognition can offer no such hope. What is at the heart of cognition and neurology is not a stable presence or identity onto which a less certain psychology could be fastened and thus strengthened, but rather the same constitutive equivocation over interpretation and empiricism that drives psychology in general. My goal, then, is not to demonstrate that cognitivism somehow lacks the ability to secure a scientific identity for psychology (where some other model of psychological functioning could), but to demonstrate that all identity must be thought through a more complex understanding of difference and the relation of inside/outside. The historical and epistemological origins of psychology (physiology over philosophy) and the ontological origins that it in turn produces (psyche as neurocomputation) are all the products of an undecidability whose generative effects have yet to be examined carefully.

In later chapters I will focus on connectionism in order to show that a different reading of psychology's relation to scientificity and interpretation is possible: a relation that does not rely on reductionism, psychical locationism, and cognitive presence for its intelligibility. This chapter lays the ground for that work by arguing that the relation between science and interpretation, empiricism and theory, neurology and philosophy is more complex and powerful than the increasingly conventionalized commentaries on cognitive and connectionist psychology allow. As far as this book is concerned, connectionism's value lies not in the potency of its scientific achievements, but in our ability to extract a different understanding of scientific psychology from it.

At the same time, an investigation of the scientific nature of psychology is important for feminist analyses of psychology. There has been a tendency for feminists to demonize, trivialize, or marginalize psychology's scientific ambitions. This has meant that feminist interventions into psychology have been clustered around those areas that are less clearly "scientific": social psychology (e.g., Wilkinson 1986), developmental psychology (e.g., Gilligan 1982), clinical psychology (e.g., Chesler 1972). It is extremely difficult to find any feminist research or commentary in areas such as perception, psychobiology, and neuropsychology, where knowledge is taken to be more objective, less interpretive, and less directly relevant to women (Wilson 1995). If feminist critiques are to become legible outside a narrow prescription of feminist psychology's proper object, method, and goals, then not only do certain feminist presumptions need to be rethought (as I have argued in chapter 1), but the nature of scientificity must be also reconsidered. This reconsideration needs to be more complex than the binarized choice often facing feminist critiques: to oppose science or to acquiesce to it; to ignore science or to adore it; to reform science or to render it inoperative. As the line between scientificity and its others (interpretation, theory) is complicated, so too will the line between feminism and its others (neurology, cognition) be transformed in productive and profitable ways.

~ Demarcation and the Constitution of the Psychological Domain

> It was in 1919 that I first faced the problem of *drawing a line of demarcation* between those statements and systems of statements which could be properly described as belonging to empirical science, and others which might, perhaps, be described as "pseudo-scientific" or (in certain contexts) as "metaphysical." (Popper 1969, 255)

These "others" to the proper domain of the empirical sciences can be known variously as pseudo-science, metaphysics, interpretation, theory, and myth. All these names can be used to denote the negative, the nonscience to Popper's privileged science. While Popper claims that a line may be drawn between science and its others, the relation between these two is more complex than the idea of a static boundary can allow. This act of demarcation, this drawing of a line that presumes to map out an epistemological territory in a benignly descriptive fashion, is in fact constitutive of that territory. In effect, Popper's demarcation proposal acts as a methodology for *constituting* rather than *elucidating* the scientific; it performs a demarcation that it claims only to describe.

The context within which Popper became aware of the necessity for demarcating between science and pseudo-science was dominated by three disparate but highly influential theories: Einstein's theory of relativity, Freudian psychoanalysis, and Marxist historical materialism. According to his own account (Popper 1969), it was the undiscriminating juxtaposition of these theories that incited the need for a system of demarcation. While all three theories laid claim to being science, Popper felt that only Einstein's theory was properly scientific. Prompted by Eddington's famous empirical test of Einstein's theory of gravitation in 1919, Popper constructed his theory of falsifiability: One could draw a line between science proper and pseudo-science on the basis that the former is falsifiable via empirical testing, while the latter is not (Popper 1969). Popper (1983b) claims that this demarcation between the scientific and the pseudo-scientific occupies the center of his philosophy of science. I have chosen to begin with Popper not only because of his influence, but also because of the distinction between the scientific and the interpretative that lies at the core of his analytical system. While there have been many debates over the validity and viability of Popper's demarcation proposal, this is not what concerns me here. I am not so much interested in the validity of Popper's proposal as in its presumptions and effects. Popper's demarcation proposal discloses what is at stake in the constitution of a scientific identity, and what needs to be done to secure and protect that identity.

Perhaps the first thing that can be ascertained about Popper's demarcation proposal is that it emerges from an anxiety that the scientific could be mistaken for the merely speculative, and vice versa. He notes, for example, that traditional verificationist principles, which demarcate between science and pseudo-science on the basis of observation and induction, would be unable to admit Einstein's speculations on relativity to the domain of science, and would be unable to exclude astrology's empirically based claims from it: "Thus there clearly was a need for a different criterion of demarcation" (Popper 1969, 256). This anxiety over the possibility of confusing the scientific with the pseudo-scientific was resolved, Popper believed, with the doctrine of falsification: Empirical falsification (or testability) became the identifying characteristic of the scientific domain. Once isolated, falsification and testability became the means by which Popper was able to circumscribe the scientific domain and separate it definitively from the interpretive, speculative, or metaphysical. More specifically, this demarcation aims to interrupt and terminate any movement between the domains of the scientific and the interpretive. As we will see, however, this termination is more apparent than real, for a certain movement between these two domains remains irreducible.

What particular criterion Popper mobilizes to effect such an interruption is less important at this point than the imperative that demands such a demarcation in the first place. The objective of demarcation is to rule out certain ideas, statements, and epistemological practices while ruling in others. To take a specific example, Popper (1983a) became concerned that some of the propositions and practices of quantum physics were more metaphysical than scientific, and that such propositions and practices threatened the scientific integrity of physics in general. Popper's explicit aim in this paper is to exclude oscillation, uncertainty, and interpretation from the scientific process. His particular concern with quantum mechanics was to remove the "mystery" of wave-particle duality and to discount the interference of the observer on subatomic particles. In short, Popper's task is to differentiate between the properly scientific nature of quantum theory and its more disruptive and excessive interpretive practices. The constitution of a scientific identity, then, is as dependent on what is ruled out as it is on what is ruled in. That is, the scientific identity that Popper champions is constructed through the exclusion and denigration of the interpretive as much as it is positively named by the doctrine of falsification. Demarcations between science and its others are always and everywhere political in their motivations and constitutive in their effects (and we need to remember that it is not only philosophers of science or scientists who wish to enact such demarcations).

What makes Popper's demarcation proposal interesting, however, is not simply that it enforces a traditionally hierarchical relation between science and interpretation (which, after all, is common to many philosophies of science), but that this system discloses how such a demarcation operates in the service of scientific integrity and authority. Unlike the (then) prevailing doctrine of logical positivism, Popper did not seek to *destroy* the nonscientific or the metaphysical; he argued against "an ill-advised attempt to destroy metaphysics wholesale" and advocated instead that we separate metaphysics from the scientific domain and try to "eliminate, piecemeal as it were, metaphysical elements from the various sciences" (Popper 1969, 264). Popper presumes that science, when properly practiced, is a self-contained domain, governed by its own set of rules (i.e., falsification) and separate from the influences of interpretation. Yet at the same time, his system explicitly acknowledges the necessity of an engagement with interpretation: The viability of this allegedly self-sufficient scientific identity is dependent on negotiation with, and exclusion of, the metaphysical and interpretive. It is the identification of metaphysical elements and their displacement elsewhere that ensures a scientific identity. A scientific identity is conceived, then, not through a set of autonomous rules, but rather through a vigilant, and seemingly endless, process of exclusion. Where the logical positivists (e.g., Schlick 1936) attempted to enable science according to some internal and completely self-referential criteria, Popper's system attests to the necessity of an engagement with the metaphysical or interpretive. What we can glean from (and against) Popper (and what could, no doubt, be excavated from logical positivism as well) is that there is an *irreducible* negotiation between scientific and interpretive identities, practices, and knowledges that is responsible for enacting and authorizing the field of science. A detour through Derrida's critique of Lévi-Strauss (below) will return me to a more thorough articulation of this irreducible, constitutive movement.

Popper's accounts of demarcation expose the complex relation between science and its others: It is the systematic expulsion of the nonscientific that allows the constitution of science as a coherent and unified field. This argument, however, needs to be extended further; these others (theory, interpretation, philosophy) do not exist as coherent, symmetrical identities against which a scientific identity is constructed. It is the distinction between science and interpretation, rather than any characteristic inherent in those domains, that controls and constrains the identities that Popper names *science* and *pseudo-science*. As always, it is the placement of a border, the declaration of a difference, that has the constitutive force in the securing of an identity. The spheres of science (as falsifiability) and interpretation (as pseudo-science) are brought into being by Popper's demarcation; it is the drawing of a line, the installation of a boundary that enables his proper and illegitimate domains. If neither the scientific nor the interpretive, as such, exists prior to demarcation, if it is their differentiation that constitutes them, then the possibility of a "choice" between one side or the other becomes non-sense. Moreover, if science and interpretation are always already asymmetrically implicated in each other, then the notion of a line will not be complex enough to describe their relation and their differences. The relation of scientific psychology to its nonscientific others (and, more concretely, the relation of neurology and cognition to interpretation, philosophy, and theory) is not one of a purely internal space to its differently located outside. If these variously named others (interpretation, philosophy, theory) are already part of the constitutive force of scientific psychology, then the nature of cognition must be thought of as something other than a discrete presence, an internally legible space distanced from its interpretive debris.

The "others" of science will be likewise complicated and refigured in this process. It is not simply the purity of a scientific identity that is at stake here; the identity and politics of interpretation, theory and philosophy have also been put into question. If, as Sedgwick and Frank (1995) argue, our current theoretical habits and procedures are mobilized through a distancing from the biological and the scientific (see the introduction to this book), then any rethinking of scientificity will also effect a rethinking of these critical positions. Not exterior to our critical methods in a simple way, questions of the scientific and the empirical—undisclosed but potent nonetheless—are at the very heart of "our" political intelligibility and viability. To this end, gestures of demarcation between science and interpretation do not operate simply in the service of scientific integrity.

~

As the story is usually told, modern academic, experimental psychology was born the hybrid child of nineteenth-century physiology and philosophy. This birth is usually celebrated as having occurred in the Leipzig laboratories of German physiologist Wilhelm Wundt in 1879 (Boring 1957). These traditional narratives of the birth of scientific psychology suggest that psychology has been grafted from the interplay of science (physiology) and interpretation (mental philosophy). This constitutive moment is considered to be a historical event, now past. However, if this interplay is considered instead to be the ongoing condition of psychology's coherence, then it becomes clear why the unequivocal realization of a scientific psychology has remained elusive in this century irrespective of its institutional and geographical location. In the first instance, I derive my account of this interplay from Boring's (1957) classic history of experimental psychology. While psychology is now diverse enough to accommodate many other histories, it is this account of the union of nineteenth-century physiology and philosophy that has come to be the history of scientific psychology in general. More specifically, it is to this history that contemporary cognitive psychology is indebted. Boring marks the emergence of an identifiable (experimental) psychology thus: "In this history of experimental psychology, we must, therefore, go back into philosophical psychology in order to see what it was that, married to physiology, gave birth to physiological, experimental psychology" (Boring 1957, 158).

This marriage of a scientific methodology to the problems of mental philosophy was not an equitable or symmetrical union. Rather, it was more the overcoming of philosophy than an active engagement with it that motivated the emergence of scientific psychology (Canguilhem 1980). The "new psychology" emerged in order to render certain metaphysical problems (specifically the mind-body problem) subservient to scientific scrutiny and resolution. Klein (1971), like many historians of psychology, argues that the crucial differentiation between mental philosophy and the new psychology was effected by the introduction of experimental procedures into the domain of psychological research (rather than, say, the introduction of philosophical questions into psychophysiological research). Progressing from the armchair to the laboratory, the new psychology endeavored to move against or beyond its philosophical heritage, and the repudiation of the metaphysical or the conceptual became the foundation for most scientific psychological research after William James. Under the influence of logical positivism, mainstream psychology (qua behaviorism) pursued an uncompromising eradication of the mental and its metaphysical correlates: "I believe we can write a psychology, define it as Pillsbury [did], and never go back upon our definition: never use the terms consciousness, mental states, mind, content, introspectively verifiable, imagery, and the like" (Watson 1913, 166).

Even with the demise of both logical positivism and behaviorism as major forces in psychological theory and research, this crusade against the metaphysical has not diminished. This struggle is waged now through the materiality of neurocognition; in particular, the brain has become the invaluable ally of scientific psychology. Offering a seemingly unequivocal grounding for the psyche, the brain is figured as the final referent for a non- or antimetaphysical scientific psychology (P. M. Churchland 1995; Globus 1995). This positioning of neurology in opposition to, or radically beyond, metaphysics will be questioned in later chapters. I will argue that neurology and computationalism, as they are usually figured in traditional analytic commentary, extend rather than displace the metaphysical presumptions of scientific psychology. Moreover, I will contend (following Derrida) that these attempts to be transported beyond metaphysical constraints by the operations of scientificity are metaphysical aspirations of the most traditional kind.

If there has been a consistent problem within the history of scientific psychology, it is this: To locate psychology's origin (and thus future) in the "choice" of scientificity over interpretation is to misread psychology's relation to science and interpretation as indecision or uncertainty, as a dilemma that requires resolution. There is a dynamic interplay between the scientific and the interpretive that is internal to psychology, and it cannot be eradicated from that domain. Psychology is not caught in an unfortunate epistemological uncertainty from which it may eventually extract itself (or from which neurology and computationalism may liberate it); rather, psychology is constituted by the difference between science and interpretation—there is no psychology before or outside the negotiation of science and interpretation. Psychology has not entered, preformed, into the field of science at a particular historical moment (e.g., at Leipzig in 1879). Rather, psychology has been enabled in the historical and epistemological movement between science and its others, and remains vitally dependent on it. As its condition of possibility, the tension in psychology between the scientific and the interpretive, between neurology and philosophy, is irreducible, irresolvable, and utterly necessary.

Perhaps one of the most interesting aspects of these traditional histories and epistemologies of psychology is the place given to psychoanalysis. Psychoanalysis, as the science of interpretation, confounds the demarcations that have been crucial to scientific and psychological identity. Accordingly, psychoanalysis has been elided from most histories of scientific psychology. Either missing altogether, or added in awkwardly, psychoanalysis disrupts the trajectory mapped out by psychology's traditional histories by disclosing the irreducibility of the movement between science and interpretation. As with psychology, scientificity has been a point of contention for the detractors and followers of psychoanalysis alike. Freud's gestures to scientificity invariably provoke a series of recuperative readings of psychoanalytic identity, which either fully envelope psychoanalysis within scientific regulation or seek to push psychoanalysis beyond empirical constraints. Because Freud's relation to scientificity is just about always read too narrowly, too literally, psychoanalysis is deemed either not scientific enough or too piously devoted to scientific tenets and procedures.

Freud bookends his psychoanalytic writings with two remarkably similar comments about psychoanalysis as a natural science. At the very beginning of his career Freud expressed his intention to "furnish a psychology that shall be a natural science" (Freud 1895, 295); in an unfinished paper forty-five years later Freud echoes this earlier sentiment by declaring that "psychology, too, is a natural science. What else can it be?" (Freud 1940b, 282). These days, such comments are usually discarded as the detritus of the infancy and senility of psychoanalysis, or as the narcissistic projections of a neurologist who had lost touch with mainstream scientific advances (e.g., Kitcher 1992). All such analyses presume that the analogy between psychoanalysis and the natural sciences works by rendering psychoanalysis stable via an association with the natural sciences. What is not often considered is how a scientific identity is refigured by such analogies. Any reading that presumes in the first instance that "a natural science" is a stable and self-evident identity onto which a more fragile psychoanalysis may be grafted will miss the subtle effect of Freud's analogy. If Freud claims that the psychoanalytic concepts of instinct (*Trieb*) or nervous energy are no less indeterminate than force, mass, attraction, and so on (1940a, 159), then why should we presume that force, mass, attraction, and so on are the ground on which the intelligibility of psychoanalysis is built? Is it not also the case that instinct and nervous energy could be the ground on which a refigured natural science could be established? If instinct is like force, is not force also like instinct? In gesturing to their similarity, not only has Freud rendered the ground of psychoanalysis natural, he has also rendered the ground of the natural sciences psychoanalytic.

There may be more in operation in Freud's gestures to scientificity than simply the attachment of the unknown and equivocal (psychoanalysis) to the known and certain (natural science). While the analogy between psychoanalysis and the natural sciences seems to shore up a psychoanalytic identity via its similitude to the natural sciences, there is another, irreducible effect of this analogy that renders the natural sciences themselves enigmatic via their similitude to psychoanalysis. The interesting question may be less "In what way is psychoanalysis like or unlike a natural science?" than "What is it about a natural science that renders it open to psychoanalytic analogy?" Unlike the proponents of computationalism and neurology in contemporary psychology, Freud's gesture to the natural sciences is never a simple gesture against interpretation and philosophy. Rather than choosing scientificity over and against interpretation, as a traditional approach to psychology would, Freud chooses both, and in the process of doing so he rewrites what both science and interpretation could be.

Psychoanalysis, by this understanding, is a more faithful, more candid psychology: It recognizes and gives itself up to the constitutive movement between science and interpretation. The openly interpretive nature of Freud's scientific methodology (e.g., the metapsychological papers of 1915) and the scientific rigor of his interpretations (e.g., Freud 1900) confound and contaminate a scientific identity as it would normally be understood. Whether psychoanalysis can best be made to fit the contemporary ideals of either scientificity or hermeneutics is less interesting than how it can be mobilized to disrupt and dislocate the demarcation between these two epistemological domains. This idea will be explored in some detail in chapters 4 and 5. By occupying and exploiting this awkward position between science and interpretation, between neurology and philosophy, psychoanalysis disturbs the traditional taxonomy of disciplines and their methodologies much more plainly than does psychology. Psychoanalysis's inability to acquiesce to this taxonomic order exposes the exclusions, the negations, and the violences that are necessary to divide knowledges into these categories of "scientific" and "nonscientific." If psychoanalysis's awkward positioning creates difficulties for scientific psychology, I would argue that these are exactly the kind of difficulties that psychology needs.

It is for these reasons that psychoanalysis will be an essential critical tool for this book. If the foreclosure of psychoanalysis has been one of the primary means by which psychology has been able to construct a scientific identity, then the return of certain psychoanalytic concepts within the domain of scientific psychology will effect a dislocation of that identity. This will also entail a rereading of the customary narrative of psychoanalysis' own genesis. Freud's "prepsychoanalytic" transition from neurology to psychology is less a giving up, a refusal, or a progression from neurology than it is an intricate interrogation of the dynamic that separates these two domains. Freud's work on the cusp of neurology and psychology (e.g., Freud 1891; 1895) is preoccupied with the reformulation of a scientific psychology. Indeed, at this particular time Freud seems to be entirely enthralled by the possibilities that such a reformulation would entail. Freud's deliberations over neurology and psychology, which are commonly taken as the "origin" of psychoanalysis (and which mirror psychology's own "originary" deliberations over physiology and mental philosophy) will be of particular interest in later chapters. Providing an opportunity for a close critical examination of the movement between scientific and interpretive domains, psychoanalysis has an unexpected resonance in contemporary cognitive and neurological theory in psychology.

~ Negotiating Empiricism and Theory

In an interview with Judith Butler, Gayle Rubin (1994) discusses the role of empirical (or "descriptive") methodologies in her own work. While she agrees with Butler that the "looking" involved in any empirical or ethnographic practice is always theoretically inflected, Rubin has a more pressing concern with respect to the relation of empiricism and theory:

> Empirical research and descriptive work are often treated as some kind of low-status, even stigmatized, activity that is inferior to "theory." There needs to be a discussion of what exactly is meant, these days, by "theory," and what counts as "theory." I would like to see a less dismissive attitude toward empirical work. There is a disturbing trend to treat with condescension or contempt any work that bothers to wrestle with data. This comes, in part, from the quite justified critiques of positivism and crude empiricism. . . . I am appalled at a developing attitude that seems to think that having no data is better than having any data, or that dealing with data is an inferior and discrediting activity. A lack of solid, well-researched, careful descriptive work will eventually impoverish feminism, and gay and lesbian studies, as much as a lack of rigorous critical scrutiny will. I find this galloping idealism as disturbing as mindless positivism. (Rubin 1994, 91–92)

For Rubin, the stigmatization of empirical research in studies of sexuality (and more generally) has meant that data have been analytically subordinated to the authority of "theory." Rubin responds to this with a defense of the value of data or descriptions for our understanding of sexuality, and she advocates a reassessment of the relation between theoretical and empirical conclusions. For example, she is concerned that "these days" analyses of sadomasochism draw too heavily on Deleuze's (1989) canonical essay on masochism. The problem for Rubin is that Deleuze's essay distinguishes between sadism and masochism on the basis of the literary styles of de Sade and Sacher-Masoch, and the analytical value of such literary analyses for an understanding of "those persons and populations who might be considered 'masochistic' or 'sadistic'" (Rubin 1994, 94) is unclear. Rubin is concerned that statements about sadism and masochism gleaned from literary, cinematic, psychoanalytic, or philosophical reflection have become authoritative statements or descriptions of what "actual masochists are, do, or mean" (Rubin 1994, 94). She infers that the former set of theoretical statements does not, or need not, correspond with the experiences or practices of the latter group of people; moreover, any attempt to make the latter legible through the former will distort, homogenize, or marginalize what actual masochists are, do, or mean. She concludes: "I have this quaint, social science attitude that statements about living populations should be based on some knowledge of such populations, not on speculative analysis, literary texts, cinematic representations, or preconceived assumptions" (Rubin 1994, 94).

While Rubin's concern about the status accorded to data is reasonable and timely, her general approach to the relation between empiricism and theory is mired in the very logic she begrudges. If data have been excluded or marginalized within certain authoritative studies of sexuality, Rubin's call for a reinsertion or restoration of data does nothing to contest the logic of oppositionality that initiated these various devaluations in the first place. Indeed, Rubin perpetuates this logic by repeating and affirming the division between data and literature, the actual and the representational, in order to remind us that there are matters of "actuality" that psychoanalysis, film, philosophy, and literature cannot contest, or to which they must acquiesce. While Rubin's understanding of ethnographic data or "descriptions" is more complicated than a crude empiricism, nevertheless there remains in data a final, authoritative connection to the actual that literature, for example, cannot have. In this way, Rubin reinstates a demarcation between empiricism and theory, the conventionalizing effects of which I have already discussed with respect to Popper. Moreover, this demarcation shuts down the "peculiar double movement" between theory and data that Sedgwick and Frank (1995) have identified as indispensable to our current critical and political viability. While ostensibly Rubin calls for a dialogue between empiricism and theory, the logic in which this call is couched determines in advance that such a dialogue will be a restrictive and unproductive replication of the very structures that need to be contested.

What Rubin's comments expose is that there is an ethical-epistemological relation between empirical and theoretical work that needs to be negotiated. Rubin has observed the current state of this relation and its effects, but because she has analytically naturalized the distinction between data and representation, she is unable to articulate a refiguration of this relation. Her comments on Deleuze, for example, already presume too much: that the experiences and practices of "actual masochists" exist prior to, or outside of, literary, psychoanalytic, filmic, and philosophic representations of masochism; that these theories re-present masochism but cannot be "actual" masochism; that empiricism is not representation; that representation is not empiricism. Until the nature of these distinctions is investigated, and the historical and epistemological contingencies that have rendered such divisions asymmetrical (for surely it is only in the narrowest of historical and political contexts that empiricism could be subordinated to the exigencies of interpretation), Rubin's difficulties with the relation between empiricism and theory will remain.

In an interview with Ellen Rooney, Gayatri Spivak (1993b) has also commented on the place of empirical work in our current critical context. This interview is concerned with the politics of essentialism/antiessentialism, and Rooney observes that there has been some confusion in the U.S. context between essentialism and empiricism. Specifically, Rooney suggests that the equation of essentialism with the reductive strategies of sociobiology, cognitive studies, and AI, for example, may have been one of the reasons why feminists in the United States have been unable to think essentialism more productively. Rooney's question discloses a widespread presumption that the discourses of sociobiology, cognitive studies, and AI are constitutionally unable to think differences adequately. Spivak acknowledges the complicity of such empirical discourses in various oppressive practices, but she resists the implication that these empirical discourses are inherently reductive or critically bankrupt. While agreeing with Rooney that it is erroneous to equate essentialism with empiricism, Spivak also rescues empiricism from a reading that is too narrow, too reductive. If empirical work and the work of "theory" are never separate, then "one has to learn how to honor empirical work" (Spivak 1993b, 17). This honoring that Spivak prefaces is different from the reclamation of data that Rubin pursues (although it is Rubin's 1975 paper that Spivak mentions as interesting with respect to such a refiguring of empiricism). In the first instance, empiricism is never opposed to interpretation: A radical or symmetrical distinction cannot be made between empirical work and theoretical concerns, or between "actual" practices and, say, literature, psychoanalysis, and philosophy. Despite appearances, empirical data is not the self-sufficient, epistemologically symmetrical other to theoretical speculation, and theoretical speculation is not detached from empirical or material exigencies. More specifically, Spivak suggests that empiricism can be grounded not in a presupposed connection to actuality, but in a catachrestic name. That is, by taking one's ontological commitments (here, data) to be susceptible to examination and to be grounded in a catachrestic configuration, one is enabled to be "thoroughly empirical" without being blindly or complacently empirical: "It seems to me that to be empirical in this way would be a much greater challenge, require much harder work, and would make people read different things" (1993b, 16). The crucial issue here may be less that empirical work requires "honoring" (on this both Rubin and Spivak agree), but rather how that honoring can take place. For Spivak, that honoring cannot take place outside a radical contestation of the ground of empiricism and interpretation, a contestation that Rubin (*pace* Spivak) seems already to have foreclosed.

Writing of the negotiation between interpretation and empirical data in the work of Lévi-Strauss, Derrida (1978b) claims that the relation between these two domains cannot be thought of in terms of a symmetrical opposition or a choice. Thus he outlines a way of proceeding differently at the juncture of empiricism and theory. Such a rethinking is pivotal, of course, to the operations and objectives of this book. If critical yet productive interventions into scientific psychology are to be formulated, they must, first of all, be able to provide a careful response to the role of empirical data. What remains elusive is the ability to address the data of the empirical sciences *and* a number of important theoretical propositions without subordinating one to the other—that is, to neither take certain empirical data to be the final word on the viability of particular theoretical procedures nor consider empirical data as secondary and supplemental to the primacy of philosophical, literary, or visual theories. The question before us now is this: How are we to recognize and respect these domains while at the same time subjecting them to rigorous scrutiny?

~

I do not believe that today there is any question of *choosing*. (Derrida 1978b, 293)

Working with and through traditional semiological and linguistic theories of the sign, Derrida (1974) presents a stunning critique of writing and signification that he names *grammatological*. Without detailing the particularities of his deconstruction of writing and the sign, we can say that Derrida names grammatology "the science of writing," although under this reformulation both science and writing have been radically dislocated. While the notion of writing, psyche, and the trace that emerges from this and other of his texts will become important in later chapters, it is the somewhat peripheral issue of grammatology as a science that I wish to pursue here.

In response to the question: "To what extent is or is not grammatology a 'science'?" (Derrida 1981, 35), Derrida offers a typically elliptical but illuminating answer: He considers that his own work is unable to choose definitively between being or not being a science. To the extent that grammatology is a deconstruction of the ontotheology, logocentrism, and phonologism that constitute the norms of scientificity, then grammatology would appear to be less a science than its interrogator. As such, grammatology "risks destroying the concept of science" (Derrida 1974, 74). At the same time, however, Derrida is careful not to install grammatology as the master of the scientific. Grammatology also draws on and is implicated in traditional scientific semiological work. Rather than constituting an epistemological crisis, as it has for psychology, this positioning between and across the division of science and interpretation is the mechanism of grammatology's critical force. In this respect, grammatology is a more radical execution of the taxonomic disruption that psychoanalysis has foreshadowed.

Grammatology effects such a disruption by invoking the traditional norms of scientificity, yet at the same time displacing the ground on which such norms would operate. By folding scientificity inside interpretation, and interpretation inside scientificity (and by acknowledging the historical and epistemological contingencies that render such foldings asymmetrical), grammatology radically refigures the morphology of scientificity. If grammatology could be said to make any choice at all between science and interpretation, it would appear to choose both. More accurately, however, grammatology has put the very idea of such a choice into question. This grammatological practice is operating in a *double register*:

> [Grammatology] must simultaneously go beyond metaphysical positivism and scientism, and accentuate whatever in the effective work of science contributes to freeing it of the metaphysical bonds that have borne on its definition and its movement since its beginnings. Grammatology must pursue and consolidate whatever, in scientific practice, has always already begun to exceed the logocentric closure. (Derrida 1981, 35–36)

By both marking and loosening the limits of scientificity, grammatology refigures and relocates the relation between science and it others. To this end, grammatology is less a new science, or a new interpretation of science, than it is the interrogation of the division between science and interpretation (a division that I have already argued is the condition of possibility for psychological research and theory). It is for this reason that Rubin's revaluing of data is only a partial response to the complexities of the relation between empiricism and theory. Her call for a revaluation of that relation remains incomplete and ineffectual as it does not directly address the logic that enforces the political and epistemological abyss between data and interpretation. Grammatology is an attempt to refigure this abyss. More specifically, grammatology works to refigure the traditional difference between a scientific project and an interpretive one. Consequently, the radical possibilities of grammatology cannot be thought by either science or philosophy: "The necessary decentering cannot be a philosophic or scientific act as such" (Derrida 1974, 92). Acknowledging that empiricism and theory have been structured as oppositional domains, yet refusing the logic, symmetry, and authority of this division, Derrida's grammatological practice offers an epistemological and political intervention that neither science nor philosophy, traditionally conceived, could realize.

As well as this more or less explicit reformulation, Derrida's critique of scientificity is already subtly prefaced in the word *grammatology* itself. As Spivak (1974) notes, the name puns on the juxtaposition of *gramme* (as trace, as origin, as the impossibility of presence, truth, and foundation) and *-ology* (as logos, science, and the desire for presence, truth, and foundation). Derrida (1974) figures this pun typographically: grammato*logy*. Through this juxtaposition (gramme/ology), science is put under erasure as an activity or a movement that is both necessary and impossible, and so grammatology's relation to the name and dominion of science remains provisional and ambivalent. Both as word and as practice, grammatology keeps alive an irresolvable contradiction, a contradiction that for my purposes could be written as the tension between science and interpretation, between empiricism and theory, and—as we will see later on—between neurocognition and philosophy. Derrida's formulation of a grammatology that can both take from and exceed the empirical sciences becomes the ground from which I may investigate cognitive psychology apart from the traditional evaluations of "for and against," "inside and outside," "critique and reformation." It is this notion of science under erasure, a science radically at odds with the binarisms that seek to control it, and which it in turn would normally seek to sustain, that I want to pursue in my account of cognitive psychology and connectionism in later chapters.

If there is a tension between empirical projects as they traditionally operate in psychology (or in studies of sexuality) and the critical projects that emerge from postmodern, poststructuralist, and deconstructive theories, then we must not be misled about the resolution of this tension. Derrida's response to this tension is not to resolve it but to exploit its productivities by "choosing" (or, perhaps more accurately, enforcing) both empiricism and theory at the same time.

This does not entail that we abandon or censure empirical projects in the light of our theoretical aspirations; but, contra Rubin, neither does it entail that data are to be reiterated as the ground of our politics and epistemology. Derrida has argued that such a paradoxical and difficult approach is the only "choice" we have: Any intervention into scientific psychology is irreducibly caught in the fields of empiricism and metaphysics, and it must acknowledge these conditions of possibility. Such an imperative enforces the paradoxical condition that one must occupy two different places simultaneously. One must be faithful to two contradictory projects; one must play a double game. In the end, one must learn to love the tension, to encourage it, to facilitate its play, rather than once again, and in the manner not unlike those structures one is moving against, attempt to repress it under regimes of unity and resolution.

~

Perhaps Derrida's most explicit engagement with the question of empiricism and theory comes in his interrogation of structure in the work of Lévi-Strauss (Derrida 1978b). It is through this engagement that a specific formulation of the general negotiation between science and interpretation can be extracted. Derrida names this negotiation *play*, although this play is not banal textual free play, an interpretive meandering without effect, or vacuous wordplay. Play operates within a tightly constrained textual relation to "structure" and functions in a manner similar to the other hinge terms in Derrida's oeuvre—trace, pharmakon, gram, *différance*, supplement. Play embodies a certain movement and dislocation within empirical structure; this notion of play permits an understanding of the relation between science and interpretation, empiricism and theory, that is more complex, and more productive, than the traditional notions of static opposition or demarcation.

While Lévi-Strauss's structuralism is a critique of anthropological empiricism, Derrida claims that this critique is not simply a negation. That is, while Lévi-Strauss critically examines empiricism, he also relies on it in order to render that critical examination viable. Derrida's analysis of this strategy in Lévi-Strauss (and in the social sciences in general) proceeds through an analysis of structure, center, and origins. I shall follow Derrida's analysis on these points only where it leads to a reformulation of the relation between science and interpretation.

Derrida begins by maintaining that the notion of structure has always been neutralized or reduced by a center that is a point of presence, an origin and a telos. The function of this center is to "orient, balance, and organize the structure" (1978b, 278). As well as providing this stabilizing and organizing effect, the center also binds what Derrida calls the play of the structure. That is, the center limits play by installing a point of presence and an origin around which play must operate, and to which it can be reduced. Consequently, this center allows only a certain, limited notion of play: "The concept of a centered structure is in fact the concept of a play based on a fundamental ground, a play constituted on the basis of a fundamental immobility and a reassuring certitude, which itself is beyond the reach of play" (Derrida 1978b, 279). While the notion of structure itself has hitherto been unthinkable without this center, it is an "unthinkable" structure, a structure without a center, that Derrida attempts to pursue in this paper. Specifically, he wants to be able to think the structurality of structure without reference to a center, origin, or presence. Through this rethinking of structurality, play, and center in Lévi-Strauss, we find our way to a reformulated notion of the relation between science and interpretation.

The opposition between nature and culture has been a central problematic in Lévi-Strauss's work. More specifically, Derrida claims that throughout this work there has been a tacit recognition of the necessity yet impossibility of this opposition. Derrida suggests that an encounter with this division and its irreducible force prompts two possible responses. First, in a response that could be named critical, "one might want to question systematically and rigorously the history of these concepts" (1978b, 284). That is, the nature/culture distinction would be subjected to a "historical" scrutiny that would seek not simply to locate these concepts philosophically or philologically, but to "deconstitute" their foundational status. The second response (and this is the response that Derrida accredits more fully to Lévi-Strauss) would consist in conserving all these old concepts within the domain of empirical discovery while here and there denouncing their limits, treating them as tools which can still be used. No longer is any truth value attributed to them; there is a readiness to abandon them, if necessary, should other instruments appear more useful. In the meantime, their relative efficacy is exploited, and they are employed to destroy the old machinery to which they belong and of which they are themselves pieces. (Derrida 1978b, 284)

That is, Lévi-Strauss borrows empirical data and methodologies that are informed by the nature/culture opposition in order to render the nature/culture division problematic. Lévi-Strauss names this procedure *bricolage*, as the bricoleur is he who uses those tools at his disposal for whatever task is at hand. Because his work is not shut off from, or in opposition to, the traditional empirical ethnography that he criticizes, Lévi-Strauss claims that his work resists totalization or certitude. That is, an incompletion or openness of a certain kind becomes inevitable within his work (and within the ethnographic domain in general) because new empirical information will always be discovered, foreclosing the possibility of a final or truthful account. For Derrida (1978b), however, this strategy does not provide a sufficiently radical displacement of empirical totalization. The notion of play entailed in bricolage remains problematic in that it is confined within an unreconstructed empirical field: It is a play delimited within a centered structure that is grounded in presence.

In response to this delimitation of play, Derrida suggests that two reasons for the impossibility of empirical totalization can be given (both of which coexist in Lévi-Strauss's work). First (as above), there is the classic formulation, which claims that because of some practical or empirical difficulty, any empirical endeavor is unable to master its subject: "There is too much, more than one can say" (Derrida 1978b, 289). This is perhaps the most common understanding of the limits of empiricism. Secondly, there is a notion of nontotalization as *play*, and this provides us with a radical dislocation of the empirical domain:

> If totalization no longer has any meaning, it is not because the infiniteness of the field cannot be covered by a finite glance or a finite discourse, but because the nature of the field . . . excludes totalization. This field is in effect that of *play*, that is to say, a field of infinite substitutions only because it is finite, that is to say, because instead of being . . . too large, there is something missing from it: a center which arrests and grounds the play of substitutions. (Derrida 1978b, 289)

In this formulation, the limits of the empirical domain are not themselves empirical; rather, the empirical field cannot achieve totalization or certitude because it does not have a center to fix and locate its epistemological play. Consequently, such play reverberates incessantly and with infinite variation within the finite parameters of the empirical field.

There are then, two interpretations of play: a narrow play, which is centered and delimited within a field of presence, and a generalized play, which is the radical dislocation of a center, origin, and presence. Derrida claims that while Lévi-Strauss brings both notions of play into action, Lévi-Strauss retains a nostalgia for origins, natural innocence, and the purity of presence that restricts the more generalized and decentered play. This produces a "saddened, *negative*, nostalgic, guilty, Rousseauistic" (Derrida 1978b, 292) play, the other side of which would be a Nietzschean affirmation, an active interpretation, which produces a play without certitude. This affirmative interpretation of play is not simply a reversal, however. Rather, the formulation of play as the affirmation of a nonorigin is situated before the division of science and interpretation, and instead of being a procedure for negotiating within the empirical domain (as with the more narrow interpretation of play), it is our means for understanding the empirical domain itself. This second notion of play is what makes the division between science and interpretation possible; coming before both absence and presence, data and theory, this notion of play constitutes the domain of empiricism as a whole.

Having formulated these two interpretations of play, one nostalgic and one affirmative, Derrida does not suggest that we are then able to choose one over the other. Rather, these two interpretations of play are "absolutely irreconcilable even if we live them simultaneously and reconcile them in an obscure economy—[they] together share the field which we call, in such a problematic fashion, the social sciences" (Derrida 1978b, 293). More specifically, it is the difference between these two types of play that defines the field of the social sciences. This irreducible, undecidable difference between interpretations is the "origin" and the "center" of the social sciences. If the center is "not a fixed locus, but a function" (Derrida 1978b, 280), then we can now name this function *play* or *différance*. For this reason, the idea of a line or a demarcation is unable to sustain the complexity of the relation between science and its others. Indeed, now we can see more clearly how drawing a line between science and interpretation is always a reductive and conventionalizing gesture. Such divisions and demarcations seek to arrest the empirical play internal to psychological structure, and in so doing they negate the dynamic of a more generalized play that brings empiricism, as such, into force. The effects of these demarcations will always be to locate, divide, and terminate the "activity" that generates and shapes the field of social science. It is perhaps for this reason that traditional philosophies of science such as Popper's and Kuhn's have had such an oppressive and ultimately unproductive effect on domains such as psychology and psychoanalysis. These readings of psychology and psychoanalysis are impoverished not only because they attempt to delimit empirical play inside a field of knowable and finite possibilities, but also because they misrecognize the more generalized play that functions within and "outside" the empirical field itself as its condition of possibility.

We will see in some detail in later chapters how, unfortunately, the same general neutralization of play is enacted with increasing frequency in commentary on connectionist theories of cognition. Specifically, the analytic commentators (who form the vast majority of those interested in the theory and philosophy of connectionism) seek to harness the functional and architectural aspects of connectionist networks in order to reinstate a center, albeit a cleverly reformulated one, within cognitive structure. On the other hand, the much smaller group of commentators who come to connectionism via the texts of Derrida, Heidegger, and Freud (see, for example,

Globus 1995) have tended to figure connectionist networks in radical excess of a structural center. Where the first group misrecognizes how any center/structure will always be undermined by the radical operations of play, the second group is unable or unwilling to negotiate how this generalized play always finds itself ensnared in, and reduced by, its relation to the traditional empirical field. Where the first group too readily reinstates the centeredness of empirical structure, the second group too readily figures connectionist networks as utopic structures radically beyond a narrow and restrictive empirical play. The difficult task ahead of me now is to read connectionism other than through these conventionalizing or utopic choices—that is, to articulate and explore within connectionist structure the constitutive difficulties and productivities of both empirical play within a finite field and the playing movement of *différance*.

~ Ontological Reduction and the Play of Natural Origins

If the notion of play has allowed us to negotiate a certain understanding of scientificity as other than an oppressive empiricism in rigid opposition to interpretation, it also allows a finer-grained understanding of the details of particular scientific discourses and their objects. In closing this chapter, I will broach some general issues about biological reductionism in order to introduce how this Derridean play can be of some use in the context of the natural, biological, or behavioral sciences. Diprose's (1991) critique of genetics as the origin of difference will be of interest in this regard. The questions of *différance* and neurology as a locatable origin that I only preface here will become increasingly important in the examination of connectionism and psychical location in later chapters.

Reductionism functions in contemporary scientific psychology to ground the complexity and intangibility of psychological phenomena in the apparent surety of biological matter. (See Valentine 1992 for an overview of recent approaches to reductionism in psychology. My approach to reductionism is more narrowly ontological, and I am not interested—as the majority of analytic commentators on psychological reductionism seem to be—in fixing a certain kind of epistemological relation between psychology and the biological sciences.) Reductionism seeks to transpose the psychically internal and unobservable into a discrete, empirically verifiable presence: The demise of behaviorism notwithstanding, it would appear that logical positivism still underpins the intelligibility of contemporary psychological research. Most often this psychological presence is grounded neurologically: Reductionism becomes (neurocognitive) localization. This search for a neurological location or origin for psychological and behavioral phenomena has generated a number of culturally and scientifically authoritative hypotheses: that the complex psychological dissociation of schizophrenia or the affective and somatic dampening of depression is reducible to synaptic biochemistry (Kramer 1994; Snyder 1980); that the perception of shape and movement is reducible to the architecture and function of cells in the visual cortex (Hubel and Wiesel 1979); that individual differences in personality are reducible to the vicissitudes of thalamocortical activity (Robinson 1987); and that the pattern of different sexualities is reducible to differences in hippocampal nuclei (LeVay 1991). While few such theories claim a complete or exact reduction of psychical or behavioral phenomena to biological locations, nonetheless in every case the reductionist tendencies of these hypotheses attribute to the biological a fundamental or irresistible psychical effect.

I will figure reductionism, in its traditional guises, as the foreclosure of play or *différance*. However, I will be keen to assert that this is not simply an epistemological foreclosure, it is also a delimitation of play within matter itself. The issue, then, is not simply that neurological, biochemical, or genetic discourses epistemologically reduce the complexity of psychological phenomena to biological explanations; it is also (and this is perhaps the more important point) that these discourses have constituted the biological as fixed, locatable, and originary. My interrogation of biological reductionism is less a critique of the reductionist drive per se (Kramer's 1994 "reductive" analysis of depression, for example, generates a series of compelling hypotheses about the nature of subjectivity) than it is a critique of the fixed and rigid ground (erroneously equated with the natural) on which that reduction takes place. It is the metaphysical desires that reductive tendencies convey, rather than the inclinations for the biological, that are my concern. What is "reduced" in biologically reductionist theories of psychology is not only the psychological phenomena involved but also biology itself. While psychological phenomena are rescued from such circumstances by critiques of reductionism, biology itself rarely is. If biology can be dislocated from the fixed and lifeless parameters set by reductionism (and this will be the focus of chapters 4 and 5), if biology can be adequately articulated as a site of play, then we have come some way toward neutralizing the effect and domination of biologically reductionist principles in psychology.

There is a convergence of deconstructive ideas, names, and strategies that will enable me to approach the issue of biological reductionism without reducing the biological. This final, brief section will begin the process of prizing biological reductionism away from its usual affiliation with the expiration of play. To pursue these ideas I will start with a detour through *différance*. "Located" in the impossible space between presence and absence, *différance* is the means by which Derrida subverts the possibility of a definitive location, presence, or origin. The critique of presence entailed in *différance* emerges, in the first instance, from Derrida's deconstruction of the Saussurian sign. The sign, as it is understood in traditional semiology, stands in for something that is not present. Thus the sign has been understood as the mark of an absent presence, a deferred origin:

> The sign is usually said to be put in the place of the thing itself, the present thing, "thing" here standing equally for meaning or referent. The sign represents the present in its absence. It takes the place of the present. When we cannot grasp or show the thing, state the present, the being-present, when the present cannot be presented, we signify, we go through the detour of the sign. (Derrida 1982, 9)

The sign, as the representative of an absent presence, is presumed to be both secondary (to the primacy of the present) and provisional (in other circumstances the thing itself can be presented). Thus the sign suggests the possibility of a movement toward the presentation of what has been temporarily deferred, toward the unmediated display of a fully present origin. The secondary and provisional formulation of the sign always signals the ontological desire that the full presence of the thing itself can be recovered.

Derrida posits "something like an originary *différance*" (Derrida 1982, 9) to contest the possibility of a fully present but deferred origin that traditional formulations of the sign imply. This critique of presence is intimately connected to a critique of identity—a critique that comes from Saussure's (1959) insight that language consists not of a collection of present identities, but of an unlocatable mobility of differences without positive terms. For Saussure, difference does not describe a comparative relation between identities that already exist; instead, difference is the constitutive production of those identities. Consequently, the identity of any one sound or idea is dependent on its difference from all other sounds or ideas in the linguistic system, which are themselves nonidentical. It is this difference, which is itself nowhere present, which has no qualities or characteristics (but is the possibility for the qualities and characteristic that mark difference), that Derrida names *différance*. This *différance* is the play, movement, or economy that produces identities and differences while refusing the popular and scientific expectation that any identity or difference can be present in and of itself, and refer only to itself:

> What is written as *différance*, then, will be the playing movement that "produces"—by means of something that is not simply an activity—these differences, these effects of differences. This does not mean that the *différance* that produces differences is somehow before them, in a simple and unmodified—in-different—present. *Différance* is non-full, non-simple, structured and differentiating origin of differences. Thus, the name "origin" no longer suits it. (Derrida 1982, 11)

The name *différance* is particular to the context of semiology, but the "playing movement" that could take the name *différance* is what defers and displaces the possibility of any origin. This playing movement can be thought of not only as semiological, but also as natural or physical—that is, as a playing movement between referents without positive terms: a natural or physical *différance* that operates with (but not *within*) semiotic play. To call this a semiosis of the natural is tautological, for the natural is already naturally semiotic, which is to say, naturally natural. We can speak of the semiosis of nature only when we are prepared to entertain, rigorously, the notion of a natural semiosis. Under the sway of *différance*, the nature of the natural or the physical is now no longer reducible to material presence, stasis, or location. As the playing movement of a nonpresent, nonoriginary nature, *différance* thwarts the reductionist's desire to reveal, in biology, the final and incontestable foundation of the psyche. Or at least, any origin so "revealed" will be non-innocent and historically contingent.

Reductionism in psychology is the attempt to establish the presence and stability of the psyche outside the play of *différance*. This reduction is usually neurological because neurology is mired in an economy of naturalized presence. As I will argue in the next chapter, this neurological economy is authorized in no small part by the conviction that neurology is cognitive matter disconnected from the predicaments of the noncerebral body. It is this conviction that has allowed certain commentators to posit neurology as the liberation from "restrictive metaphysical assumptions." However, as Derrida notes with reference to semiological origins (but which we could analogize to the revelation of natural origins), the attempt to terminate the play of *différance* is a metaphysical gesture of the most traditional kind:

> It could be shown that metaphysics has always consisted in attempting to uproot the presence of meaning [or referent], in whatever guise, from *différance*; and every time that a region or layer of pure meaning or a pure signified [or a pure referent] is allegedly rigorously delineated or isolated this gesture is repeated. (Derrida 1981, 32)

However, such metaphysical gestures are unable to be fully enacted: There is no delineation of a neuropsychological origin that is not exceeded by the play of its elements. And this, as we have seen with Lévi-Strauss, is the condition of the scientific domain in general. Its incessant and always incomplete productions are not the effect of an elusive or infinite empirical domain; rather, they are the effect of a natural economy that always already exceeds its own ontological constraints.

Rosalyn Diprose (1991) has carefully demonstrated how this ontological reduction is enacted, and defeated, in the discourses of pure and applied genetics. It is widely assumed that the genetic code is the origin of biological differences, and perhaps more controversially even of psychological differences (see Jensen 1972; Herrnstein and Murray 1994). More than perhaps any other scientific domain, genetics represents to the popular and scientific imagination the final grounding of interpretation: The genetic code is the origin of biological differences and the delimitation of biological play.

Diprose's argument is not simply that there can be no direct link between the genetic code and its expression (i.e., a disjunction between genotype and phenotype), as many of the liberal critics of genetics have contended, and indeed as is already presumed in genetic theory itself. Rather, she contends that there is no originary code from which such expression could arise. She argues that a genetic origin is always deferred and dispersed through difference and otherness. This dispersal of the genetic origin operates on a number of levels. First, the expression of genetic material is determined not by the nucleotide bases per se, but by the pairing and contiguous relation (or ordering) of these bases. Phenotypic expressions of difference and sameness are not solely the effect of a particular piece of genetic material, but also of the interval between genetic elements. A genetic origin grounded in a present genetic material is thus deferred via relational spacing. Second, the spacing of nucleotide bases is deferred temporally via a process of translation and doubling that never returns to an original code. In order for the "originary" DNA code to become operative, it must first be replicated into a mirror image of itself. This process is then reversed. However, this reversal does not lead us back to the "original" nucleotide code but instead to "the other of the other" (Diprose 1991, 72), which is never identical to its "origin." The process of DNA-RNA transcription effects a double deferral: from the nucleotide bases to their interval, and from their interval to a series of transcriptions that never return to the origin. It is the processes of spacing, differ-ence, and translation without original—rather than the repetition of the same from a present origin—that determines genetic effect. It is this trace of a trace, rather than a present and locatable code, that is the genetic "origin."

Diprose's analysis of the nonorigin of the genetic code disrupts a scientific hierarchy of reduction that seeks to ground itself in a fixed biological location: in the gene itself. She shows that genetic differ-ence is grounded nowhere—it has no origin except as *différance*. Thus genetic difference is not an expression from an origin, but instead an iterative play that produces its own origin. Even here, in biological matter that most potently represents the possibility of ori-gins, presence, and determinable effects, play is incessantly opera-tive. A genetics that is unable to accommodate or articulate this movement will always misread and attenuate the natural play of molecular differences.

My goal, then, will not be to prohibit the biological within the do-main of psychology; it is not the case that psychology should not or cannot approach certain genetic, neurological, and biological do-mains. However, where such approaches are made, they need to be dislocated from traditional reductionist desires about the nature of genetic, neurological, or biochemical matter. In the coming chapters, I will pursue the vicissitudes of neurological matter as they deter-mine the psyche and cognition. My goal is to rethink the place of neurology in the psychological domain such that it need not rely on location, presence, and an origin. Despite its usual placement at the origin of psychology, neurology will be found to operate in excess of the tight scientific constraints of neurocognitive reductionism.

~ Conclusion

This chapter has been an attempt not to rescue the scientific or the natural from criticism, but rather to locate them more productively within our current critical milieu. Specifically, I have attempted to situate (the epistemological and ontological origins of) scientific psychology within a critical space that does not reify, or fetishize, or negate, the scientific and the biological.

In the first instance, this has required a detailed examination of the relation between the interpretive and empirical forces that animate psychology. Produced within an irreducible historical and epistemological negotiation between science and interpretation, scientific psychology is at once deeply equivocal and thoroughly conventionalized. This play between equivocation and conventionalization is constitutive: A more careful practice will not be able to correct or stabilize psychology. At the same time, we are unable to withdraw from this disorderly pursuit of the scientific. Psychology is not possible except through this difficult and incessant mediation between science and interpretation. While this indeterminacy is figured most often as a crisis of identity, and as the constraining limitation of psychology's possibilities, I have argued that it is the very condition that enables and maintains psychology's productivity.

The Derridean questions that have been advanced here to articulate this equivocation-conventionalization do not promise a new mode of scientific practice. Contra Kurtzman (1987) and Globus (1995), there is no Derridean or deconstructive psychology that could be formulated and performed as a better, less metaphysical, more interpretive science. While the deconstructive arguments about presence/absence, structure/play, and empiricism/interpretation have provided unique tools for intervening into the epistemological and ontological aspirations of scientific psychology, they do not posit an alternative to current psychological practice. And while these arguments seek to refigure empiricism at its base, they do not seek to destroy the possibility of a scientific psychology in general.

I have chosen cognitive theory in general and connectionist theory in particular as the means by which I can pursue this generative undoing of scientific psychology. However, connectionism will not offer a utopic resolution to the problematics of neurology, psychology, and reductionism. But then again, neither will deconstruction. Instead, it will be my task to read each against the other, to manipulate both their points of conjunction and their points of incommensurability. In the chapters that follow, I will pursue a reading that is not reducible to purely connectionist or purely deconstructive concerns, but that draws on and encourages the incessant negotiation between these two terrains.

chapter three

Morphologies
of Mind

There is very little written about psychology in a contemporary scientific context that does not in some way invoke either
the computer or the brain. On the one hand, it may be that the mind
is considered to be analogous to a digital computer—a highly complex, but essentially rational, information–processing machine
(Newell and Simon 1972; Pylyshyn 1984). This approach has already been announced whenever the phrase "psychological processing" can be used intelligibly. On the other hand, there is a wealth of
neurological research that has been able to map cortically various
psychological functions (Geschwind 1979; Luria 1973), although
this approach has been more concerned with the clinical implications of topographical localization than with a theory of the psyche
per se. Broadly speaking, there have been two general approaches to
contemporary scientific studies of psychology: the *computational*,
which takes the mind to be the formal manipulation of symbolic information, and the *neurological*, where psychological capacities are
located in delineated cortical and subcortical regions.

These two approaches offer different and incommensurate
accounts of psychology. Emerging from the recently developed field

of cognitive science, the computational approach has eschewed the idea of neurological plausibility, aiming instead to produce a theory of cognition that exists independently of biological constraints. Within the neurological approach, a theory of the mind is presumed rather than explicitly formulated. It is the neurological location of observable psychological and behavioral capacities that has been of interest, not an account of the mental relation between these capacities. Consequently, these two approaches have been separate and divergent paths in psychological research. Neurological data have had no impact on traditional cognitive theories of memory, perception, attention, and so on, and cognitive theory appears to have had little relevance to empirical work on brain structure and function (Churchland 1986).

More recently, however, these two different paths have been converging. Bringing neurological data to bear on cognitive theory, and vice versa, this convergence of interests has produced a domain that I will call the *neurocognitive sciences* (but is sometimes referred to as cognitive neuroscience or computational neuroscience). A hybrid field that can no longer be contained within traditional disciplinary boundaries, neurocognitive science encompasses a wide range of cognitive and neurological research on the psyche (see Baron 1987; Churchland 1995; Churchland and Sejnowski 1992; Gluck and Rumelhart 1990; Kosslyn and Koenig 1992). What differentiates this hybrid domain from either of its constituent traditions is the view that neither neurology nor cognitive theory, taken in their usual form, can furnish us with an adequate account of psychology. The psychological processing exemplified in traditional cognitive theory—subject more to formal logic than to the constraints of embodied cognitive systems—is being materialized as neurologically plausible cognition (e.g., What are the neurological constraints to the idea of separate memory stores such as short-term memory and long-term memory?). Likewise, neurological accounts of psychology are being disciplined within the parameters of known cognitive dynamics (e.g., Is there a clear dissociation between verbal and spatial capacities, as theories of hemispheric specialization suggest?). Connectionism is exemplary of this neurocognitive approach: Merging both cognitive theory and neurological constraints, connectionism offers theories and models of psychological processing that differ in important ways from earlier cognitive and neuropsychological accounts (McClelland, Rumelhart, and Hinton 1986).

This chapter will offer a critical account of the two traditions that have merged to form this new neurocognitive field. This is not an exercise in explicitly comparing and contrasting these two traditions, as if to adjudicate their weaknesses and strengths and then determine a viable hybrid from the two. Nor is it my goal to draw a historical lineage that would map the discursive or institutional convergence of these two domains. Rather, this chapter will examine some of the theoretical presuppositions of each tradition, so that the extent to which these presuppositions have been rewritten or carried through into the "new" neurocognitive sciences may be ascertained. While there are a number of different theoretical avenues that could be explored in these two traditions, I will focus on the problematics of morphology and embodiment. I will argue that there is a certain morphological structure (logocentric and phallic) that has underwritten traditional computational and neurological theories of psychology. I will propose that computationalism and neurologism have been successful in psychology not because of the veridicality of the computer and brain metaphors, but because what is presupposed by embodiment in each case fits with certain masculinist and logocentric presumptions about psychological functioning. Nonetheless, within both the computational and neurological traditions there is a certain morphological volatility that resists this logocentric and phallic containment. This volatility—drawn from the very heart of these theories—will become the means by which these traditions may be realigned against the constraints of stasis, presence, and location.

Before I start this account, a few words about terminology. I will use the words *mind, cognition*, and *psyche* separately and differently. I take the idea of mind to be indebted primarily to a traditional analytic philosophy of mind, which has usually posited mind in opposition to a certain static and conventionalized account of the body. I take cognition to be the contemporary scientific instantiation of mind, referring to the quantifiable processes of thinking, reasoning, problem solving, or pattern recognition that occupy cognitive psychology. The terms *mind* and *cognition*, as I use them, refer explicitly to the idea of psychology that is entailed in these traditions. I take psyche to be a rather old-fashioned term that has lost currency in many contemporary contexts. Drawing on the lexicon of psychoanalysis, I use psyche where I am attempting to cut across the narrow morphologies of psychology entailed in theories of mind and cognition.

~ "Loving the Computer": Cognition, Embodiment, and the Influencing Machine

In principle, it is possible to be a cognitive scientist without loving the computer; but in practice, skepticism about computers generally leads to skepticism about cognitive science. (Gardner 1987, 40)

The emergence of cognitive psychology goes hand in hand with the development of a more broadly based cognitive science. It has been usual to trace the beginnings of contemporary, mainstream cognitive science to September 1956, when the Symposium on Information Theory was held at MIT (Newell and Simon 1972; Gardner 1987). The program at this symposium included Newell and Simon's presentation of the Logic Theory Machine, Chomsky's new grammar based on information theory, and George Miller's influential paper on the capacity of short-term memory (the "magic number seven"). This symposium was widely seen as having brought to fruition the promised new science that had been evident since the Lashley, von Neumann, and McCulloch papers at the Hixon Symposium at the California Institute of Technology in 1948 (Jeffress 1951). This new science brought together research from cybernetics, computer technology, information theory, formal logic, neurology, and linguistics to form an authoritative hybrid domain. In the forty years since, cognitive science has influenced each of these disciplinary knowledges and has become a powerful, lucrative, and highly productive interdisciplinary field in its own right.

This "cognitive revolution" has been felt acutely in psychology. The increasing importance of a cognitive paradigm in psychology since the 1950s has been attributed to a variety of causes, the most popular of these being the inevitable decline of behaviorism's theoretical and experimental authority, advances in computer technology, and the consequent development of an information-processing model of cognition (Gardner 1987). By offering the first sustained argument (within psychology) for the modeling of psychology on computational processes, and differentiating such an approach from psychodynamic, behaviorist, and neurological accounts, Neisser is usually seen as the founder of cognitive psychology:

> A book like this one might be called "Stimulus Information and its Vicissitudes." As used here, the term "cognition" refers to all the processes by which the sensory input is transformed, reduced, elaborated, stored, recovered, and used. It is concerned with these processes even when they operate in the absence of relevant stimulation, as in images and hallucinations. Such terms as *sensation, perception, imagery, retention, recall, problem–solving,* and *thinking,* among many others, refer to hypothetical stages or aspects of cognition. (Neisser 1967, 4)

In such a system, there is a one-to-one mapping between human thinking and the computation of a machine: Both the mind and the computer "accept information, manipulate symbols, store items in 'memory' and retrieve them again, classify inputs, recognize patterns and so on" (Neisser 1976, 5). Many cognitive psychology textbooks figure this information-processing model textually: The chapters are laid out—in a systematic progression from the sensible to the intelligible—to follow the transition from perception and sensation, to memory and attention, and to the higher-order processes of language, problem solving, and reasoning (see Lindsay and Norman 1977; Neisser 1967; Rumelhart 1977 for early examples of such textbooks, and Best 1992; Kosslyn and Andersen 1992; Solso 1995 for more recent examples of the same tendency). The cognitive turn in psychology has been a very prosperous one. Like behaviorism before it, cognitive psychology now dominates scientific psychology to the exclusion of any other approach. Psychology has become cognition.

I will not become directly involved in the arguments for and against modeling the mind on computers, as they are already well rehearsed in the literature: Churchland (1986), Dreyfus (1979, 1992), and Searle (1980) have all argued against the computer metaphor of mind, although for different reasons, while Fodor (1990) and Pylyshyn (1984) give strong support for the essentially computational nature of mind. These arguments have perhaps run the course of their natural critical life, relying as they do on early (i.e., nonneurological) understandings of computation. By synthesizing cognitive and neurological constraints, computational neuroscience has refigured the early ground of AI on which such arguments were conducted (see Churchland and Churchland 1990). Nonetheless, what remains underexamined in all these debates is the constitutive nature of the analogy that is drawn between computation (be it classical, parallel, or neurological) and cognition. What will be at stake in my argument is not whether early computational theories and models adequately describe or simulate the mind, but rather how psychology, qua cognition, has been constituted through computation. If it can be said that cognition is *like* computation, what are the morphological foundations of this similarity?

~

We need not be too concerned about the legs, eyes, etc. (Turing 1950, 456)

If the isomorphism of computation and cognition is taken seriously, then the problematic of a thinking machine becomes a pertinent consideration. In a paper that has been seminal to contemporary cognitive science, Alan Turing (1950) outlines a means for assessing the question "Can machines think?" This test (the so-called Turing test) has set out the parameters within which most subsequent scientific formulations of cognition have been made. Certain axioms about the computational nature of thinking are being articulated here, and by proposing a working definition of human and machine thinking that "satisfies nearly everyone" (Haugeland 1985, 6), Turing's test has laid down the philosophical foundations for most cognitive research that has followed. I will examine Turing's test in order to ascertain the morphology of these widely satisfactory foundations: What presumptions about the body and about sexual difference have been installed by Turing as axiomatic to cognitive intelligibility?

The Turing test is a game of imitation. The conditions for a thinking machine are met when its responses to a set of problems cannot be differentiated from those of a thinking man. Initially the test is set up using three people—a man (A), a woman (B), and an interrogator of unspecified sex (C). The interrogator is in a separate room from the man and the woman, and it is his or her task to determine which of the two is a man and which is a woman on the basis of their (written) answers to certain questions (e.g., "What is the length of your hair?"). It is A's task to confuse the interrogator (and thus he may lie), and B's task to help (although her truths will be indistinguishable from A's lies). The test proper comes into play by swapping the man (A) with a machine. If the interrogator makes the same sort of judgments, deductions, and guesses after this swap as before, that is, if the interrogator is unable to distinguish the machine's answers from the answers of a man, then this particular machine is said to have passed the Turing test.

There are two things to note here. First, the Turing test is conducted via written or couriered information between the players; there is no bodily, visual, or aural contact between the participants. Very early in the paper Turing impresses upon his reader that this arrangement has the particular advantage of being able to draw "a fairly sharp line" between a man's physical capacities and his intellectual capacities. That is, by separating the players bodily, Turing claims to be able to test a purely intellectual exchange:

> No engineer or chemist claims to be able to produce a material which is indistinguishable from the human skin. It is possible that at some time this might be done, but even supposing this invention available we should feel there was little point in trying to make a "thinking machine" more human by dressing it up in such artificial flesh. The form in which we have set the problem reflects this fact in the condition which prevents the interrogator from seeing or touching the competitors, or hearing their voices. (Turing 1950, 434)

The thinking that Turing promotes need not be dressed up in flesh; the mind can be known directly without detour through real or artificial bodily material. We need not see, hear, or touch our respondents in order to access their cognitive processes. Of course, this desire to draw a sharp line between mind and body, between sensation and intellectuality, lies at the heart of traditional Cartesian dualism. If one of the primary objectives of cognitive science after Turing has been to resolve the Cartesian division of mind and body (i.e., to provide a material account of the mind), then the coherence of this objective is founded in its opposite: the desire for a radical distinction between cognition and flesh. Certain critics of cognitive science may be surprised only at the open declaration of such a desire, for has it not always been clear, they might argue, that computation and cognitive science are invested in the pursuit of bodiless virtual spaces and encounters? Is Turing's declaration not exactly the kind of body-phobia that we have come to expect from the fathers of computational and cognitive science?

An analysis of the morphological foundations of cognitive science will need to be more circumspect that this. Despite Turing's careful plans and intentions, the foundations of cognition are not noncorporeal; the absence of the body is not the means by which cognition's intelligibility is assured. This paradox of anti-Cartesianism being founded on Cartesianism is the key to a more thorough understanding of the ways in which the body is administered in cognitive theory. That is, the relation of the body to cognition in Turing's paper is less a radical negation than it is a careful and generative disavowal. Questions of the flesh, far from being peripheral or dispensable to the nature of cognition, are its most preciously repudiated foundation. Whenever the desire for a separation between cognition and flesh surfaces, what is put into action is not the expulsion of the body but its deliberate restraint. For example, toward the end of his paper, Turing departs on a reverie about the possibility of producing a child-machine and educating it in a manner similar to that of a human child. Turing advises us that as far as the education of the computer-child is concerned, we need not be concerned with legs, arms, or the body in general. Instead, he proposes a learning method that does not presuppose any sensibility or feeling in the machine. In this educational regime, where bodies and sensibility are dispensable, rewards and punishments would be directly intellectual. In contrast to the behaviorist paradigms on which Turing draws, learning (and so cognition in general) would bypass the body altogether. Somewhat surprisingly, however, Turing endorses his argument about the optional nature of legs, eyes, and so on for the cognizing child-machine by comparing its education to that of Helen Keller—as if her deaf, blind, and mute body were no body at all. A more careful consideration of the education of Helen Keller would perhaps demonstrate that she was completely dependent on her ostensibly noncognitive body (particularly her hands) for thought and communication. Helen Keller's body was not the secondary vehicle for cognitive processing that had been animated elsewhere; rather, it appears that her hands were the generative organs of cognitive possibility.

There is a curious logic at work in Turing's example, then, that cannot be reduced to a uncomplicated refusal of the body. What seems evident is that as much as the explicit negation of the body appears to be foundational to the crisp formulation of cognition, this negation always fails. Specifically, Turing argues for the dispensability of the body to cognition via a figure who demonstrates exactly the reverse. Nonetheless, Turing's analogy is not analytically useless (to him or us) for having enacted such a contradiction; what this "failed" analogy discloses is not simply that cognition arises from the body, but that it arises from a particular kind of bodily substance. In the case of Helen Keller, Neisser's list of cognitive attributes—sensation, perception, imagery, retention, recall, problem solving, and thinking—must be located in the flesh. Turing's neglect of this substantive effect for Helen Keller does not signal the exclusion of the body, but rather the inclusion of *a certain kind of body*: a cognitively blind, mute, and deaf body. To this end, the body is never radically absent from Turing's field of cognition; rather, it has been fabricated and naturalized as a benignly noncognitive entity. Turing's fantasy of a discrete cognitive domain and of pure intellectual communication between cognizing subjects is premised not on the eradication of the body, but rather on an attentive constraint and management of corporeal effects.

Second, there is a subtle but crucial transition in the players in Turing's game. Specifically, there is a double displacement of the female player and the corporeality she comes to represent. The Turing test starts with a comparison between the intellect of a man and a woman. This coupling is displaced, and the test proper is enacted through a comparison of the absented man and the machine that has replaced him—the female participant having become peripheral to the main focus of the test. This displacement is enacted a second time later on in the paper when Turing—without explanation—replaces the female respondent with a man. What was initially a differentiation between a man and a woman, and then between a man and a computer (the female respondent having been sidelined), is now streamlined further by ridding the test of the female respondent altogether. She is replaced by a male respondent, and the test is now a direct comparison by the interrogator between this man and a computer. Once this change has been effected, Turing considers "the ground to have been cleared and we are ready to proceed to the debate on our question 'Can machines think?'" (Turing 1950, 442). But by what means has the ground been cleared, and to what effect?

It would seem that Turing fine-tunes the test in this way because the female participant has become excessive and distracting to the goals of the test. The difference between a man and a woman is an initially self-evident but eventually intolerable choice for Turing's game. In the first instance, sexual difference seems to be a straightforward, uncontroversial comparison—reducible, perhaps, to the length of one's hair. More specifically, the difference between a man and a woman seems to be more acute, more readily ascertained than the difference between, say, one man and another. Sexual difference is mobilized as being exemplary of all difference, and thus as the starting point of this thinking game.

However, the utility of sexual difference collapses once the test itself is operative. While it may initiate the test, sexual difference rapidly threatens to undermine the purity of the intellectual exchange that the test performs. If the goal of Turing's test is to establish the parameters within which thinking may be thought, then the female respondent is not merely dispensable to these requirements; she is in excess of them. That is, the particularity of the female respondent threatens to breach the sharp line that Turing has drawn between the players' intellectual and physical capacities. Specifically, the female respondent carries certain bodily differences into the test that are not respectful of a cognitive exchange. The exclusion of the female respondent reveals one of the foundational presumptions of Turing's thinking: The computer and the man are morphologically alike. In the absence of the female player (i.e., in the presence of bodily similarity) it is thought that what differentiates the man and the computer is only a question of intellectuality.

Cognition has been generated in this morphological reflection between man and his selfsame computer; it has been animated through an embodiment that can be shared by a computer and a man but not by a woman. For Turing, cognition is rendered identifiable and intelligible at the moment when the female participant becomes the receptacle for noncognitive corporeality and is excluded from the homo-computational pact of thinking beings. This process is not simply incidental to the constitution of cognition; rather, this projection of a certain, restrictive corporeality onto the female respondent and its subsequent displacement are the very means by which cognition is generated and rendered generative. It is the management of the body of the female respondent, rather than its radical exclusion, that allows the similitude between computer and man to be established. Turing's selfsame cognitive morphology emerges from the interminable movement of the female respondent's body in and out of the field of cognition. Necessary yet intolerable, the body of the female respondent is more central to cognitive intelligibility than Turing, and the tradition that follows from him, would suppose. This is no simple anticorporealism. Rather, the contemporary logic of cognition has been established within a tightly constrained set of bodily corrections and identifications.

~

Turing's account establishes the sexed and bodily structure of cognition. As he is more concerned with the nature of thinking in general, Turing does not examine the way in which information is processed within this structure. The transfer of information is a simple and methodical transportation between players, and presumably the processing of information within each player follows a similar pattern. This direct, discrete, and orderly mode of information transfer and processing is simply the internal reflection of the general morphology that Turing has already established. Once cognition is situated within particular information-processing models (e.g., of memory), however, it becomes clear that this notion of an exact and contained exchange cannot be fully sustained.

Perhaps the exemplary information-processing model in psychology is Atkinson and Shiffrin's (1968) classic (but now outdated) multistore model of memory (see Figure 1). Drawing on the flow diagram paradigm brought from information theory to psychology by Broadbent (1958), Atkinson and Shiffrin model human memory processes through a distinction between structure (which is analogous to computer hardware) and control processes (analogous to computer software). Briefly, information is assumed to enter the information processing system via the senses, and these sensory data are immediately registered by the *sensory register*. Information is held in this store for only a very short period of time (up to a few hundred milliseconds). Information is either lost entirely from the system or transferred to the next stage—*short-term store* (or working memory). As in the sensory register, information is held here only for very short periods of time, although it can be retained longer than in the sensory store, especially if the information is "rehearsed" (i.e., repeated, as in the repetition of a phone number long enough for it to be written down or dialed, and after which it is forgotten). From short-term memory, information is either lost from the system or transferred to the last stage—*long-term store*, where information can be stored permanently.

While the architecture of Atkinson and Shiffrin's model of memory is conventional, the movement of information within this structure is less bound by traditional expectations about the nature of cognitive processing. The transfer of information within this cognitive structure is not the transportation of fully present data, or fully present meanings, from one store to the next. The flow of information within the system is not a process of passive conduction, where the information is carried along as if on a conveyor belt. Rather, information moves between stores as an effect of serial copying:

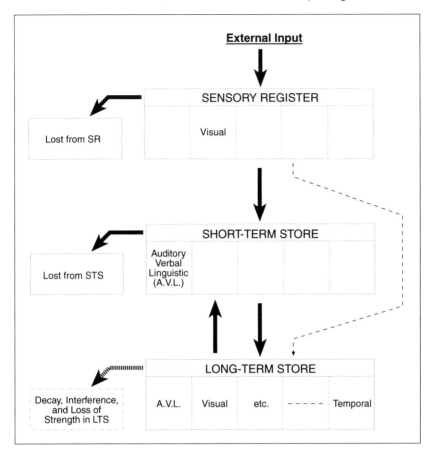

Figure 1 *Atkinson and Shiffrin's (1968) model of memory.*
From R. C. Atkinson and R. M. Shiffrin, Human memory: A proposed
system and its control processes. In K. W. Spence and J. T. Spence (eds.),
vol. 2 (New York: Academic, 1968), 93.

> Note that by information flow and transfer between stores we refer to the same process: the copying of selected information from one store into the next. This copying takes place without the transferred information being removed from its original store. The information remains in the store from which it is transferred and decays according to the decay characteristics of that store. (Atkinson and Shiffrin 1968, 94)

It is in this description of serial copying that the most volatile but least exploited aspect of theories of cognition becomes visible: Cognition is an active and iterative process. The activity of a cognitive system was one of the key differences between the old behaviorist paradigm of psychology and the new cognitive models (Neisser 1967). Where previously the organism and its behavior were the passive effects of stimulus-response associations, these new cognitive models posited a system that actively transforms the information presented to it. Moreover, as Atkinson and Shiffrin suggest, information is transformed (rather than faithfully repeated) through the processes of serial copying and transfer.

This transformation has two faces in Atkinson and Shiffrin's model: one that they formulate explicitly and another that remains latent, but is perhaps the more unruly of the two. First, Atkinson and Shiffrin argue that information is selected and copied as a effect of what is already deemed to be important by the cognitive system as a whole. They attribute the culturally, socially, and individually specific features of memory to the effects of other cognitive systems already in operation (e.g., systems of language or attention, and already established beliefs and expectations). This displacement of cognitive function onto other preexisting internal and external cognitive systems has generated a theory of cognition that is less static and autonomous than that promised under the rubric of formal symbol manipulation. Atkinson and Shiffrin's model provides a way of encompassing the effects of wider social, cultural, and psychical contexts on cognitive function, and in so doing they establish cognition not as the direct translation of sensory data, but as a more broadly interpretive process.

Without dismissing the importance of this dissemination of cognitive function, it should also be noted that cognition remains a self-present and originary process in this model. As Atkinson and Shiffrin envisage it, the displacement of cognition via other systems is a secondary effect visited on an otherwise autonomous procedure of information processing. However, there is another, more radical cognitive displacement already encapsulated in this system, which Atkinson and Shiffrin do not exploit: The mnemic traces in the various memory stores are iterative rather than re-presentational in nature. Where Turing's early cognitive structure presumes the pure and contained transportation of information, Atkinson and Shiffrin's model demonstrates that the cognitive trace is manufactured by the transformative vicissitudes of iteration. That is, cognition is generated through a repetition that is not the re-presentation of a fixed and stable origin. As information is copied and transferred through different memory stores, the cognitive trace (or the mark of processing) is continually being remade. In the sensory store, "a visual stimulus leaves a more or less photographic trace which decays during a period of several hundred milliseconds and is subject to masking and replacement by succeeding stimulation" (Atkinson and Shiffrin 1968, 95). This more or less photographic trace is then copied, transferred, copied, and transferred before it reaches long-term memory. Traces in long-term store are then subject to interference and decay, and their accurate retrieval cannot be guaranteed. To this end, there is no one trace that persists throughout processing. And the trace that is laid down in long-term store has an iterative rather than direct relation to the "original" environmental stimulus. In Atkinson and Shiffrin's model, any cognitive trace is always already a copy: first a copy, in the sensory store, of an external stimulus, and then a copy, in subsequent memory stores, whose "origin" has long since decayed. In chapter 5, I will return to a more detailed examination of this cognitive trace. In the meantime, Atkinson and Shiffrin's model offers the first indication of a cognitive process that is built not on the logic of on/off, presence/absence, original/copy, but on the logic of a interminably transcriptive process.

If the tradition of information processing has been unable to predict reliably, explain, or simulate anything but the most basic (and frankly, uninteresting) aspects of human psychology (as Neisser 1976 has argued at length), this is not because this science is not yet fully developed. The difficulties here are not empirical, they are conceptual: The limits of these cognitive models are reached because they pursue an inert and corporeally restrictive psyche. Powerful as such models are, they will always be dislocated by their own internal and excessive iterative processing. If Atkinson and Shiffrin had been able to more fully elucidate this aspect of their model, cognition might have emerged in a form different from that we know today. Cognition might have become the iterative production and deferral of meaning, rather than the self-present processing of information. As we will see in later chapters, this deferred, differing cognitive trace latent in Atkinson and Shiffrin can be more fully exploited in recent connectionist models of cognition.

~

Under Atkinson and Shiffrin, cognition could be figured a process of active iteration that, by its very nature, resists reduction to unitary determination. However, while empirical models such as this push us toward a recognition of cognition's iterative nature, cognitive theory in general has failed to capitalize on this recognition. While every psychological model of memory since Bartlett (1932) establishes the essentially reconstitutive processes of memory, cognitive theorists still insist on placing a noniterative process of direct translation at the center of their models (e.g., Baddeley 1990). There has been a general tendency toward stasis in cognitive psychology, a stasis that fixes both the structure and processing of cognition within a contained morphology.

The love of the computer has been central to all these formulations. It has been the computer (or, as we will see more fully in later chapters, a certain notion of the computer entailed in traditional AI) that has narrowed the morphology of cognition to an articulation of discrete cognitive traces inside fixed cognitive spaces. There is a fertile nexus between morphology, technology, affect, and cognition that is worth pursuing briefly in relation to these concerns. It is no secret, nor does it appear to be cause for serious concern, that the mind has been modeled on a series of different technological objects (e.g., hydraulic machines, the telephone switchboard, the hologram) before the computer emerged as the current darling of the cognitive science (Gardner 1987). Moreover, as the neuropsychologist Karl Lashley has astutely observed, there is a curious parallel between the history of such theories and the delusions of paranoia: "In Mesmer's day the paranoid was persecuted by malicious animal magnetism, his successors by galvanic shocks, by the telegraph, by radio, and by radar, keeping their delusional systems up to date with the latest fashions in physics" (Lashley, cited in Cobb 1960, xix).

If there is a link between technology and delusion, there is also a link between technology, delusion, and projective fantasies of the body. Victor Tausk (1992), in an accomplished psychoanalytic interpretation of the influencing machine in paranoid delusions, hypothesizes a close relation between the nature of the influencing machine and the patient's own body. An influencing machine is a delusionary device, usually located some distance from the patient (e.g., in another city), that the patient claims is influencing his or her thoughts and actions. Influencing machines are almost always mechanical, and at the time of Tausk's writing (1919) seemingly always operated by men. Tausk was fortunate enough to observe the genesis and transformation of an influencing machine in a young woman—a process that revealed the corporeal foundation of the influencing machinery. Initially manifest in humanlike form, over the course of some weeks the patient's influencing machine became more and more mechanical until it lost any resemblance to her own body.

This transformation suggested to Tausk that every influencing machine is a projection of the patient's own body onto the world. Moreover, the libido motivating the original projection has regressed to an infantile, pregenital stage where the body is shaped by a number of erotogenic zones. More precisely, for Tausk the entire body in this pre-oedipal stage is libidinized, and so the whole body is a genital (thus this body is pregenital in only a very restricted sense of genitality): "The construction of the influencing apparatus in the form of a machine, therefore, represents a projection of the entire body, now wholly a genital" (Tausk 1992, 564). That the influencing body becomes an influencing machine is a defense against this libidinal investment, and its infantile, genital determination: "The patient obviously seeks not to recognize herself in the influencing machine, and thus, in self-protection, she disinvests it of all human features; in short, the less human the appearance of the delusion, the less does she recognize herself in it" (Tausk 1992, 552).

Without wanting to make too much of the similarities between paranoid delusions and the processes of scientific discovery, it is worth noting that the processes of projection and disavowal cannot be contained within the domain of psychopathology. We have already seen in Turing that the human computational machine is a projection of a certain fantasy of embodiment—specifically, the possibility of a noncognitive body, or (in what amounts to the same thing) the possibility of cognition unencumbered by the body. A historical analysis of the metaphorical lineage from hydraulic machine to computer would no doubt find a certain similarity in these objects that makes them so appropriate for the task of representing cognition—specifically, a contained and affectless structure, a functional autonomy, and a direct, observable, and measurable cognitive cause and effect that requires no appeal to unconscious or infantile motivations, all of which we are compelled to recognize as morphologically phallic characteristics. Embodying a masculine infantile genital wish (for control, linearity, autonomy, and passage in the world of men), the computational machine of cognitive theory is an influencing machine of sorts. Disinvested of its bodily features, the computer serves a similar purpose to the paranoiac's machine: The machinery of cognitive theory expresses, in disguised form, a variety of infantile, phallic wishes about the world and about the self. As Tausk himself argues, "The machines produced by man's ingenuity and created in the image of man are unconscious projections of man's bodily structure. Man's ingenuity seems to be unable to free itself from its relations to the unconscious" (Tausk 1992, 569).

~ Location and Decapitation: The Mind-Brain-Body Problem

Nobody has ever doubted, from the time of Epicurus down to the present day, that men think by means of their heads, as they walk by means of their heels. (Anonymous, 1806, cited in Clarke and Jacyna 1987, 220)

It has become a popular and scientific orthodoxy that thinking can be located in the head. Such an idea has keen support from everyday, introspective evidence and from a wealth of neuropsychological research. This part of the chapter will canvass the particular relation of mind and brain to the body that sanctions this orthodoxy in neuropsychology. Like cognitive science, neuropsychology has a constitutive investment in distancing the body from the mind (or, more specifically, the body from the brain), even as it claims for itself an irreducible materiality. As with cognitive science, this produces a psychical (and here, neurological) morphology that is restrictive and moribund. I will be concerned in the first instance with the efficacy of neuropsychology as a scientific response to mind-body dualism: Is the neuropsychological brain the resolution of mind-body dualism or its more subtle redeployment? While the relation of the brain to the mind has been explored extensively, what can be said of the relation of the brain to the body, and how would this impact on a theory of the psyche?

As the sciences of the mind (phrenology, neurology, psychology, psychiatry) gathered data and authority in the nineteenth century, the special metaphysical status accorded to the mind by Cartesian dualism was slowly revoked. It was the development of the computer and the establishment of the brain sciences in the twentieth century that finally rendered the mind material and mechanistic, and thus amenable to scientific and empirical investigation (Flanagan 1991). While not all neuropsychologists would argue a reductive materialism, there is a binding assumption across the field that the materiality of the brain holds a critical place in the determination of psychological function. If, by the late twentieth century, there has been no decisive resolution to Cartesian dualism, there would at least seem to be a general consensus that any serious scientific study of mind must be founded on a materialist antidualism. Despite the enthusiasm with which neuropsychology has been embraced as an antidualist account of the mind, it is my contention that neuropsychology is consonant with, rather than a refutation of, Cartesian dualism. Turning to Descartes's formulation of the brain, a clear and uninterrupted line of inheritance can be deciphered between it and contemporary neuropsychology.

While Descartes separates mind and body as ontologically distinct entities, he is also careful to stress their interrelation. The "I"
that cognizes is separate from the body, but it is also tightly bound to
it: "I and it form a unit" (Descartes 1954, 117). The body is not simply the vessel that contains the mind, and the body is not just one
object among others: Descartes recognizes that there is some special
relation (a close or intimate one) between mind and the body. The
difficulty for Descartes is how to administer communication
between two entities that he has already set up as ontologically distinct and mutually exclusive. This problem is never convincingly
resolved, but his first solution is to mobilize the brain (more specifically, the small pineal gland) as conduit between the immaterial
mind and the material body: "Next, I observe that my mind is not
directly affected by all parts of the body; but only by the brain, and
perhaps only by one small part of that—the alleged seat of common
sensibility" (Descartes 1954, 121). At the end of the "Sixth Medita-
tion" (on the existence of material things and the real distinction
between mind and body), Descartes turns to the brain as a means of
explaining how (bodily) sensation interacts with (conscious) intellect. While he is careful not to suggest that the brain could be equated with the mind (i.e., monism), neither does he equate the brain
with the body in general. Already in Descartes, then, neurological
matter is partitioned off from the rest of the body and is attributed a
special corporeal status and a privileged position with respect to the
operations of the mind.

The pineal gland is named as the part of the body that carries out
some special function with respect to the mind. The pineal gland is
moved by the soul, and through the action of animal spirits on the
nerves, intellect is transmogrified into physical events such as the
movement of limbs. In explaining how an unextended or nonphysi-
cal mind can be made present in the body, Descartes seems to
attribute to the pineal gland a capacity above and beyond the mechanism of the body in general. In some unexplained way, the pineal
gland acts as the relay station between the immaterial mind and the
material body. While not clearly spelled out by Descartes, this suggests that neurological matter has a special ontological status with
respect to the mind-body distinction—it seems to have the capaci-

ties of both, or at least the capacity to translate between the material and the immaterial. Cartesian dualism, then, is mediated by the operations of the brain: The division of mind from body pivots on the plausibility of the brain as an organ of extraordinary corporeal stuff. Here we see, in embryo, a tripartite distinction (mind-brain-body) that emerges with full force in contemporary neuropsychological theories of the mind.

~

The brain of contemporary neuropsychology is presumed to induce a disintegration of Cartesian dualism (Kosslyn and Koenig 1992). By being both ghost and machine, the brain renders this division impossible, and mind-body is collapsed into a monist materialism. The mind comes to be equated with (Armstrong 1990), mapped onto (Luria 1973), or reducible to (P. M. Churchland 1990) the brain. These are mappings or reductions that leave no mental excess: The mind is what the brain does, and the last vestiges of the immaterial and free Cartesian mind are eradicated. Yet what of the Cartesian body in these accounts? Is the brute, mechanical, noncognitive body of Cartesian dualism subject to critique in neuropsychology, or is it merely being reinstated elsewhere? And how effectively has Cartesianism been displaced if its restrictive accounts of the body are still in uncritical circulation? While most commentators on contemporary neuropsychology have focused on mind-brain reductionism, I am more concerned with brain-body reductionism. That is, before we can assess the operations of a mind-brain reduction, we must first of all understand the condensation that has allowed the brain to stand in for, but aside from, the body in general. What type of embodiment does this brain entail? What is the cost to the body in general, and to neurology in particular, of this materialization of the mind through the brain?

If what differentiates scientific mind-brain reduction from Cartesian mind-body dualism is the materialization of the mind, then what unites them is the displacement of the body from the scene that determines the mental. Contemporary neuropsychology rescues only the central nervous system (and then only a small part of that) from Cartesianism; the rest of the body is readily abandoned to brute, noncognitive mechanization. While the brain becomes an organ blessed with a wondrous capacity—it becomes the cradle of cognition—the extraneurological body is relinquished to the psychologically barren reflex arc and is rarely an object of neuropsychological discussion. The problem here is not that there may be two or more kinds of bodily material (and that certain disciplinary distinctions may follow from that), but rather that the divisions between these kinds of material are Cartesian in character. That is, the extraneurological body is not simply nonneurological; more pointedly, it is noncognitive, nonconscious, nonintellectual, nonrational.

The extraneurological body that is implied in contemporary neuropsychology, but never explicitly discussed, is the same degraded, unthinking, unknowing body that is to be found in Descartes's philosophy of mind, and on which that philosophy is founded. This is a body that can be approached via physiology, biomedicine, biophysics, microbiology, biochemistry, and so on but it remains inarticulable as a cognitive or psychical corpus. No innocent division of bodily matter, the sequestration of cognitive effects in the brain and the concomitant evacuation of psychical effect from the body enforces an ontology that is violent and restrictive in its effects. More specifically, it is the preservation and containment of Cartesianism in the extraneurological body that allows the Cartesian capacities of consciousness, rationality, and intellect—which have never been seriously in question—to be conferred on neurology. The nature of neurological matter as cognitive, then, is directly attributable to a Cartesianism that has been repositioned but not resolved.

The instantiation of the brain as mind impels not a termination of dualism but its careful redeployment; not a generalized materialism but a *decapitation*. The neuroscientific brain, as the scientific heir to consciousness, rationality, and intellect, has been disconnected from the rest of the body. Through this decapitation, the disembodied brain (and often the head in general) becomes the seat of the intellect, and the headless body becomes the home of sensation and the guardian of the passions. No monist materialism, this is simply Cartesianism in material form. In a powerful turn of events, traditional mind-body dualism has been displaced and disguised through *embodiment*: The body itself, dichotomized between upper (brain, sight, voice) and lower (genitals, digestion, excretion, and the derogated sense of touch), becomes the material-scientific sphere of Cartesianism. Contemporary neuropsychology dissolves a superficial mind-body opposition via the materiality of the brain but redeploys its cognate couplings (intellect-sensation, reason-emotion) in the division of brain and body. In this way, the goals of neuropsychological materialism seem to fall more in line with raising the cortical regions of the body to the lofty heights of consciousness, rationality, and intellect than with dragging the mind through the mud of a generalized embodiment.

If the logic of decapitation generates a restrictive extraneurological body, it also formulates neurology itself according to a static and delibidinized morphology. Simon LeVay's (1991; 1993) controversial hypothesis concerning the biological substrates of sexuality is exemplary in this regard. It would not be unreasonable to expect that the conjunction of neurology and sexuality might reorient the conventional morphology of neurological matter, but in fact LeVay's study further promulgates a static, hygienic, and contained neurology. The first presumption of LeVay's study—as with neuropsychological research in general—is that the brain is a solid and quantifiable organ that offers itself readily as the originary ground to which sexuality could be assigned. This solid, originary ground is generated, in the first instance, by the distance that LeVay places between neurological matter and the body. Explicitly positioning himself in opposition to the Freudian accounts of perverse and normal sexuality, LeVay gives an account of sexuality from which the body is almost entirely absent. The bodily material of Freud's accounts of sexuality—the hand, the skin, the mouth, the anus, the genitals—is put aside in favor of hypothalamic nuclei. Nonetheless, it is not these neurological inclinations per se that present difficulties. What does emerge as a problem is that the character, intent, and effects of such neurological inclinations are established through a recoil from certain forms of bodily matter. Opening a book-length defense of his hypothalamic hypothesis with a quote from *Romeo and Juliet*, LeVay makes this brain-body separation explicit: "Mercutio offers Romeo an explanation for his amorous feelings that is as inaccurate as it is romantic. Yet in one respect Mercutio was closer to the truth than many of his contemporaries: he located these feelings, not in the heart, liver, or bowels, but in the brain" (LeVay 1993, xi).

The generative paradox at the center of LeVay's research is that the materialization of sexuality requires a distancing from the body. Moreover—and this seems all the more curious in a study of sexuality—this distancing from the body is a deliberate distancing from affect, sensation, and libido. LeVay's reductive division of sexuality into male-typical and female-typical behavior follows naturally from this libidinal foreclosure. If the body, its organs, and its libidinal effects can be so quarantined outside the scope of neurological matters, then the brain is shored up as neutral, stable, asexual ground. It is this distancing from bodily effects that divests the brain of its corporeal and erotic potentialities. The brain may administer sexuality, but erotics are external to its nature. It is clear that the sexuality doctored by LeVay is risibly simple in its orientation. So too, the neurology that circulates in LeVay's research is sterile and inert. By thinking neurology as the nonsensational, nonaffective arbiter of sexuality, LeVay reinstates in neurology the privilege accorded to Cartesian mind: stasis, self-presence, and rationality. Even the arrival of sexuality has failed to pervert the conventionalized, upright morphology of the brain. Far from reorganizing a conventional neurological morphology, LeVay's coupling of neurology and sexuality produces its most successful instantiation.

While Freud is figured by LeVay as the father of psychological theories of sexuality, Freud was also a neurologist, and curiously enough, the neurology that Freud championed did not entail the repudiation of the body, affect, and libido that is central to LeVay's research. Importantly, those neurologists this century who have been most aware of the relation of neurology to body (e.g., Goldstein 1995; Head 1920; Schilder 1950) are directly influenced by (although not necessarily acquiescent to) Freudian psychoanalysis. The clinical origin of studies of neurosis in the study of the nervous system has meant that there is a careful negotiation of the relation of psyche to neurology in Freud's work. Unlike the sterile nature of LeVay's neuroscience, Freud's neuroscience was more carefully tied to the movements and affects of the body. In the next two chapters, Freud's 1891 and 1895 accounts of neurology and psychology will

be one way of exploiting a different kind of neuropsychological morphology, as it is to be found in connectionist theories and models.

~

While contemporary neuropsychology was given its conditions of
possibility in Descartes, the shift from mind-body dualism to mind-
brain reductionism was more actively pursued in the nineteenth
century by the new physiologists and neuropsychologists such as
Flourens, Broca, Wernicke, Hughlings Jackson (Young 1970), and
through phrenology, evolutionary theory, and the establishment of a
scientific psychology. Within the period of time from Descartes to
the late nineteenth century, the focus of inquiry shifted from the
interior of the brain (the pineal gland) to the outer surfaces of the
brain (the cortex). Somewhat precociously, Gall's craniology took
this trend out past the brain itself to the skull: Psychological faculties were presumed to be located in the brain, and the more
endowed one was with a particular faculty, the larger was one's
brain at this point, and the greater the swelling of the skull to accommodate its presence.

> *Seat and external appearance of the organ of Circumspection:*
> The convolutions marked . . . constitute the surface or final
> expansion of this organ, on the two hemispheres of the brain. A
> large development of these convolutions raises the superior-
> posterior outer portion of the parietal bone into a lateral promi-
> nence, so that, to the eye, or the touch, the head presents a very
> broad surface in its superior-posterior lateral region. On the
> contrary, the head will be very narrow in this region, when the
> organ is little or moderately developed. This last shape is met
> with in inconsiderate, precipitate, heedless men, and very gen-
> erally in beggars and people who voluntarily engage in doubt-
> ful enterprises. (Gall 1835, 202)

Through this method it was maintained that all the qualities of
a Cartesian intellect, rather than merely being *translated* via an interior organ, could be physically *located* in the brain itself. Cartesianism itself remained intact, and was perhaps fortified by this materialization of the mind. While Gall is commonly taken as a psycho-

logical charlatan, such a reputation may be unwarranted; it was Spurzheim's popularization of organology, rather than Gall's own work, that led to the fanciful speculations for which phrenology is remembered today (Clarke and Jacyna 1987). While Gall's organology quickly dissipated into quackery, the central tenets of his science flourished more or less unchanged throughout the rest of the nineteenth century. In fact, Gall's organology contains some of the key empirical and philosophical concerns that have shaped contemporary neuropsychology. Specifically, it has been the debates over localization (can the mind be located in circumscribed areas of the brain?) that have shaped the direction of neuropsychological research in the period since Gall.

In the 1880s Broca and Wernicke announced the discovery of circumscribed cortical regions responsible for language production and comprehension (Clarke and Jacyna, 1987). Following these discoveries, there was a flurry of activity to find the neurological locale of other psychological centers. Where the phrenologists had looked for avarice, quick-wittedness, and criminality, these neurologists searched for centers for writing, concept formation, mathematical calculation, reading, and orientation in space, and they attempted to locate these centers not on the skull but in the outermost layer of the brain, the cortex (Luria 1973). Typically, these early localizationists claimed that there was a one-to-one relation between a particular anatomical feature of the brain and a particular psychological faculty. While less openly speculative than Gall, and more respectable in their methodologies, these localizationists were no less invested in the idea of the psyche as a locatable neurological presence.

While localization theory dominated nineteenth-century neuropsychology, its claims did not go uncontested. As early as 1824, Flourens (cited in Kosslyn and Koenig 1992) demonstrated, using the brains of birds, that recovery of function was possible irrespective of where the nervous system had been damaged; there seemed to be no one-to-one relation between locale and function. This type of empirical evidence has been put forward repeatedly since then to refute extreme localizationism. In this century, Lashley (1960a) and Luria (1973) were perhaps the most active proponents of an antilocalizationist view of brain function. Lashley's work is exemplary of the tendency toward holism that has marked the reactions to localization. He replicated Flourens's finding that damage to large areas of cortex (this time in the rat) did not disrupt previously acquired habits and did not inhibit further learning. Similarly he was unable to find any local connections that determined specific cognitive functions. In reviewing some twenty years of his experimental research on learning, Lashley (1960c) concluded that the search for an isolated and localizable psychological trace (the engram) was in vain. He suggested that the engram is represented in a distributed fashion throughout a cortical region; this idea made an important contribution to the rise of contemporary theories of connectionism (Valentine 1992).

The nineteenth-century localizationist project, while tempered somewhat, has continued as the dominant theory of the mind-brain in the twentieth century. Penfield's (1959) cortical exploration of epileptic patients briefly encouraged a return to a more extreme localization. By electrically stimulating very small areas of the cortex, he was able to elicit quite specific cognitive responses from conscious patients. From these responses he was able to map localized function in the motor cortex, the association cortex, and the hippocampus (which elicited the most remarkable responses of highly specific and evocative memories). More recently, however, an extreme localization has given way to a more compromised understanding of function; it is now assumed that while some "lower" processes such as motor abilities and vision may indeed be acutely localized (e.g., Hubel and Wiesel 1979), the "higher-order" processes, such as abstract thinking, reasoning, and memory, are distributed throughout the cortex (Luria 1973; Kosslyn and Koenig 1992).

Theories of neurological localization, even in their current distributed form, present a number of philosophical difficulties. In the first instance, they presume a self-present neurological trace, center, or pathway to which certain psychological capacities can be ascribed. This question of psychophysical traces in the brain is a complex one, and it will be dealt with in more detail in the final chapters. Freud's (1891) early critique of neurological localization established a certain orientation to the nature of neurological presence that will be indispensable to my later analysis of contemporary neurocognitive theories. To anticipate those discussions briefly here: How is the trace, center, or pathway made present in the brain when clearly the brain reuses the same neurons for different functions? How can memory (or the permanent storage of traces) be possible if the psyche is required to be fresh constantly for new sensory impressions? Are there present and locatable traces in the brain, or are they the effect of more subtle and powerful processes of difference and deferral?

As well as bringing these logocentric pressures to bear on the neurological trace, theories of neurological location implicate the brain as a whole in certain dualistic divisions. The localization of psychological function has allowed the characteristics of Cartesianism to be deployed and embodied in the brain itself. Evolutionary theory, for example, has contributed substantially to the intelligibility of mind–brain reductionism (Clarke and Jacyna 1987). Despite Darwin's oft-cited note to himself to never use the terms *higher* and *lower*, the brain has been divided cognitively and topographically according to such a hierarchy—into the interior, or "reptilian," regions, which humans share with lower animals, and the outer, more phylogenetically recent cortical surfaces. The lower brain is widely considered to be responsible for more "primitive" psychological faculties, such as hate, love, fear, and sexual behavior, and the basic life functions, such as breathing, eating, and cortical tone (Luria 1973). This part of the brain is sometimes called the emotional brain (Lashley 1960b). The cortical surfaces are understood to be primarily involved in "higher" psychological functions such as reasoning, spatial skills, language, and so-called creative or nonverbal skills, such as dance, music, and art. We can glimpse the force of these divisions and localizations in Simon LeVay's comments on the hypothalamus, which is a subcortical structure:

> People tend to stay away from the hypothalamus. Most brain scientists (including myself until recently) prefer the sunny expanses of the cerebral cortex to the dark, claustrophobic regions at the base of the brain. They think of the hypothalamus—although they would never admit this to you—as haunted by animal spirits and the ghosts of primal urges. They sus-

pect that it houses, not the usual shiny hardware of cognition, but some witches' brew of slimy, pulsating neurons adrift in a broth of mind-altering chemicals. (LeVay 1993, 39)

In the same way that Cartesian dualism becomes embodied through a division and hierarchization of the body and the head, so too a dualism is localized in, and constitutive of, the brain. The highest achievements of intellect are housed in the neocortex, which has been separated (physically and developmentally) from the rest of the body. Below this (anatomically, developmentally, and evaluatively) reside sensibility and passion. The higher one moves up the brain stem and the evolutionary ladder, and the further away from the rest of the body, the less embodied and more cerebral (literally and figuratively) the cognitive processes become. We can find evidence for this localized dualism in almost every neuropsychological text: Gall, for example, considered that the vital forces were housed in the brain stem, while the intellect was housed in the hemispheres (Clarke and Jacyna 1987). Broca instantiated a more finely tuned hierarchy within the cortex itself: "The most elevated cerebral faculties such as judgment and reflection, the faculties of comparison and abstraction, have their seat in the frontal convolutions, while convolutions of the temporal, parietal and occipital lobes are affected by sentiments, predilections and passions" (Broca, cited in Schiller 1979, 179–80).

While Luria's (1973) general system differs markedly from Broca's in that he moves against a narrow localization of function, nonetheless he enacts a dualistic division in the brain similar to Broca's. Luria separates the brain into three principal functional units, wherein the progress from the brain stem to the cortex charts the progress from passion to reason.

Rather than being simply inscriptive over an otherwise innocent organ, these mappings are constitutive of the brain itself. It is the hierarchical effects issuing forth from a generalized mind-body dualism that have materialized the neuropsychological brain as intelligible matter. The brain of contemporary neuropsychology is not a simple factual object. It has been constituted scientifically via the division of body from brain, and between upper cortex and lower brain stem; so too it is constituted via the dualistic relations of mind and body, intellect and emotion. The topography and internal morphology of the brain suggest that the brain is not simply the locus of the mind; more pointedly, it is the materialization of certain masculinist and ethnocentric desires about the mind and their attendant anxieties about the (psychologically and culturally) primitive body.

~ Conclusion

The cognitive machinery of scientific psychology is neither innocent nor neutral. The desire to be free from the body, to be rid of sexual difference, and to create computer-children outside the constraints of flesh and femininity are, of course, the aspirations of a peculiarly masculine logic. Likewise, the containment of cognitive traces within the logic of direct and translatable processing generates an economy of containment, presence, and reserve that operates at the expense of the psyche's interpretive mobility. The introduction of neurology into the field of cognition further complicates the pattern of these aspirations. The materiality of neurology seems to emerge within a system that implicitly, and not accidentally, censures the body. The efficacy of neurology as a resolution to philosophical concerns of mind and body, psychology and biology is circumscribed by this system of censure. Moreover, the anatomical and topographical space that neurology exemplifies is confined with a logic of location and hierarchization.

These concerns will be discussed in the coming chapters in relation to connectionism's computational-neurological morphology. While connectionist architecture and function offer a powerful critique of a locatable, contained, and hierarchical cognitive morphology, it is by no means clear that such a critique has been, or indeed can be, decisively enacted.

chapter four

Projects for
a Scientific Psychology

Freud, Derrida, and Connectionist
Theories of Cognition

There are a number of uncanny points of convergence between Freud's (1895) *Project for a scientific psychology,* Derrida's (1978a) reading of the *Project,* and recent connectionist theories of cognition in psychology. The similarities in their approach to cognition, memory, the trace, and psychical writing offer an opportunity for developing a critical, but productive, interrogation of contemporary cognitive psychology. Specifically, it will be hypothesized that the juxtaposition of these Freudian, Derridean, and connectionist projects permits a reassessment of the conventional relation between neurology and psychology. While the neurological is usually thought of as the self-present origin of the psyche, there is a strategic movement in all three of these projects that disperses this origin through a system of differences and deferrals. Under the force of these projects, a psychoneurology can be forged that exceeds the limits of both neurology and psychology as they are usually conceived.

I will begin by reassessing the import of the *Project* to the identity of psychoanalysis and scientific psychology: To what extent is the division of neurology from psychology the founding moment of psychoanalysis? What is it about neurology that has made this division so easy to enact? And in what ways are more recent psychoneurological projects in scientific psychology still struggling with the same problematic of neurology and psychology that is so passionately articulated in Freud's *Project?* Through Derrida—and in some respects in spite of Derrida—I wish to evaluate these possibilities not only in the *Project*, but also in contemporary neurocognitive theory.

~ "Psychology for Neurologists": Freud and the *Project for a Scientific Psychology*

A man like me cannot live without a hobbyhorse, without a consuming passion, without—in Schiller's words—a tyrant. I have found one. In its service I know no limits. It is psychology, which has always been my distant, beckoning goal, and which now, since I have come upon the problem of neuroses, has drawn so much nearer. I am tormented by two aims: to examine what shape the theory of mental functioning takes if one introduces quantitative considerations, a sort of economics of nerve forces; and, second, to peel off from psychopathology a gain for normal psychology. . . . During the past weeks I have devoted every free minute to such work; have spent the hours of the night from eleven to two with such fantasizing, interpreting, and guessing, and invariably stopped only when somewhere I came up against an absurdity or when I actually and seriously overworked, so that I had no interest left in my daily medical activities. It will still be a long time before you can ask me about the results. (Freud, letter to Fliess, May 25, 1895, in Masson 1985, 129)

This duckbilled platypus of a scientific psychology . . . (Krell 1990, 151)

To many commentators, Freud's *Project for a scientific psychology* (1895) is an early, abortive attempt to give a neurological explanation of the psyche. In Krell's words, it is a "monstrous regression" (1990, 105) in the development of psychoanalysis—the last stand of

Freud's dying neurological interest. As such, the *Project*'s interest to a psychoanalytic audience has been primarily a developmental or chronological one: In the *Project* we can document Freud's last struggle with neurology, and we can find, in embryo, some of the central constructs of psychoanalytic theory. In this chapter I want to upset this comfortable placement of the *Project* and the implications concerning the relation of neurology to psychology that it has institutionalized.

In 1895 Freud wrote a series of letters to his dearest friend, Wilhelm Fliess, in which he spoke not only of his attempts to lay down his emerging psychological theories in primarily neurological terms, but also of his fears and aspirations surrounding such a project. In a letter on April 27, 1895, Freud first refers to this new project. He writes:

> Scientifically, I am in a bad way; namely, caught up in "The Psychology for Neurologists," which regularly consumes me totally until, actually overworked, I must break off. I have never before experienced such a high degree of preoccupation. And will anything come of it? I hope so, but it is difficult and slow going. (Freud, letter to Fliess, April 27, 1895, in Masson 1985, 127)

In the following months, Freud mentioned his "Psychology" frequently in his correspondence to Fliess. However, it was not until after their congress in September of 1895 that Freud began a draft with the intention of setting down the details of his project for Fliess's scrutiny. This draft, contained in two notebooks, was sent to Fliess on October 8, 1895; it is this draft that was published posthumously as the *Project for a scientific psychology*.

Freud's work on the *Project* was marked by a vacillation between preoccupation and disinterest, enthusiasm and dismay. It was a piece of work that drove him obsessively from its inception and from which he eventually retreated in disillusion. After an initial period of delight and enthusiasm upon completing the drafts for Fliess, Freud expresses frustration with his project in the letter of November 8, 1895:

I have packed up the psychological manuscripts and thrown them into a drawer, where they shall slumber until 1896. This came about in the following way. At first I put psychology aside in order to make room for infantile paralysis, which must be finished before 1896. Next I began to write about migraine. The first points I discussed led me to an insight which again reminded me of the topic I had put aside and which would have required a lot of revision. At that moment I rebelled against my tyrant. I felt over worked, irritated, confused, and incapable of mastering it all. So I threw everything away. . . . Since I have put the ψφω aside, I feel beaten and disenchanted; I believe I am not at all entitled to your congratulations.

I now feel a void. (Freud, letter to Fliess, November 8 and 10, 1895, in Masson 1985, 150–51)

However, the *Project* was not easily abandoned in a drawer. In late November Freud writes of the allegedly banished psychology:

I no longer understand the state of mind in which I hatched the psychology; cannot conceive how I could have inflicted it on you. I believe you are still too polite; to me it appears to be a kind of madness. (Freud, letter to Fliess, November 29, 1895, in Masson 1985, 152)

The manuscripts must have been woken from their slumber a little earlier than the new year, as Freud's last attempt at a revision of the *Project* comes in a letter to Fliess on January 1, 1896, where he adds an extensive postscript to the notebooks.

From this point on, Freud abandoned the expression of these ideas in this form. In 1896 he diverted his attention to Fliess's theories of periodicity, the sexual etiology of neurosis, his self-analysis, and the draft of *The interpretation of dreams* (Masson 1985). While the strictly neurological framework of the *Project* was never repeated, the ideas contained therein continued to resonate throughout Freud's work for the next forty years. The mark of the *Project* is most notably evident in the final extraordinary chapter of *The interpretation of dreams* (1900); in the metapsychology papers of 1915; in *Beyond the pleasure principle* (1920); and in "A note upon the 'Mystic Writing-Pad'" (1925a). This continuity has been documented in a number of commentaries on the *Project*: Derrida 1978a, Holt 1965, Krell 1990, and Strachey 1966 all suggest that the *Project* is seemingly both abandoned and retained by Freud. They take the *Project* to be the most explicit manifestation of Freud's strong ambivalence about the relation of neurology, biology, or physiology to the psyche: "His real interest lay elsewhere [from children's neurology], in two fields—or rather in two manifestations of a single problem—which alternatively occupied the first place in his mind. These were anatomy of the brain and research into hysteria" (Kris 1954, 18). This ambivalence never again provokes the levels of anxiety that are evident in and around the *Project*, but nonetheless Freud's ambivalence is not ever finally put to rest. The viability and desirability of chemical, neurological, biological, and physiological explanations of psychoanalytic constructs are raised periodically throughout the remainder of Freud's career (see Holt 1965).

Kris has speculated that the connection between physiology and psychology was a particularly important one in initiating and sustaining the Freud-Fliess relationship. Fliess was more thoroughly trained in physiology than was Freud, yet Freud's interests were always more clearly psychological. The link between biology and psychology that is so desperately sought in the *Project* (and the libidinal energy with which that coupling is pursued) in many ways mirrors the Freud-Fliess relationship itself (for a nuanced and comprehensive account of that relationship, see Boyarin 1995). The successful convergence of psychology and biology would reflect a similar agreement and compatibility between the two men. The impossibility of the *Project* is thus the same impossibility of the Freud–Fliess relationship:

> Your letters . . . contain a wealth of scientific insights and intuitions, to which I unfortunately can say no more than that they grip and overpower me. The thought that both of us are occupied with the same kind of work is by far the most enjoyable one I can conceive at present. I see how, via the detour of medical practice, you are reaching your first ideal of understanding human beings as a physiologist, just as I most secretly nourish

the hope of arriving, via these same paths, at my initial goal of philosophy. (Freud, letter to Fliess, January 1, 1896, in Masson 1985, 159)

The posthumous publication of the *Project* opened up a number of different avenues for approaching Freud's work, and not surprisingly it has often played a pivotal role in the skirmishes over Freud's identity and the proper interpretation of psychoanalysis. The ambitious scope of the *Project* readily incites all manner of revisionist claims. Starting with some basic principles of biophysics dealing with the discharge and accumulation of energy, the *Project* moves on to explain (among other things) the psychoneurology of pain, consciousness, satisfaction, sleep, dreams, and remembering; the structure of the ego; the psychopathology of hysteria; and finally normal psychological processes. The *Project* does not submit easily to a definitive reading on any criteria, for it is positioned undecidably between neurology and psychology, refusing a simple reduction to either domain. While the *Project* is clearly not a psychoanalytic text, as normally understood, neither is it simply a neurological text. It is, as I will argue with more force in the following sections, a psychoneurological text of the most unusual kind. It is a text that, consciously or otherwise, undoes the purity of its neurological aims. For my purposes, the *Project* becomes a crucial text in the taxonomic division of psychology from biology, psychoanalysis from neurology, and interpretation from science.

To press this point a little further: As I have already suggested, one of the most common assessments of the *Project* is that it is a prepsychoanalytic document. In particular, a strong demarcation is often made between the *Project* (1895) and *The interpretation of dreams* (1900), which many commentators (and perhaps Freud himself) see as the first "proper" psychoanalytic text. In being named prior and seminal to psychoanalysis proper, as Derrida (1978a) does implicitly and as Strachey (1966) does explicitly, the *Project* is reduced in status to a precursor or a prototheory, which is abandoned in the light of the theory proper that follows: a catalyst that is effaced in the wake of the reaction which it has initiated. The specifics of the *Project*'s strategies and effects are consequently subordinated under the narrative of psychoanalytic progress and development. Psychoanalysis is divorced from neurology, and an interpretive method is separated from a scientific one. I shall treat with suspicion these attempt to separate the *Project* (historically or theoretically) from the proper body of psychoanalysis. Any notion of a smooth gestation of psychoanalytic theory can be sustained only through a very partial reading, for the period from 1880 to 1900 is full of contradictions (on topography), ambivalence (between neurology and psychology), false starts (the seduction hypothesis), and dead ends (periodicity). The allegedly neurological *Project* is written after the *Studies on hysteria* (Freud and Breuer 1895), which is primarily a psychological text. Similarly, the ideas of the *Project* had only just been "abandoned" when they were resurrected in the final chapter of *The interpretation of dreams*.

The *Project* presents an uncomfortable chronological glitch in psychoanalytic history. Without the Fliess papers, there is a dutiful historical and theoretical progress of psychoanalytic ideas away from neurology—starting with the *Studies on hysteria* and moving smoothly through to *The interpretation of dreams* and beyond. The neurological aspirations of the *Project* upset this tidy narrative and have initiated a series of revisionist and recuperative interpretations of Freud's neurological interests. On one side, there are the attempts to restore the repressed biologism in the later Freud (e.g., Sulloway 1979; Holt 1965; Pribram 1965), and on the other, the attempts to explain away these perverse neurological ambitions (e.g., Derrida 1978a; Krell 1990; Strachey 1966). I hope to be able to negotiate my reading somewhere between these two positions. The *Project* never reaches the potential of its stated neurological aims, yet nonetheless it is a text that does not slip quietly into the prehistory of psychoanalytic theory. It manifests a certain dilemma (of mind and body, neurology and psychology) that a hundred years later is no closer to being addressed properly inside psychology.

~

At the very beginning of the *Project*, Freud states that his intention is to "furnish a psychology that shall be a natural science: that is, to represent psychical processes as quantitatively determinate states of specifiable material particles" (Freud 1895, 295). In other words, he aims to give an explanation of the psyche in terms of neural activity. His objective, then, appears to be one of classical mind-brain reductionism. However, every time Freud calls certain reductionist biological principles into action in the *Project*, he almost immediately dismantles or decenters their effects on the psyche. There are a number of critical places where the *Project* undoes the presumptions of biological reductionism at exactly the moment it seems to be elucidating their necessity. This maneuver is what Spivak identifies as "the typical sleight of hand of 'sous rature' [erasure]" (1974, xli); that is, the *Project* advances a neurological explanation that is both necessary but impossible. Rather than obliterating or repressing the import of neurology to the psychological, Freud accords to neurology the effects appropriate to biological reductionism, but at the same time he displaces these effects in such a way that this reductionism (although not neurology itself) becomes untenable. To paraphrase Spivak (paraphrasing Derrida), this putting of neurology under erasure means that it is written down but it is also crossed out: ~~neurology~~. Because a neurological origin is inaccurate, it is crossed out; because it is necessary, it remains legible. If the *Project* is interpreted as presenting neurology under erasure, rather than neurology as the foundation of a biologically reductionist model, then the role of neurology in the constitution of the psyche has been profitably reoriented, and the psychoneurological struggle that the *Project* entails can be revalued.

At the very beginning of the *Project* Freud sets up two theorems that serve as the bearings for the rest of the text. In the first of these Freud postulates that neurons tend to divest themselves of quantity (Qn), Qn being the stimulation that impinges on the neurons, originating from either an external source or a somatic one. Any system moves to divest itself of Qn, because constant or excessively high levels of excitation are destabilizing or injurious to the organism. Freud names this the principle of neuronal inertia. The discharge of Qn is the primary function of the nervous system, but this process is also subjected to a secondary (and contradictory) function. This secondary function is the accumulation of Qn, necessary in order for the organism to address what Freud calls the "exigencies of life": that is, to give flight from external stimulation, or to change the environment such that internal, somatic stimulation ceases. The organism is thus caught in an irreducible dilemma—the need to discharge Qn, and the need to accumulate Qn.

> In consequence, the nervous system is obliged to abandon its original trend to inertia (that is, to bringing the level [of Qn] to zero). It must put up with [maintaining] a store of Qn sufficient to meet the demand for a specific action. Nevertheless, the manner in which it does this shows that the same trend persists, modified into an endeavor at least to keep the Qn as low as possible and to guard against any increase of it—that is, to keep it constant. All the functions of the nervous system can be comprised either under the aspect of the primary function or of the secondary one imposed by the exigencies of life. (Freud 1895, 297)

Freud too is caught in the same sort of irreducible dilemma. He implies that the secondary function is developmentally second, or supplemental, to the primary function; yet at the same time he recognizes that no organism can function with only the primary function (i.e., discharging all the energy that it receives). Life requires some accumulation of energy: The organism needs the "exigencies of life" as much as it demands the discharge of all energy. Consequently, the so-called primary and secondary functions always and necessarily occur together, and thus the very idea of their primariness and secondariness is rendered provisional. This is the first example of an empirical-theoretical maneuver that is typical of Freud's early neurological work. Freud postulates a biological doctrine that on closer inspection becomes not unsustainable, outmoded, or contradictory, but carefully seditious. For this reason, it is rarely an issue of whether or not the empirical sciences have progressed past the parameters of Freud's own scientific expertise, or even whether Freud has misread or misunderstood such parameters as they were presented to him at the time; these readings prove themselves to be too simpleminded (Laplanche 1989; Spivak 1974).

Rather, it is this sleight of hand—a careful and effective twist at the core of scientific theory—that is the operative maneuver in Freud's "biologism."

The second theorem that Freud lays down at the beginning of the *Project* is his theory of neuronal activity, specifically the contact-barrier hypothesis. Starting with the secondary function, which calls for the accumulation of energy, Freud postulates that there must be resistance in neurons that prevents the discharge of energy. He hypothesizes that this resistance must be located in the contacts between the neurons rather than in the neurons themselves. Thus the primary function manifests neurologically as a moving (discharging) current of stimulation, and the secondary function manifests neurologically as contact barriers between neurons that work to oppose discharge. From this rather simple hypothesis, Freud constructs an elaborate model of the psyche that in its basic premises bears a strong resemblance to contemporary connectionist theories of cognition (a resemblance to which I will return later in this chapter).

How does Qn move through this system of contact barriers? Do the contact barriers resist the discharge of Qn completely or only partially? Freud is able to complete his psychoneurological model with a formulation of the principles of the movement and discharge of Qn. Central to this formulation is the need to resolve the paradox that neurons are altered by stimulation, yet they must also remain unaltered for future stimulations: "The process of conduction itself will create a differentiation in the protoplasm and consequently an improved conductive capacity for subsequent conduction. . . . Nevertheless it cannot be disputed that, in general, fresh excitations meet with the same conditions of reception as did the earlier ones" (Freud 1895, 298–99). That is, the psyche must have the capacity to be altered permanently by a single event (and thus the possibility of memory), yet also to remain "unprejudiced" for new excitations. Freud confesses that he is unable to "imagine an apparatus capable of such complicated functioning" (Freud 1895, 299). This apparatus arrives belatedly in the unexpected form of the child's toy in "A note upon the 'Mystic Writing-Pad'" (1925a). In the meantime, Freud saves his model by postulating two classes of neurons: those that are permanently altered by excitation (mnemic cells) and those that are fresh for new excitation (perceptual cells).

Freud hypothesizes that this first group of neurons (the mnemic cells) are impermeable. They have contact barriers, and so Qn passes through them with difficulty or only partially; they resist Qn. Freud names them the ψ (psi) neurons. In the second group of cells (the perceptual cells), excitation passes through them as if there are no contact barriers. They are permeable, offering no resistance to Qn, and operate in the service of perception. Freud names them the ϕ (phi) neurons. Freud has no histological evidence to support his hypothesis of two different classes of neurons. He therefore attributes the differences between the ϕ and ψ neurons not to a static biological essence, but to the differences in quantities of excitation with which they have had to deal. The ψ neurons are considered analogous to the gray matter of the brain and receive excitation only from endogenous sources, whereas the ϕ neurons are analogous to the gray matter of the spinal cord and receive excitation from external sources. It is this difference of *placement*, rather than of *essence,* that determines the nature and function of the neurons: "Therefore let us . . . attribute the differences [between the ϕ and ψ neurones] not to the neurones [themselves] but to the quantities with which they have to deal" (Freud 1895, 304). Freud claims that if the two neuronal systems were swapped, so too would their functions be swapped, and each would adapt accordingly to their new placement: "A difference in their essence is replaced by a difference in the environment to which they are destined" (Freud 1895, 304).

Neuronal effect, then, is a function of differences in Qn: The biological essence of the neuron is displaced as the effect of spacing. Different psychical action is not inherent in the neuron, but is the effect of differential anatomical placement. It is this move to dislodge a strict biological essentialism from the neuron that gives us our first (incomplete) glimpse of a critique of neuropsychological localization. Having no biological essence, the neuron is unable to carry the origin of the psyche. This responsibility is displaced onto excitations—more specifically, the difference between excitations (as we will see in a moment). Freud's claim radically undermines any reductionist tendencies that might be attributed to the *Project;* it is never simply the case that Freud has mobilized neurology in this text in order to establish a fixed and immobile origin for the psyche. Rather than recruiting neurology to render the psychological intelligible, Freud has inverted this trajectory and uses the psyche to render traditional neurology enigmatic.

With these moves, Freud enacts the *Project*'s first major displacement of neuronal effect. A traditional mind-brain reductionism would normally be content with the successful isolation of a neural mechanism for a particular psychological process. While Freud's model mobilizes these traditional reductive strategies and presumptions, in the end he undermines the certainty of the neuronal explanation by deferring the origin from the neuron to the external and endogenous excitations of Qn. That is, the origin is removed from its comfortable and discrete housing in the neuron and scattered among the vicissitudes of endogenous and external excitation. It is not simply that the neuron is now excluded from the origin (a kind of antireductionism); rather, it is the very notion of an origin of the psyche or a final explanatory ground that is contested. Dislocated, but nonetheless essential to the constitution of the psyche, a neuronal origin of the psyche is placed under erasure.

Having established this displacement, Freud goes on to introduce the ω neurons, and with them the possibility of quality and consciousness in a quantitative system. In a fashion similar to that above, the ω system is constituted not through any locatable essence, but through the rhythms and vicissitudes of periodicity. That is, the ω system, because it receives no Qn directly, produces qualities and consciousness from the *period* of Qn. Here the psychical effects of ω are constituted through a temporal displacement rather than the spatial displacement of the ψ system. This formulation of Qn and the $\psi\phi\omega$ system provide Freud with the building blocks for his model in the *Project*. One further issue, and perhaps the most crucial one—facilitation—will be introduced in the following section. I shall break off from Freud's account at this point in order to pursue the matter of neurology and psyche in Derrida's analysis of the *Project*.

~ Neurology Breached: Derrida and Scientific Psychology

The paper published as "Freud and the scene of writing" is devoted to an examination of the mutual debts owed between psychoanalysis and deconstruction. This is a careful negotiation on Derrida's behalf, and it is implicated in forging a certain identity for deconstruction: "Despite appearances, the deconstruction of logocentrism is not a psychoanalysis of philosophy" (Derrida 1978a, 196). At the same time that he expresses a reticence to use Freudian concepts except in quotation marks, as "all of these concepts, without exception, belong to the history of Western Metaphysics" (1978a, 197), Derrida seeks out those aspects of psychoanalysis that, like deconstruction, disrupt a metaphysics of presence: "Our aim is limited: to locate in Freud's text several points of reference, and to isolate, on the threshold of a systematic examination, those elements of psychoanalysis which can only uneasily be contained within logocentric closure" (1978a, 198). Specifically, Derrida pursues the metaphorics of writing in Freud's texts. Derrida claims that throughout his career Freud borrowed models of the psyche that are irreducibly graphic: The contents of the psyche are written traces, and the structure of the psyche eventually becomes a writing machine. Derrida's investigation of the metaphor of writing follows Freud over a thirty-year period, from the *Project for a scientific psychology* (1895) through *The interpretation of dreams* (1900) to *Beyond the pleasure principle* (1920) and "A note upon the 'Mystic Writing-Pad'" (1925a). Derrida announces a progression in this work that starts out with the problematics of neurological facilitation (in the *Project*) but which increasingly conforms to a metaphorics of a written trace (fully realized in "A note upon the 'Mystic Writing-Pad'") that Derrida takes to be incongruous with the earlier "neurological fable."

I have two interests in Derrida's analysis. First, Derrida's interpretation of facilitation opens up, in more detail, the thesis that neuronal effect proceeds through difference and deferral—a notion that I have already begun to address in relation to Freud. This reformulation lays the ground for my commentary on connectionism and the discussion of psychical locality in chapter 5. Second, I will argue that neurology has not been fully incorporated into the narrative of a metaphorics of writing that Derrida traces across Freud's work. I will pursue a less dismissive interpretation of the neurological aims of the *Project*, so that the productive conjunctions between Freud, Derrida, and neurocognitive theories in psychology may be broached.

~

As Freud's notion of *Bahnung* is crucial to Derrida's reading of the *Project*, an initial note on the translation of *Bahnung* (lit., "path breaking") will be useful. *Bahnung* has been translated by James Strachey as "facilitation," following the standard translations of nineteenth-century neurology textbooks. Alan Bass, Derrida's translator, uses the more awkward (and less neurologically oriented term) "breaching." Bass claims that for the purposes of translating Derrida's text (rather than Freud's, for which he gives Strachey's standard-edition translation), "it is crucial to maintain the sense of the *force* that breaks open a pathway and the *space* opened by this force" (translator's note in Derrida 1978a, 329). Thus in the Bass translation of "Freud and the scene of writing," *facilitation* and *breaching* are used to refer to the Freudian and Derridean projects, respectively. This difference in translation, and the tension that it creates in the text, is not inconsequential to the analysis that I wish to construct around Freud, Derrida, and neurology. Where one translation (*facilitation*) perhaps remains true to Freud's neurological ambitions, it misses the aspects of spacing and temporization that Derrida exploits with *breaching*. Likewise, the effect and power of Derrida's *breaching* seems to be premised on its distance from these neurological ambitions. This discontinuity is no mere linguistic incommensurability; it suggests a critical tension between the Freudian and Derridean projects.

Before I relate how Derrida reads *Bahnung* as "breaching," let me return briefly to Freud to give an account of his model of facilitation. In the ψ system (which, for Freud, represents the psychical processes in general), the contact barriers between neurons are permanently altered by the passage of excitation. These neurons thus have the capacity for representing memory. The effect of this alteration is that the ψ contact barriers become more capable of conduction, less impermeable, and ultimately more like the φ system: "We shall describe this state of the contact-barriers as their degree of *facilitation [Bahnung]*" (Freud 1895, 300).

At this stage, Freud's model is not unlike a contemporary neurocognitive model, which searches for the traces of psychological processing in the neuronal system (as in, say, the visual record of cognitive activity in a PET scan). In such models the visualization and examination of facilitations gives an indication of the type and/or intensity of the psychical process involved. However, having set up these traditional reductive expectations, Freud immediately removes the certainty of a direct signifying or causal relation between neural facilitations and the psyche—memory is represented not by a single facilitation, but by the difference between facilitations:

> If we were to suppose that all the ψ contact-barriers were equally well facilitated, or (what is the same thing) offered equal resistance, then the characteristics of memory would evidently not emerge. For, in relation to the passage of an excitation, memory is evidently one of the powers which determine and direct its pathway, and, if facilitation were everywhere equal, it would not be possible to see why one pathway should be preferred. We can therefore say still more correctly that *memory is represented by the differences in the facilitations between the ψ neurones.* (Freud 1895, 300)

It is here, in the difference between facilitations, that the Derridean reading of breaching as *différance* begins in earnest. Derrida's reading proceeds through an analysis of the two faces of *différance*—difference and deferral. Etymologically, *différance* draws on the two senses of the French verb *différer*, which can mean either "to differ" or "to defer." It thus draws simultaneously on the notions of spacing (to differ) and temporization (to defer). Moreover, *différance* confounds the logic of presence and absence, and the oppositionality of difference and identity. A difference, as normally understood, operates between two separate and distinct entities. These entities, or identities, are said to be primary, and present in and of themselves. Thus a difference between facilitations is normally understood as a spacing between two entities whose identity exists prior to that relation. In contesting this understanding of difference and identity, Derrida draws on Saussurian pure difference, wherein (linguistic) identities are constituted not in and of themselves, but through their difference from each other; in language, there are only differences without positive terms. Expanding on this semiological analysis, Derrida claims that any entity (here a signified concept) is "never present in and of itself, in a sufficient presence that would refer only to itself. Essentially and lawfully, every concept is inscribed in a chain or in a system within which it refers to the other, to other concepts, by means of the systematic play of differences" (Derrida 1982, 11).

Likewise, the identity of any facilitation is not to be attributed to a single plenitude of quantity, but to the difference between facilitations: a systematic play of neurological differences. *Différance*, that ungraspable yet unerasable difference between facilitations, is what constitutes the psyche; it is difference and delay (*différance*) that are at the origin. Under Derrida's tutelage, simple and self-present neurological facilitation has become breaching, a movement intolerant of the notion of full and present quantities. Memory and the psyche in general are not created by a single passage of Qn (i.e., a single breach), but by the differences between quantities: "An equality of resistance to breaching, or an equivalence of the breaching forces, would eliminate any *preference* in the choice of itinerary. Memory would be paralyzed. It is the difference between breaches which is the true origin of memory, and thus of the psyche" (Derrida 1978a, 201). However, even with the psyche displaced into this gulf between breaches, the nature of these breaches must also be displaced. Without further comment, we may be led to conclude that there are full quantities between which difference is established. Derrida is careful to assert that there can be no pure breach (i.e., a breach that is present) before difference:

We then must not say that breaching without difference is insufficient for memory; it must be stipulated that there is no pure breaching without difference. Trace as memory is not a pure breaching that might be reappropriated at any time as simple presence; it is rather the ungraspable and indivisible difference between breaches. (Derrida 1978a, 201)

There is no pure, singular, present, originary breach against which the occurrence of a second breach creates a difference. It is not that a single breach is insufficient for memory, but that there is no breach without that difference.

The displacement in the *Project,* then, is twofold: The psyche is displaced from present quantities onto the difference between quantities, and these quantities themselves no longer are self-present but rather are constituted through an incessant play of differences. The trace, under Derrida, is thus something other than the empirically fixed entity that the neurologist would hope for. The neuropsychical trace escapes the containment of measurement and visibility pursued in contemporary neurocognitive technologies and methodologies. The trace is material—it is the effect of breaching and somatic excitation—but it resists both intelligibility (it is ungraspable) and sensibility (it is unlocatable). Confounding both a faithful scientism and a reactionary antineurologism, this trace exceeds the logic of empiricism versus antiempiricism by invoking an irreducible, non-present materiality. The extent and radicality of this resistance of the trace to empirical ambitions will be the focus of chapter 5.

There is another facet to Derrida's formulation of breaching as *différance.* This is the idea of deferral (temporization), which is indivisible from the movements of difference (spacing): "All these differences in the production of the trace may be reinterpreted as moments of deferring" (Derrida 1978a, 202). For Derrida, *Nachträglichkeit* (delayed action) and *Verspätung* (delaying) govern the entire Freudian system; delay, temporality, and periodicity manifest throughout the *Project.* Having already contested the constitution of breaches and their relation to the psyche through the notion of difference—an issue of spacing and locality—Derrida moves on to interrogate the temporal relation between breaches.

Repetition does not *happen to* an initial impression; its possibility is already there, in the resistance offered *the first time* by the psychical neurones. Resistance itself is possible only if the opposition of forces lasts and is repeated at the beginning. It is the very idea of a *first time* which becomes enigmatic. (Derrida 1978a, 202)

That is, repetition is not the effect of the second breach—the possibility of repetition is already there in the first breach: "In the *first time* of the contact between *two* forces, repetition has begun" (Derrida 1978a, 202). Derrida displaces the primariness of the first time (a displacement that he claims is reflected in the relation of the secondary processes to the primary processes): "It is thus the delay which is in the beginning" (1978a, 203). Freud "complies with a dual necessity: that of recognizing *différance* at the origin, and at the same time that of crossing out the concept of *primariness*" (Derrida 1978a, 203).

By bringing these two faces of *différance* into play, the Derridean notion of breaching accounts for the psyche in terms of topographical spacings of nonempirical quantities and temporal delays. It is the former of these two displacements that will be of most use to me. By resolutely deflecting a conventional topographical location to the psyche, breaching provides the possibility of radically reformulating neurology and psychology. The irreducible relation between neurology and breaching that is formulated here allows neurology to be thought of as something other than the stable bedrock of reductionism. Through breaching, neurology breaks the banks of its scientific confinement, exceeding the conventional biological formulations of stasis, presence, and location.

~

Despite my enthusiasm about the possibilities of Derrida's reading of Freud for an investigation into contemporary neurocognitive theory, I have reservations about certain aspects of that reading. There seems to be a reactive move in Derrida's text against the viability or propriety of neurological models for his own deconstructive project. It appears, at times, that it is Derrida's construction of a certain type of neurology and then its almost immediate exclusion that allows him to construct and enforce his narrative of a metaphorics of writing in Freud's work—neurology becomes the excess in Derrida's reading of Freud. My concern is not that such a move is outside the rules of fair interpretive play (it is not), but rather that one of the effects of this gesture is to further distance science and neurology from our own critical habits and procedures, a move that renders neuroscientific discourse (and neurology itself) monolithic or unalterably crude and thus beyond the reaches of productive critical intervention. I pursue these moments in Derrida's text not from any punitive motivation, but in order to extract and exploit the (latent) connection between Derrida's project and scientific psychology. If Derrida's reading of Freud (and thus the identity of deconstruction) proceeds through a certain distancing from neurology, then an examination of that inclination will enable me to more accurately ascertain what will be at stake—for both psychology and our own critical habits—in an analysis of contemporary neurocognitive science.

These are Derrida's opening comments on the *Project*:

From the *Project* (1895) to the "Note on the Mystic Writing Pad" (1925), a strange progression: a problematic of breaching is elaborated only to conform increasingly to a metaphorics of the written trace. From a system of traces functioning according to a model which Freud would have preferred to be a natural one, and from which writing is entirely absent, we proceed toward a configuration of traces which can no longer be represented except by the structure and functioning of writing. At the same time, the structural model of writing, which Freud invokes immediately after the *Project,* will be persistently differentiated and refined in its originality. All the mechanical models will be tested and abandoned, until the discovery of the *Wunderblock*, a writing machine of marvelous complexity into which the whole of the psychical apparatus will be projected. The solution to all the previous difficulties will be presented in the *Wunderblock*, and the 'Note,' indicative of an admirable tenacity, will answer precisely the questions of the *Project*. The *Wunderblock,* in each of its parts, will realize the apparatus of which Freud said, in the *Project*: "We cannot offhand imagine an apparatus capable of such complicated functioning" (SE, I, 299), and which he replaces at that time with a neurological fable whose framework and intention, in certain respects, he will never abandon. (1978a, 200)

The narrative that Derrida constructs in these opening comments is surprisingly traditional in its historicity. Derrida positions himself above Freud's desk, commenting on the unfolding genius of Freud's writings, and rushing ahead in time in order to verify the narrative Derrida himself creates: "In letter 52 (6 Dec. 1896), the entire system of the *Project* is reconstituted in terms of a graphic conception as yet unknown in Freud" (Derrida 1978a, 206). In keeping with the most orthodox of historical commentaries, Derrida places himself at the conclusion of a historical episode, and through him we are able to observe an orderly unfolding of events: namely the "progression [from the *Project*] . . . to a metaphorics of writing" (1978a, 200), "the transition from the neurological to the psychical" (1978a, 206). In many ways, Derrida's uncharacteristically conventional critical demeanor is an effect of the difficulties with historically placing the *Project*. Krell, for example, pauses to consider the issue of the historicity of the *Project*. Commenting on Freud's difficulty in maintaining the present tense in the *Project*, Krell hypothesizes that even at the time of their creation these "sketches toward a scientific psychology are already relics of the past" (1990, 110). Krell, like Derrida, draws on the future tense when describing the *Project*, as though its entire value lies in what it initiated rather than what it actually attempts to do.

The placement of the *Project* is an important consideration: In which tense and at what chronological point should the *Project* be apprehended? Where both Krell and Derrida take the *Project* to be the beginning, an origin left behind in the development of a more sophisticated system, this beginning could just as easily be overturned, the standard chronology inverted, and the *Project* positioned as the conclusion of psychoanalysis. That is, if the *Project* is considered within its publication chronology, it becomes the last work that Freud published. The *Project* is then extracted from its conventional placement as protopsychoanalytic and will more forcefully resist both neurological and mentalistic recuperations. The *Project* is undecidably both the first and the final word—it could be equally both psychoanalysis in embryo *and* a summary of the field, the final introductory lecture (indeed, the *Project* is perhaps most intelligible when read as a summary, where the reader is already acquainted with psychoanalytic and metapsychological theory). No more is lost in the *Project* as a summary than is yet to be found in the *Project* as an origin.

The difficulty that the *Project* presents to the accepted (or desired) reading of psychoanalysis has tended to be suppressed in the service of a particular narrative. In Derrida's case this narrative is the development of the metaphorics of writing (and thus the instantiation of a deconstructive identity). He suggests that the *Project* does not "conform" to a metaphorics of writing. It is only after the *Project* that a truly Derridean metaphor of writing emerges; the system of traces in the *Project* is a natural one "from which writing is entirely absent" (Derrida 1978a, 200). The hypothesis of breaching, for example, becomes remarkable "as soon as it is considered as a metaphorical model and not as a neurological description" (Derrida 1978a, 200). Simply put, Derrida is suggesting that in the *Project* we have the origin of certain ideas that reach their full and *proper* expression only at a later date, as if the neurological model is too crude or heavy-handed to deal with the subtleties that a graphic model offers and so is destined to be jettisoned in the service of writing. This inclination in Derrida's assessment of the *Project* has necessitated a concomitant move (by Derrida) to jettison neurology from Freud's later texts. However, as I will argue in some detail in chapter 5, it is simply not the case that Freud has "renounced" neurology, as Derrida suggests. Neurology is again and again brought into play in the very same papers in which Derrida excavates writing. Important references to neurology can be found in *The interpretation of dreams*, *Beyond the pleasure principle*, and the metapsychology papers. Derrida's pursuit of the metaphorics of writing is paralleled by Freud's own pursuit of the placement of neurology in a psychical system. Rather than displacing or disregarding such neurological pursuits, I want to examine the purchase that such insertions may have in Freud's formulation of metapsychology.

For Derrida, the break from neurological frameworks is one of the crucial constitutive moments in forging an identity for psychoanalysis and deconstruction. The unfortunate effect of this divorce is an increasing bifurcation between science and deconstruction, neurology and interpretation. In problematizing this inclination in Derrida's analysis of the *Project*, I wish to avert this partitioning of neurology and psychology and return to a critical examination of neurology, under breaching, in contemporary scientific psychology: What could we expect if, contra Derrida, we accede to the neurological intentions of Freud's hypothesis? What happens if we move Derrida's general project of breaching into the neurocognitive domain?

~ Connectionism: Neurology for Psychologists

There are a number of features in connectionist models that make them quite different from traditional models of cognition, and which allow comparisons not only to Freud's model in the *Project* but also to Derrida's reading of the psyche, memory, and the trace. In order to facilitate that discussion, I shall take a brief detour and offer an outline of the architecture and function of a simple connectionist model (I draw this condensed version from a number of very good introductions to connectionist architecture: Bechtel and Abrahamsen 1991; Churchland 1989; Churchland and Sejnowski 1992; Hinton 1992; Rumelhart, McClelland, and the PDP Research Group 1986).

In its most simple instantiation, the architecture of a connectionist network consists of three layers: input units, output units, and a layer of hidden units between these two (see Figure 2). Like a neuron, each of these units receives and propagates activity. Thus, the input units receive stimulation from outside the network (and are analogous to sensory neurons, or to Freud's ϕ system), while the output units propagate a signal to the outside of the network (and are thus analogous to motor neurons or to the associative cortex). Between these two layers lie the hidden units (of one or more layers), whose function is to internally propagate and transform activity in the network. Unlike a traditional cognitive system, these individual units have no representational status as such; it is the overall

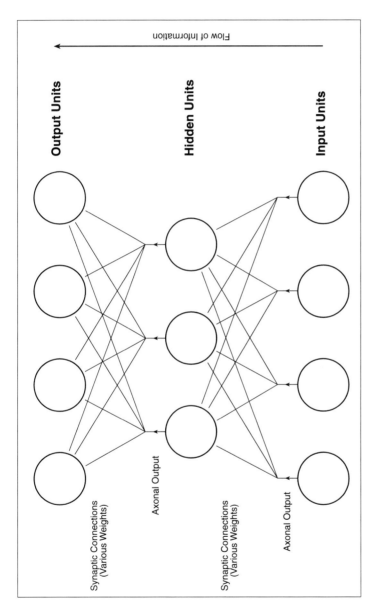

Figure 2 *A simple network.*
From P. M Churchland, *A neurocomputational perspective: The nature of mind and the structure of science* (Cambridge, MA: MIT Press, 1989), 162.

pattern of activity across the network in total that determines a particular "cognitive" output.

Activity is propagated and transformed across the network according to two parameters: the input-output function of each unit and the weightings of the connections between units. Each unit in a network has an input-output function, which determines the level and the manner in which activation is transformed as it moves through a unit. This function may be linear, threshold, or sigmoid. In the linear function, output is directly proportional to input; in the threshold function, input must reach a certain value before output is initiated; and in the sigmoid function, output varies systematically but nonlinearly to the input. This sigmoid function is the most neurally plausible of these functions. The input-output function is a constant feature of any network. The second parameter within which activation is determined is the weighting of the connections between units, and this varies over time. Units and layers are wired together by connections in a massively parallel fashion: Each unit is connected to many other units in the layers above and below it, and is thus receiving and transmitting activation across a web of associative linkages. Like the Freudian model, it is these connections that play a crucial role in the functioning of the system. Each connection carries a weight, varying from 0 to 1, which determines the level of activity that can be propagated through that path. The strength of that weight determines the extent to which each unit influences all other units to which it is connected. The differential weighting of connections, like the differential permeability of Freud's contact barriers, determines the spread of activity in any particular network. Moreover, as with the changes in permeability of Freud's "neurones," these connection weights undergo change over time (becoming more or less weighted) as a function of previous activations. These changes in the connection weights are the crucial determinate of cognitive functioning in a network.

This system of input-output functions and weights forms the basic architecture of a network. More broadly, the spread of activation is controlled by modification rules (external algorithms) which govern (i) the summation of input activations received by a unit, and the combination of this with the unit's activation level to produce a new output for the unit (the activation rule); (ii) the manner in which activation is propagated through a network's connectivity (the propagation rule); (iii) the modifications to weights as a result of previous activations (the learning rule).

It is this last rule that points to the most remarkable feature of connectionist networks: their ability to learn. That is, after being presented with a number of trial input vectors, and under the influence of modifications to weights ("training"), a network is able to produce the desired output in response to entirely new data without reference to a central program or memory. This is because new "knowledge" is accumulated not as stored sentential elements, but "in" the distributed and differential pattern of connection weights. Simply put, a network can extrapolate new information without the aid of centrally stored universal rules. For example, given the task of recognizing visual patterns such as letters of the alphabet, or the aural patterns of speech, rather than needing such patterns to fit a preprogrammed template exactly (as in traditional AI), the network is able to recognize a very wide set of variations of visual or aural pattern as lying within a particular class (e.g., the different visual patterns are all the letter *A*; the different pronunciations are all the word *cat*). In such networks there is no stored original against which comparisons are made; rather, the network is weighted in a manner that allows the recognition of vicissitudes and approximations in the absence of a template.

This outline presents only the most rudimentary aspects of connectionist architecture and function. However, my general goal is less one of producing an exhaustive account of connectionism than it is one of mobilizing certain aspects of connectionist theory in order to effect a rethinking of cognition, neurology, and location. Below I will indicate some of the differences between these connectionist networks and conventional models of cognition.

Connectionist models are "neurally inspired."

The units of a connectionist network are said to be modeled on an ideal neuron, the axons being represented by the connections and weights between units (McClelland, Rumelhart, and Hinton 1986). Where cognitive psychology traditionally has operated at a higher, more abstract level (a top-down approach) and has assumed that cognition is the processing of symbols in a manner similar to that in computational programming, connectionist networks are much more obviously committed to a neurophysiological (or bottom-up) approach to cognition. Moreover, there is a certain similarity between these units and the "neurone" as Freud constructs it in the *Project*. Indeed, Freud's "neurones" are perhaps more like these artificial, neurally inspired units than they are like "real" neurons. While neuroscientists themselves were initially skeptical at the biological plausibility of neural networks, an increasing amount of work is now being done on the applicability of PDP models to brain function (Churchland and Sejnowski 1992; Gluck and Rumelhart 1990). The strength of the commitment to such a bottom-up approach often depends on the disciplinary affiliation of the researcher (e.g., the physiological approach is often more attractive to neuroscientists than it is to psychologists). Some connectionists, following Smolensky (1988), claim that connectionist models fall somewhere between these two levels of explanation, incorporating aspects of both the top-down and bottom-up approaches. Sejnowski, for example, claims that his models work from the "middle out" (cited in Allman 1989, 180).

Cognitive processing is distributed and parallel.

Traditionally, theories of cognitive functioning rely on the idea that cognitive information flows in a linear and sequential manner (e.g., Atkinson and Shiffrin's [1968] model of memory). In connectionist models there is a move away from simplistic notions of causal linearity and toward synchronically and diachronically connected units and networks. Connectionist models are composed of a web of interconnections between units or between groups of units rather than being arranged in simple linear systems. Thus cognitive processing is assumed to be distributed and parallel rather than sequential and linear. In such networks, it is not simply that there are many sequential processes happening at one time; rather, cognitive processing is the product of mass parallel processing distributed throughout a network. This parallel processing renders connectionist models more similar to the stochastic and parallel functioning of the brain than traditional cognitive systems.

Architecture.

Traditional AI models of cognition are inspired by the universal Turing machine and realized in the von Neumann architecture of the modern computer. In a von Neumann machine, the rules that govern processing are literally written out in sentential or propositional form and stored inside the computer program (Bechtel and Abrahamsen 1991). Thus there is a crucial distinction between software and hardware in traditional AI: It is the software that determines cognitive function, whereas the hardware is the machine on which that program is implemented. In principle, all hardware is much the same, and so the particularity of the machine is irrelevant to the functioning of the software. More specifically, the influence of information theory in cognitive science meant that "it became possible to think of information apart from a particular transmission device: one could focus instead on the efficacy of *any* communication of messages via *any* mechanism, and one could consider cognitive processes apart from any particular embodiment" (Gardner 1987, 21). Cognitive models that rely on an analogy to von Neumann architecture have assumed that there is a distinction between a cognitive program (mind) and the machine (body-brain) on which it is run. Cognition is taken to be a universal process that always operates in the same way irrespective of its embodiment in a particular machine-brain. This distinction between hardware and software is rejected in connectionist models. The structure and wiring of a network instantiates the functional ability of that network. Embodiment is irreducible: There is no universal connectionist machine.

Rules and executive programs.

Traditional approaches to cognitive processing have replicated many other features of the von Neumann-influenced computational paradigm. Conventional cognitive models include, or at least imply, a central executive (or central processing unit), which controls cognitive functioning at a higher level. Given its resemblance to a psychological homunculus, such executives have been problematic for these cognitive accounts. In a connectionist architecture, there are no central processing units and no implied homunculi in cognitive processing. Instead, cognitive functioning is controlled by the difference in weights between units, the general wiring pattern of the units, and the learning rule (see Selfridge's [1959] "pandemonium" model for an interesting dissemination of the homunculus in a protoconnectionist schema). Like Freud's psychoneurological schema, a connectionist network is a machine that appears to function on its own (see Freud, letter to Fliess, October 20, 1895, in Masson 1985, 146). Similarly, conventional cognitive models have assumed that human cognition is the manipulation of symbols or representations in accordance with stored rules. In connectionist models, there are no stored rules on which a central executive would operate; rules are implicit in the structure of the network. That is, "cognitive rules" are materially instantiated, but they are distributed through the vicissitudes of connections and changing weights rather than stored as locatable propositions. In a connectionist model "rules no more need be explicitly represented than do the principles of aerodynamics honored in the design of the birds' wings" (Dennett 1991, 25).

Knowledge is distributed rather than local.

As a consequence of the move away from sequential linearity and stored rules, there is a concomitant move away from structural, store-based models of cognition, and away from the idea that knowledge is anatomically or cognitively locatable in any straightforward sort of way. Models of memory, for example, have traditionally suggested that information flows through a number of different stores: for example, sensory memory, short-term memory, and long-term memory. Memory traces are held in these stores, and it is from here that they are retrieved (Atkinson and Shiffrin 1968). At least implicitly in this type of theory, we have to assume that these stores are located somewhere in the brain; that is, particular cortical regions store and process particular cognitive functions. In connectionist models, knowledge (and, by extension, the psyche) is not locatable in this way. Knowledge is implicit, stored in the connections rather than the units. More accurately, knowledge is stored in the spatial and temporal differences between connection weights. Like the displaced cognitive rules, knowledge is material but unlocatable in any direct sense. The full philosophical implications of such a model of knowledge have not been fully addressed in the connectionist literature; the distributed nature of knowledge in a connectionist network is considered noteworthy by most connectionists simply because it produces a more viable cognitive model (e.g., McClelland, Rumelhart, and the PDP Research Group 1986).

The psychical trace.

Not only are there problems with (cortical) location in the traditional cognitive models, there is also a major problem with the constitution of the cognitive traces (e.g., memory traces) themselves. The general assumption in traditional models is either that there are neuronal representations (or traces) of a memory in the brain or, more abstractly, that there are cognitive traces in the mind. Either way, memory is taken to be the function of self-present, locatable traces. By moving the focus away from the properties or contents of units in a network to the weights between units and to activation as it moves across a network, the connectionist models posit an entirely different type of cognitive trace. Here, cognition is not the effect of a self-present trace, but rather the effect of differences between weights, between units, and between networks. In a connectionist network, a memory is not a property of the unit or a group of units (i.e., a store), but the effect of relational differences in the activation between units and across a network. This concurs with Freud's hypothesis that "memory is represented by the differences in the facilitations between . . . neurones" (Freud 1895, 300), an idea to which he returned in later texts: "Ideas, thoughts and psychical structures in general must never be regarded as localized in organic elements of the nervous system but rather, as one might say, *between* them, where resistances and facilitations [*Bahnungen*] provide the corresponding correlates" (Freud 1900, 611).

The connectionist trace, like Freudian facilitation, displaces psychical effect into the space *between* connections. Cognition arises out of the spatial and temporal differences between connections, rather than from any one individual connection. Thus there is a dou-

ble displacement: from the locale of the unit or store to the connection, and then again from the connection to the spaces between connections. But there is one more displacement that is effected in connectionist architecture: None of the elements in the network (the
units and the connections) can be thought of as present and locatable. As Smolensky (1988) points out, neither the units nor the connections of a connectionist network are spatially located or present
in any straightforward way. Like each of the elements in Saussure's
linguistic system, these connectionist elements have no identity
except through their difference from other elements in the system.
Connectionist units are not self-present, discrete entities, like the
stores of the traditional cognitive approach. Each unit gains its identity not through any essential characteristics (as is the case in Atkinson and Shiffrin's [1968] multistore model, for example), but
through its placement in the connectionist architecture. Like
Freud's deferral of a neurological essence into the vicissitudes of
anatomical placement, input, output, and hidden units gain their
identity as such only by virtue of how they are wired into the system. Likewise, the connections of the connectionist network are not
themselves neurocognitively present or potent; their effect is constituted through the spatial arrangement of the connectionist architecture and the temporal vicissitudes of the activation rules.

This dislocation of the trace will be what occupies me in the next
chapter. There I shall outline more fully how the convergence of
Freud, Derrida, Saussure, and connectionism provides a general critique of cognition, location, and neurology. I will argue that the connectionist project offers an occasion for a critique of a self-present,
originary, locatable psychical trace. Moreover, this critique is deliv-
ered (surprisingly) through the processes of traditional scientific
inquiry. Via connectionism, the embodiment of the psyche is enacted not through present cortical traces, but through the deferral and
difference of a material trace that is nowhere locatable. Similarly,
connectionist models replace the propositional logic of the Tur-
ing/von Neumann machine with the differential functioning of a
"Saussurian machine." Saussurian pure difference is instantiated in
the architecture and functioning of the web of interconnected units.
In the same way that each element of the linguistic system is instan-

tiated not through its own self-given identity but rather through a system of differences, so too each unit and connection of a neural network is dependent on every other unit and connection in the net for its cognitive effect. The connectionist model, as Saussurian machine, generates psychological effects through the systematic and lawful play of nonpresent neurocognitive differences.

~ Conclusion

> I do not believe in decisive ruptures, in an unequivocal "epis-
> temological break" as it is called today. Breaks are always, and
> fatally, reinscribed in an old cloth that must continually, inter-
> minably be undone. This interminability is not an accident or a
> contingency; it is essential, systematic, and theoretical. And
> this in no way minimizes the necessity and relative importance
> of certain breaks, of the appearance and definition of new
> structures. (Derrida 1981, 24)

In the preceding section I have argued that there are a number of important and irreducible differences between the computational-ism of connectionist models and that of traditional cognitive psy-chology. As such, connectionist models offer the possibility for a generative reading of cognition. What I have *not* argued—and this is a crucial component of the analysis that I wish to build—is that these connectionist models are a better or more accurate version of cognition. While connectionism enacts a disruption of the con-straints of traditional computationalism, it is never separate from, or in radical opposition to, such constraints. As Derrida would remind us, connectionism is still systematically inscribed in a cloth that "must continually, interminably be undone." The issue, as I see it, is neither to pursue decisive ruptures in cognitive theory under the name of connectionism nor to narrate the ways in which connec-tionism fails to deliver such ruptures.

Gordon Globus (1992; 1995) is one of the first commentators to give a sustained investigation of the convergence of Freud, Derrida, and connectionism. However, despite his enthusiasm for a decon-structive approach, his analysis is unable to sustain the critical bearing that Derrida demands, and he rushes too quickly into an uncritical affirmation of connectionist theory. Specifically, Globus is too concerned with finding a one-to-one mapping between neural networks and deconstruction, as if to show that connectionism is the empirical validation not of analytic theories of mind but of deconstruction's critical pursuits (there is a similar tendency in Miers, who suggests that connectionism offers us a "neural recipe for representation" [Miers 1992, 954], which will effect a rewriting of "postmodern theory" as it currently operates).

Specifically, Globus attempts to map connectionism onto deconstruction without concern for the excess and tension that such a mapping necessarily creates. The purpose of this mapping is to effect what Globus calls a "deconstruction of the brain," a task he considers central to any critical investigation of the cognitive sciences. For Globus, this necessitates an articulation of how the stochastic nature of brain activity entailed in connectionist models undermines the computational logic of traditional models of mind-brain. This in turn allows a cozy alliance between a connectionist brain and deconstruction: "There is, I suggest, a strong affinity between Derrida's vision of continental anti-rationalism and a connectionism whose fundamental process is dynamical, self-organizing, stochastic and holistic." Globus argues that if the computational brain of traditional AI is the "metaphysical brain," then the "spontaneous, unpredictable, self-organizing, holistic" entity of connectionist science is the "deconstructed brain" (Globus 1992, 193). However, the status of Globus's deconstructed brain remains unconvincing; this spontaneous, unpredictable, self-organizing, holistic brain simply *opposes* the previous properties of computational order, stasis, and rationality, and is not in any way "deconstructed." Globus correctly differentiates between the traditional computer-brain and the neurological connectionist brain, but this difference in itself does not constitute a deconstruction. Moreover, Globus is unable to explain what it is about this "deconstructed brain" that has made it so readily and widely assimilable to conventional accounts of neurology and computation.

Deconstruction never offers the possibility of a move beyond or outside what it interrogates. Deconstruction is always a small, internal movement that acknowledges our enclosure within a field even as we attempt to undo that containment. *Deconstruction cannot produce or unequivocally support a new cognitive theory.* More specifically, the process of "deconstructing" the brain is interminable, and does not find its final resolution in an empirical paradigm such as connectionism. The brain's relation to both mind and body remains uncontested in Globus's paper—its role as the origin of the psyche, for example, remains axiomatic. Connectionism, under Globus, remains faithful to the same general philosophical presumptions of traditional cognitive science: solutions to the question of the origin. The end effect of Globus's paper is to lend deconstructive credence to what remains primarily a realist scientific project (see Cilliers 1990 for a more careful examination of the relation between Freud, Saussure, Derrida, and connectionism).

Globus's project mirrors Pribram and Gill's (1976) earlier attempt to investigate Freud's *Project* in the light of (then contemporary) cognitive theory. Pribram and Gill were looking to simply merge the neurological and psychological aspects of the *Project* without investigating the critical tensions between them. They were interested in integrating control theory with the *Project*; this required a certain amount of correction for both cognitive and Freudian theory. They saw the *Project* as the empirical translation of psychoanalysis, wherein all the major aspects of psychoanalytic theory are given operational definition. Consequently, they attempted to rewrite both psychoanalysis and traditional cognitive psychology in order to create a more advanced "neuro-psychoanalysis." Theirs is a dialectical model: "We propose that we examine the basic concept as it appears in the *Project* in the light of today's neurochemical findings to see how that concept relates to current knowledge and then develop a more appropriate version" (Pribram and Gill 1976, 43).

My orientation differs significantly from that of both Globus and Pribram and Gill. I want to juxtapose connectionism, Freud, and Derrida, but I have no advanced or integrated cognitive theory to offer, nor do I claim that connectionism is a more accurate account of cognition by way of its intersections with certain deconstructive notions. The value of an analysis of this juxtaposition is neither to demonstrate that connectionism is the empirical application of deconstruction (which is to position philosophy as the origin of scientific theory) nor to argue that deconstruction is an elaboration of an already established scientific paradigm (which is to position empiricism as the adjudicator of philosophical analysis). Rather, I am interested in connectionism in order that the relation between empiricism and philosophy may be figured other than through the tired divisions of theory/application, data/explanation, primary/secondary. If I remain suspicious of Globus's too easy fraternization of Derrida and connectionism, this is because I wish to keep the nature of the relation philosophy-science open to investigation, and through this enact a critical reorientation to psychology's scientific projects. This is what will be pursued more fully in the final chapter.

chapter five

Locating Cognition

Force, Topography, and the Psychical Trace

The points of intersection between connectionism, Derrida, and Freud offer a number of opportunities for an interrogation of cognition. In this chapter I shall focus on only one particular issue that arises from this reorientation to cognition: the status of the psychical trace in cognitive theory. Specifically, I am interested in the issue of the location of this trace. My hypothesis is that traditional cognitive theories attempt to locate the psychical trace as a present and fixed entity within the mind-brain. I will respond to such reductive tendencies with an examination of the negotiation between cognitive force or mobility, on the one hand, and cognitive topography or location, on the other, arguing that the cognitive trace (and thus the structure of cognition in general) is conventionalized in cognitive theory through a determined refusal of this interchange between force and topography. Derrida has warned of "the danger involved in immobilizing or freezing energy within a naive metaphorics of place" (1978a, 212); a warning that he instantiates in the nature of breaching as both the force that forges a pathway and the space generated by this force. Here I shall investigate the stultifying effects of a cognitive trace that, disavowing its debt to an economics of force, is constituted through a pure locality.

The connectionist trace will help in articulating this conventionalization, and it will become the means by which an intervention into its operations can be made. The central tenets of connectionist theory displace and defer the psychical trace through a system of differences, undermining the empirical drive toward a pure cognitive location. More specifically, the connectionist trace, as irreducibly both force and topography, effects a radical disruption of the distinction between trace and structure that is at the heart of traditional cognitive intelligibility. While connectionism has been reducible, in part, to traditional scientific and philosophical expectations about the static and locatable nature of the cognitive trace (see, for example, Bechtel and Abrahamsen 1991), it nonetheless operates in excess of these tendencies. I will argue that Freudian, Derridean, and Saussurian tools are necessary to deploy adequately connectionist theories as a critique of traditional cognitive morphology.

~ The Cognitive Trace and Location

> Mental states of every kind—sensations, feelings, ideas— which were at one time present in consciousness and then have disappeared from it, have not with their disappearance absolutely ceased to exist. Although the inwardly-turned look may no longer be able to find them, nevertheless they have not been utterly destroyed and annulled, but in a certain manner they continue to exist, stored up, so to speak, in the memory. We cannot, of course, directly observe their present existence, but it is revealed by the effects which come to our knowledge with a certainty like that with which we infer the existence of the stars below the horizon. (Ebbinghaus 1885, 1)

> Remembering is not the re-excitation of innumerable fixed, lifeless and fragmentary traces. It is an imaginative reconstruction. (Bartlett 1932, 213)

Ebbinghaus's (1885) experiments on memory were important in establishing the parameters within which current psychological theories of cognition operate. Along with Fechner, Helmholtz, and

Wundt, Ebbinghaus is credited with founding the experimental tradition in psychology (Boring 1957; Hilgard 1964). Where Helmholtz had successfully measured the speed of nerve transmission, Ebbinghaus took the next step and attempted to demonstrate that higher cognitive processes themselves could be submitted to empirical measurement. The direct influence of Ebbinghaus's experiments on later developments in cognitive psychology cannot be underestimated—his formulations of memory have been carried through to the present day almost unchanged (Klix and Hagendorf 1986). In particular, his notion of a discrete and stable memory trace is the backbone of the information-processing model of contemporary cognitive psychology.

Unlike the measurement of a nerve impulse, however, a determination of memory traces can only be ascertained incompletely. The empiricist is foiled by the fact that such cognitive traces are not directly observable or measurable—we know them only through their effects. Ebbinghaus is thus compelled to pursue memories via indirect, inferential and mediated means. On the one hand, then, memories are presumed to be present, discrete, and locatable entities existing in some sort of psychical storehouse and awaiting retrieval, but on the other hand, these entities are unable to be brought directly into contact with the senses; memories are psychically present yet empirically elusive. Herein lies the central difficulty of contemporary cognitive psychology: how to scientifically study a trace that defies empirical location.

Despite these difficulties in bringing a memory trace into line with scientific demands, or perhaps because of such difficulties, Ebbinghaus formulated the memory trace through the ideals of empirical inquiry: presence, location, stability, quantification. Ebbinghaus built his study on the presupposition that cognitive traces of perception are stored permanently in the psychical system, and when reactivated these stored inscriptions are experienced as memories. While many of these traces may not be instantly accessible, they do continue to exist elsewhere in the psychical landscape. Consequently, recall is formulated as the transportation of a past event into the presence of consciousness. Drawing on the Platonic metaphor of memories as birds in an aviary, Ebbinghaus described the voluntary retrieval of a memory thus: "Among the representations is found the one [memory] which we sought, and it is immediately recognized as something formerly experienced. It would be absurd to suppose that our will has created it anew and, as it were, out of nothing; it must have been present somehow or somewhere. The will, so to speak, has only discovered it and brought it to us again" (Ebbinghaus 1885, 1–2). In a manner completely consistent with the dominant philosophical metaphors of memory (Krell 1990), Ebbinghaus takes memory to be engrammatical—that is, made up of locatable inscriptions of set and finite dimensions that lie dormant until reactivated in the processes of retrieval. It is this formulation that fashions the memory trace as a suitable object for scientific psychological inquiry.

Some fifty years after Ebbinghaus's experiments, a British psychologist published an extensive theoretical and experimental critique of what by then had become known as "the Ebbinghaus tradition." Bartlett's (1932) text was a lone critical voice against the methodological and theoretical dominance of Ebbinghaus's work, and unfortunately it was soon buried by both behaviorism and the authority of already established experimental norms. Largely ignored by the histories of psychology (Boring 1957; Kantor 1969; Leahey 1992), Bartlett's text provides an incisive examination of the theoretical assumptions that underwrite the experimental and cognitive traditions in psychology. His general thesis—that memory is an active, reconstructive process, not the reactivation of fixed and lifeless traces—was fairly simple, but it has a number of far-reaching implications for psychological theory and methodology.

Underlying all Bartlett's theoretical and empirical criticisms was a concern with the discrete and individual nature of the memory trace as proposed by Ebbinghaus:

The traces are generally supposed to be of individual and specific events. Hence, every normal individual must carry about with him an incalculable number of individual traces. Since these are all stored in a single organism, they are in fact bound to be related one to another, and this gives to recall its inevitably associative character; but all the time each trace retains its essential individuality, and remembering, in the ideal case, is simple re-excitation, or pure reproduction. (Bartlett 1932, 197)

Bartlett proposes that "the past operates as an organized mass rather than as a group of elements each of which retains its specific character" (1932, 197), and that any particular memory is a reconstruction from this mass. This idea of an "organized mass" was drawn from Sir Henry Head's work on body posture and movement. Head had rejected the hypothesis that skilled bodily movement and body posture are controlled by a series of stored images or cortical traces, and he posited instead the notion of a bodily schema (Head 1920, cited in Bartlett 1932). This schema is a postural model of ourselves that is dynamic and which determines the *psychological* parameters of bodily posture and movement. New movements are assimilated into one's schema, change that schema, and then become part of the general determining force of bodily posture and movement. Incoming stimuli are always interpreted according to the already existing schemata; thus the registration of every sensation is always influenced by what has gone before. Bartlett (1932) generalized this idea of a bodily schema to cognition in general: Cognition is the operation of schemata that assimilate perceptual and intracognitive information, and which are in turn transformed by those assimilations. Specifically, these schemata are organized chronologically (rather than spatially) and according to various laws of association, and they are mediated by appetite, instinct, interest, and ideals. Intrapsychically they become interconnected and are thus interdependent; the pattern of interconnections between schemata forms what is called temperament or character. Schemata are also intrinsically social (as shown by the forces of conventionalization in serial recall)—their content, and the reactions that they elicit, are constantly checked and facilitated by others. These schemata, which are individual yet culturally shared and constrained, determine and actively sustain cognitive processing. For Bartlett, then, cognition cannot be simply the possession of an individual, but is the effect of a web of determination between individuals, and between an individual and the social.

Even though Bartlett draws his understanding of cognitive schemata from Head, he remains critical of Head's allegiance to the Ebbinghaus tradition. While Head had rejected the notion of individual traces controlling bodily movement, he nonetheless invoked a more generalized storehouse of impressions that precede and establish the bodily schema:

> But, in addition to its function as an organ of local attention, the sensory cortex is also the storeroom of past impressions. These may rise into consciousness as images, but more often, as in the case of special impressions, remain outside of central consciousness. Here they form organized models of ourselves, which may be termed "schemata." Such schemata modify the impressions produced by incoming sensory impulses in such a way that the final sensation of position, or of locality, rises into consciousness charged with a relation to something that has happened before. Destruction of such "schemata" by a lesion of the cortex render impossible all recognition of posture or of the locality of a stimulated spot in the affected part of the body. (Head 1920, cited in Schilder 1950, 11–12)

For Head, a bodily schema is a cortically located aggregation of traces and impressions. Against such a formulation, the idea of cognitive schemata that Bartlett advances is an attempt to undermine radically a locatable cognitive element, be it a schema, a trace, or a perceptual fragment. Explicitly rejecting Head's inference of a cortical location for schematic traces or the schemata themselves, Bartlett (1932) insists on a more dynamic use of schemata. For Bartlett, the essential part of a schema is activity and mobility, not location: "The organized mass results of past changes of position and posture are actively *doing* something all the time; are, so to speak, carried along with us, complete, though developing, from moment to moment" (Bartlett 1932, 201). Consequently, memory is formulated as a force, rather than a fixed or locatable structure.

Bartlett privileges an organized, dynamic mass of past experiences over a passive framework of individual memory traces:

> There is not the slightest reason, however, to suppose that each set of incoming impulses, each new group of experiences persists as an isolated member of some passive patchwork. They have to be regarded as constituents of living, momentary settings belonging to the organism, or to whatever parts of the organism are concerned in making a response of a given kind, and not as a number of individual events somehow strung together and stored within the organism. (Bartlett 1932, 201)

So memory neither produces something completely new, nor simply reproduces something that already exists. Instead, memory is "literally manufactured" (Bartlett 1932, 202) within or between already existing schemata. Memory is never the re-presentation of an element stored elsewhere; it is always an "imaginative reconstruction," a constant variation without a discrete origin. If Bartlett was to posit a memory trace, then this "trace" would be constituted in the act of remembering; it does not preexist and determine retrieval, but is the effect of the processes of schematic reconstruction.

For these reasons, Bartlett's notion of schema is perhaps closer to Schilder's (1950) idea of the body image. While both Bartlett and Schilder were working at the same time and drawing heavily on Head's work, neither seemed to be aware of the other's work. The gap between Bartlett's empirical commitments and Schilder's psychoanalytic commitments was perhaps sufficient to keep them at a distance from each other. Both men moved away from the strictly neurological course that Head maintained, and its concomitant locationism, and moved toward explicitly psychological schemata. In Schilder's case, the body image is formulated through a careful negotiation between the domains of neurology and psychoanalysis. Schilder's body image is a multisensory self-concept that, like Bartlett's schema, is irreducibly the product of one's interactions with others. While mediated through the cortex, the body image cannot be located as such. Instead it is the product (and producer) of the space between self and other, between sensations over time, between the inside and the outside, between and through bodily movements. (A more extensive discussion of the production and effects of the body image can be found in Grosz 1994b.)

While never as explicitly and radically corporeal as Schilder's body image, Bartlett's schemata are nonetheless indebted to a similar displacement of psychical locality and determination. In particular, the fact that Bartlett draws on a theory of the body, and its postures and movements, to articulate his theory of memory, and that he occasionally formulates the processes of memory as isomorphic with bodily movement should not go unnoticed. For Bartlett, the body offers movement and dynamism to a theory of memory that cannot be so easily extracted from the more sedentary theories of mind–brain. Specifically, the notion of bodily movement defies the localizing effects of inert individual traces. If memory is metaphorized through bodily movement, then it cannot be so easily reduced to discrete, fixed, and lifeless traces.

In Bartlett's formulation, a schema is not a storehouse of traces, but a living, constantly developing organization of knowledge; moreover, such schemata are not locatable as delineated and static cognitive structures. No longer fixed and lifeless, locatable and measurable, the cognitive trace is displaced in Bartlett's account in favor of a dynamic system regulated by social and intrapsychic forces. By exploiting the tension between psychical place and psychical force, Bartlett's schemata exceed the fixed structuration of the Ebbinghaus tradition that problematically constitutes cognition through a "fundamental immobility and a reassuring certitude" (Derrida 1978b, 279).

~

Neisser's (1967) textbook of cognitive psychology is widely regarded as the first authoritative account of contemporary cognitive psychology (Best 1992; Eysenck and Kean 1990). This was one of the first experimental psychology texts to defy the behaviorist orthodoxy about mental processes, and to construct a radically new approach to psychological explanation. As the self-appointed heir to Bartlett's hitherto buried legacy, Neisser was primarily interested in the complex social and psychical systems that interpret and transform sensory information. Like Bartlett, Neisser postulates a cognitive system that is always reconstructive and always dependent on its psychical and social context.

Despite his place in the history of cognitive psychology, the central tenets of Neisser's approach to cognition (the influence from Bartlett, his interchanges with Freudian psychoanalysis, his insistence on the lived reality of cognitive processes) have all been repudiated by later cognitive psychologists in favor of the traditional experimentation to which both Neisser and Bartlett were so vehemently opposed. In general, it has been an examination of a fixed cognitive trace within an information-processing machine, rather than an explication of the social, reconstructive, and dynamic nature of such processing, that has been central to cognitive psychology's empirical concerns. Given Neisser's strong influence on the emerging field of cognitive psychology and his equally strong convictions concerning the appropriate subject matter and methodology of that field, why were his central concerns so quickly and easily overlooked? What was it in Neisser's position that allowed his ideals to be redeployed in the service of the tradition he disdained?

One answer, at least, can be found in Neisser's (1967) formulation of the cognitive trace. Despite his overt allegiance to Bartlett-like schemata, Neisser betrays the essence of Bartlett's system by reintroducing fragmentary cognitive traces as the building blocks of schemata. In so doing, Neisser authorized a certain amalgamation of the Bartlett and Ebbinghaus traditions that subordinates the critical purchase of Bartlett's work to a more restrictive and orthodox empiricism. It is this move to a fragmentary schematic trace that allowed those who followed Neisser to ignore the radical implications of Bartlett's critique of trace theory and to build a cognitive psychology more faithful to the locationism of the Ebbinghaus tradition.

Concerned by the absence of any "raw material" in Bartlett's process of memory reconstruction, Neisser (1967) posits a trace prior to the processes of reconstruction. Unable to tolerate Bartlett's erasure of the trace through the processes of schematic reconstruction, Neisser introduces a prototrace out of which memories are built:

> It must be admitted that this kind of theorizing [i.e., Bartlett's construction of memory] deals at best with half the problem. Even if the constructive nature of the memory is fully acknowledged, the fact remains that information about the past must be somehow stored and preserved for subsequent use. Today's experience must leave some sort of trace behind if it is to influence tomorrow's construction. (Neisser 1967, 280)

Concerned that Bartlett's hypotheses suggest that memory is constructed out of nothing at all, Neisser, like Ebbinghaus, proposes that perception produces traces that then become the raw material for the reconstructive processes of memory. Bartlett's careful use of schemata as an argument against a theory of present, locatable traces, be they cognitive or perceptual, is thus disregarded, and the always already activated schemata are reduced to originary or constituent traces. Bartlett's thoroughgoing critique of the structure of memory is simplified by Neisser and transformed into a routine critique of representation in British empiricism (i.e., the notion that ideas are isomorphic copies of experience):

> The notion that the stored information consists of ideas, suspended in a quiescent state from which they are occasionally aroused, has a very long history in psychology. It seems to me so important—and so misguided—that it deserves a special name. Here I will call it the "Reappearance Hypothesis," since it implies that the same "memory," image, or other cognitive unit can disappear and reappear over and over again. (Neisser 1967, 281–82)

Against this "reappearance hypothesis," Neisser promotes a "utilization hypothesis" (1967, 284). Here Neisser ventures that acts of perception and previous acts of cognition generate traces of their activity. Rather than these traces forming full-blown empiricist memories, they are simply the building blocks out of which memories are built (although we should note that this notion is not so very different from J. S. Mill's associationism, and particularly his idea of mental chemistry). For Neisser, cognition becomes analogous to paleontology:

> The model of the paleontologist . . . applies also to memory:
> out of a few stored bone chips, we remember a dinosaur. . . .
> The present proposal is, therefore, that we store traces of earli-
> er cognitive acts, not of the product of those acts. The traces are
> not simply "revived" or "reactivated" in recall; instead, the
> stored fragments are used as information to support a new con-
> struction. (Neisser 1967, 285–86)

At this moment, then, Neisser reintroduces the locatable, fixed,
static origin in the trace fragment that Bartlett was at pains to relin-
quish. Like Head's subschematic impressions, Neisser's prototraces
are no less implicated in the problematic of location: The fragmented trace belongs to the same ontological economy as the full-blown
memory trace. The end effect is to distribute, but not displace, the
effect of a psychical presence.

In the years following 1967, Neisser has become increasingly dis-
illusioned with contemporary experimental cognitive psychology.
Like Bartlett before him, Neisser has become particularly concerned
that cognitive psychology is unable to apply itself to behavior other
than that elicited in a laboratory environment (Neisser 1976; Neisser
and Winograd 1988). However, it would seem that the cognitive psychology that blossomed after, and seemingly against, his 1967 text is
already latent in Neisser's original formulations. As much as Neisser
wanted to expose cognitive psychology to the perceptual and psychical flux within which the subject operates, he sowed the seeds
for the attenuation of this system in his representation of the cognitive trace. Specifically, Neisser has deflated the tension between
psychical place and psychical force that was evident, although not
fully exploited, in Bartlett's theory of memory. By establishing and
authorizing the psyche through discrete and inert paleontological
traces, Neisser effectively obstructs an understanding of cognition as
anything other than machinistic, immobile, and self-present.

While Bartlett's notion of schema has become one of the key conceptual tools of contemporary cognitive psychology, such schemata
now always function through the reconstruction of atomistic traces.
Consequently, while most cognitive psychologists do indeed accept
the reconstructive nature of cognition, they avoid, and are protected

from, Bartlett's strong antitrace criticisms. Even with the theoretical shifts in cognitive psychology away from store-based models of memory (e.g., Atkinson and Shiffrin 1968) to more active, processual models (e.g., Tulving 1972; 1985), the commitment to a fixed and locatable memory trace persists. Relying as they do on local representations of memory, traditional cognitive theories of memory are concerned with the manipulation of already existing psychical entities. The influential "levels of processing" model (Craik and Lockhart 1972), for example, refers explicitly to individual cognitive traces; it is the type of processing these traces undergo, and the effects of elaboration of these traces, that determine the nature and function of memory (Cermak and Craik 1979). Only with the advent of connectionist models of memory has it become possible inside psychology to think the memory trace in a way more faithful to Bartlett's original formulation and less subservient to the dominant empiricist and experimental traditions (Le Voi 1993).

~

While it is extremely difficult to find any major cognitive psychology text that pauses to give a definition of the cognitive trace (in general, most texts take the cognitive trace as a priori), such a definition can be ascertained obliquely through the definitions of what it is not. Specifically, most cognitive texts make the distinction between a cognitive and a neurological trace the means by which the cognitive trace is defined:

> We are not primarily interested in the way information is physically stored by the brain. Psychology deals with the organization and use of information, not with its representation in organic tissue. (Neisser 1967, 281)

> It's true that there is always the possibility that specific relationships may be found between specific neural activities or locations, and particular mental events. . . . However, despite this, cognitive psychologists working in the information-processing tradition maintain that there are no guarantees that a specific, discoverable neural code underlies all specific mental events. (Best 1992, 22)

> Though the appeal of PDP models is definitely enhanced by their physiological plausibility and neural inspiration, these are not the primary bases for their appeal to us. We are, after all, cognitive scientists, and PDP models appeal to us for psychological and computational reasons. (McClelland, Rumelhart, and Hinton 1986, 11)

In general, cognitive psychology has been either indifferent to, or agnostic about, the role of neurology in psychological theory. Cognitive psychologists are often at pains to point out that their trace is not the same as a neurological trace. Differentiating themselves from neurologists, neurological reductionists, eliminativists, neuropsychologists, and even cognitive neuropsychologists, cognitive psychologists are keen to preserve the essentially psychological nature of the cognitive trace. Cognitive psychologists are usually highly skeptical of any one-to-one correspondence between psychology and physiology, claiming that the psychological cannot be contained within, or explained by, a science of biological or neurological inscriptions.

Nonetheless, there can be no doubt that the cognitive trace is in some crucial way indebted to the neurological trace. This debt is not only historical (the neuropsychological trace discursively predates the cognitive trace), but also philosophical. The notion of psychical inscription, which defines neuropsychology, is also a constituent part of the cognitive trace. As much as cognitive psychology has sought to distance itself from neurological inscription, the very idea of a "trace" necessarily invokes inscription, and in so doing insists on a certain materiality of cognition. Given the dominance of mind-brain reductionism in twentieth-century cognitive science, the cognitive trace is always marked, and delimited, by the neurological trace.

Specifying the similar philosophical and empirical commitments in neurology and psychology has typically led to the hope of reducing the latter to the former. This is not my goal here. If, as I shall argue in the following two sections, the psychical trace can acknowledge its debt to a certain mode of inscription that exceeds location, then no biological reductionism or determination need ensue. What is gained through such cognitive tracing is the instantiation of the material and mobile nature of the psyche, but without an imperative for locationism and reductionism. Freud helps us some way down this path with his transformation of psychical place and locality. An understanding of these aspects of the Freudian system, along with a contribution from Derrida, Saussure, and connectionism, allows us to envisage just such a material yet unlocatable trace. In the following section I introduce Freudian topography and the Derridean trace as the means by which such an intervention can be initiated.

~ Freudian Topography and the Transformation of the Cognitive Trace

And when he renounces neurology and anatomical localizations, it will be not in order to abandon his topographical preoccupations, but to transform them. (Derrida 1978a, 205)

Topography (the word comes from the Greek for "place," *topoi*) is a theory of places. In Freud's texts, the term *topography* refers specifically to psychical places. While his topographical formulations are always explicitly psychological, the notion of topography came to Freud primarily through the discourses of neurology, physiology, and psychopathology that dominated his medical training and practice (Laplanche and Pontalis 1973). At the end of the nineteenth century the notion of topography was intimately tied to theories of cerebral location, wherein complex psychological functions, particularly language, were thought to be located in specific areas of cortical tissue. It is through, rather than against, this connection to discourses of anatomical location that Freud eventually transformed the term topography into a critique of psychical space and psychical location.

Topography is one of three crucial components of Freud's metapsychology: "I propose that when we have succeeded in describing a psychical process in its dynamic, topographical and economic aspects, we should speak of it as a *metapsychological* presentation" (Freud 1915, 181). Where the dynamic approach deals with the conflicts of instinctual forces, and the economic with the circulation and distribution of psychical energy, the topographical approach is concerned primarily with the spaces and structures within which these processes are "located." Freud proposed two quite different topographical models: the systems of the unconscious, preconscious, and conscious (Freud 1900; 1915) and the agencies of the id, ego, and superego (Freud 1923). It is the first of these models (unconscious, preconscious, conscious) that is of primary interest to me here. This topographical model, which has its roots in Freud's transition from neurology to psychology, was given its first public explication in chapter 7 of *The interpretation of dreams* (Freud 1900), although a similar approach to the psychical system was already evident in the *Project* (Freud 1895) and in Freud's letters to Fliess (especially the letters of January 1, 1896, and December 6, 1986, in Masson 1985). Emerging on the cusp of neurology and psychology, it is this model that provides Freud's most incisive critique of psychical locality.

A critique of psychical and cortical location can be found in the very earliest of Freud's texts. In the preface to his translation of Bernheim's *De La Suggestion*, Freud offers a categorical response to claims for a strictly cortical location for hypnotic symptoms: "[Consciousness] is not a thing which is bound up with any locality in the nervous system" (Freud 1888, 84). While still enmeshed in his neurological practice, Freud was critical of the paradigm of cortical location derived from Wernicke's and Broca's discovery of language centers in the left hemisphere of the brain. In *On Aphasia*, Freud (1891) gives a complex and well-grounded critique of Wernicke's and Lichtheim's localized theories of aphasia. Heavily influenced by the writings of the English neurologist John Hughlings Jackson (1958), Freud argued that the prevailing theory of aphasia, which posited localized centers and cortical pathways, should be replaced with a functional model. Freud rejected the assumption that language can be found within certain circumscribed areas of the cortex, and that aphasias are the disruption of the pathways between these areas. Freud argued that the brain is arranged not topographically (i.e., there is no one-to-one projection of the body surface on the cortex) but functionally, and so he hypothesized that aphasia is due to "a change in the functional state of the speech apparatus rather than a localized interruption of a pathway" (Freud 1891, 29).

Freud (1891) provides a critique of not only the location of psychical space but also the existence of discrete and localized psychical traces within that space. He contested the notion that cortical centers contain localized ideas, images, or traces (e.g., sound word images, glosso-kinesthetic word images). More specifically, he disputed not only the empiricist heritage of localized ideas, but also the scientific "advance" that posits the presence of atomistic elements of images out of which full psychological entities are made (as, for example, in the position taken by Neisser 1967):

> Considering the tendency of earlier medical periods to localize whole mental faculties, such as are defined in psychological terminology, in certain areas of the brain, it was bound to appear as a great advance when Wernicke declared that only the simplest psychic elements, i.e., the various sensory perceptions, could be localized in the cortex, the areas concerned being those of the central terminations of the sensory nerves. But does one not in principle make the same mistake, irrespective of whether one tries to localize a complicated concept, a whole mental faculty or a psychic element? (Freud 1891, 54–55)

According to Stengel, not only was Freud "the first in the German speaking world to subject the current theory of localization to a systematic critical analysis" (1953, x), but this is also the first Freudian text that deals with the contradiction between functionalism and locationism. This antagonism between Wernicke's localized topographical model and Hughlings Jackson's functional explanation is the same antagonism that drives the tension between the dynamic and topographical modes of Freud's metapsychology (see below). This engagement of dynamism with stasis, and function with locale, becomes crucial to Freud's later formulation of psychical space and locality.

In these early texts, the term *topographical* has problematic resonances for Freud. It is a term used, in a somewhat derogatory fashion, to describe a purely localized system. When presenting his new schema of psychical systems in a letter to Fliess, Freud is careful to label it "not necessarily topographical" (Freud, letter to Fliess, December 6, 1896, in Masson 1985, 207). Yet at some point around this time Freud came to realize that a notion such as topography would bring substantial theoretical purchase to his psychological formulations. In a manner that marks many of his theoretical innovations, Freud takes a commonplace notion and folds it back on itself. Here he takes one of the key tenets of locationism—topography—as the means by which he constructs a radical critique of psychical locality. In this short text on aphasia, Freud begins the task of reorienting the relation of topography to (cerebral) location. From this period onward, Freud embarks on a stronger and stronger recuperation of topography. From the *Studies on hysteria* (Freud and Breuer 1895) onward, the psyche is topographically differentiated, although it is not until 1900 that a full-blown topographical model was put forward with any confidence. From 1900, topographical models of some sort play an important role in the theoretical foundations of psychoanalysis.

Freud's primary consideration in the transformation of topography is to loosen it from a fixed and localized anatomy. Wherever topography is introduced, Freud clearly and repeatedly distances his model from too literal an association with anatomy:

> What is presented to us in these words is the idea of *psychical locality*. I shall entirely disregard the fact that the mental apparatus with which we are here concerned is also known to us in the form of anatomical preparation, and I shall carefully avoid the temptation to determine psychical locality in any anatomical fashion. (Freud 1900, 536)

> [While] mental activity is bound up with the function of the brain as it is with no other organ . . . every attempt to go on from there to discover a localization of mental processes, every endeavor to think of ideas as stored up in nerve-cells and of excitations as traveling along nerve-fibers, has miscarried completely. The same fate would await any theory which attempted to recognize, let us say, the anatomical position of the system *Cs.*—conscious mental activity—as being in the cortex,

and to localize the unconscious processes in the sub-cortical parts of the brain. (Freud 1915, 174)

The subdivision of the unconscious is part of an attempt to picture the apparatus of the mind as being built up of a number of *agencies* or *systems* whose relations to one another are expressed in spatial terms, without, however, implying any connection with the actual anatomy of the brain (I have described this as the *topographical* method of approach). (Freud 1925b, 32)

However, the relation of Freudian topography to the discourses of anatomical location of function should not be thought of simply as negative critique: The issue of anatomy is never fully banished from the scene of topography. Freud repeatedly returns to anatomical metaphors to describe his psychical topography—as, for example, in the comparison of the system *Pcpt–Cs.* to the outer crust of the cerebral cortex (Freud 1920). Similarly, he takes the reflex arc as his schema for the psychical system in general: "Reflex processes remain the model of every psychical function" (Freud 1900, 538). As Laplanche and Pontalis (1973) point out, this schema of the reflex arc is neither literal nor simply metaphorical. It is not so much an effort to map the psyche directly onto the reflex arc that concerns Freud in these theoretical-empirical productions (although a certain similitude is necessary and profitable); rather, the reflex arc is mobilized in order to mediate the impossible space between biology and psychology that psychoanalytic topographies inhabit. As such, certain biological and neurological formulations become indispensable to psychoanalytic metapsychology. It is not renunciation of anatomy and neurology, but its transformation, that drives the Freudian topography. To reformulate the quotation from Derrida that opens this section: *When Freud announces his topographical preoccupations, it is not in order to abandon neurology and anatomy, but to transform them.*

The unconscious is the first, and perhaps the most radical, of Freud's topographical formulations (Freud 1900; 1915). Moreover, in the unconscious we find a thoroughgoing critique of location. Not only is the conscious system displaced as the locale of the psyche, but the unconscious itself is located nowhere. The contents of the unconscious do not exist as such (like stars below the horizon). They are not full and present entities kept, temporarily, from the gaze of the conscious mind. Derrida says of the text of the unconscious:

> There is no text *present elsewhere* as an unconscious one to be transposed or transported. . . . There is then no unconscious truth to be rediscovered by virtue of having been written elsewhere. . . . There is no present text in general, and there is not even a past present text, a text which is past as having been present. The text is not conceivable in an originary or modified form of presence. The unconscious text is already a weave of pure traces, differences in which meaning and force are united—a text nowhere present, consisting of archives which are *always already* transcriptions. Originary prints. (Derrida 1978a, 211)

Freud's topographical unconscious radically undermines any notion of psychical presence and locality. This other scene—always displaced and deferred—is a place without location. For Spivak and Derrida, this radical displacement of psychical locality is accomplished through the irreducible negotiation of the topographical (place) and economic (force) components of Freud's metapsychology:

> Freud does not put the psyche under erasure merely by declaring it to be inhabited by a radical alterity; nor by declaring perception and temporality to be functions of a writing. He does it also by his many avowed questionings of that same topological fable of the mind that he constantly uses. It does not seem correct to unproblematize Freud's different models for the psychic system and call them "varying 'points of view' used by Freud to represent the psychic system." The point is that Freud uses the dynamic (play of forces) or functional picture of the psyche almost to annul the topological one; yet gives the topological picture greatest usage; the typical sleight of hand of "sous rature." (Spivak 1974, xli)

In an attempt to think place and force simultaneously, Freud pits each against the other, effecting a displacement of the purity of both place and force within his psychical models. Across a number of pivotal texts, Freud oscillates between the spatial and economic models of the psyche. In the final sections of chapter 7 of *The interpretation of dreams* (Freud 1900), the topographical model, which has held sway throughout, is momentarily defeated by the economic model. Freud announces that when an idea forces its way through into the conscious, this should not be thought of a change in locality—it is energy that is mobile, not the idea itself. In the end it is the topographical model that prevails, but now topography has been recast through an irreducible debt to force.

In his most detailed elucidation of the unconscious, Freud (1915) returns to the same problem: Should the transposition of an idea from the unconscious to the conscious be viewed as a spatial transposition (i.e., moving an idea from one psychical location to another) or as a change of state? Freud suggests that the first of these is "doubtless the cruder but also the more convenient" model, while the second is "*a priori* more probable, but it is less plastic, less easy to manipulate" (1915, 175). A decision between the two is never made, and is instead deferred through the introduction of a third hypothesis about the hypercathexis of the word-presentation and the thing-presentation in the different topographical systems. As Spivak (1974) argues, this oscillation is not inconsistency or indecisiveness on Freud's behalf, but rather a concerted attempt to negotiate between two necessary but impossible views on the psyche; it is the process of putting psychical locality under erasure. Neither fully present nor absent, neither freely mobile nor totally static, the psyche's placement remains undecidable. Derrida claims that for Freud the psyche cannot be contained within "familiar and constituted space, the exterior space of the natural sciences" (Derrida 1978a, 204). Freud's formulation of the unconscious, poised undecidably between force and space, between dynamism and location, constantly reminds us that our thinking of the psyche "can neither dispense with topography nor accept the current models of spacing" (Derrida 1978a, 204).

~

The notion of the psychical trace is less well developed than that of psychical space in the Freudian system. Indeed, Freud occasionally regresses into uncritical empirical formulations of the memory trace (see, for example, Freud 1925a). Nonetheless, as Laplanche and Pontalis claim, the Freudian memory trace is distinct from the engram of empirical psychology, despite these occasional lapses. They propose that Freud adopted the conventional notion of a memory trace because he needed "to assign memory a place within a topographical schema and to provide an explanation of its functioning in economic terms" (1973, 247). While it is less apparent than in his articulation of psychical space, it is still this negotiation between force (economics) and place (topography) that structures the Freudian trace.

Laplanche and Pontalis (1973) suggest that the neurophysiological orientation of the *Project* should furnish Freud with his clearest opportunity to present the memory trace as an empirically graspable presence. However, it is here that the notion of the memory trace as static engram is most carefully displaced. Indeed, as Laplanche and Pontalis attest, it is his later, less neurophysiological (and more psychological) works that are most likely to reproduce the conventional empirical notion of the memory trace. Specifically, it is an attenuation of the effects of an economics of force in these later works that reduces the Freudian trace to a problematic locality. While there is no doubt that the systems and functioning of the psyche become more sophisticated in Freud's texts after 1900, it is through an engagement with neurophysiology that the most interesting formulation of a psychical trace (qua breaching) emerges. That is, neuropsychical breaching, as both the force that forms a psychical space and the space itself, keeps the negotiation between force and topography operative. Specifically, it is the negotiation with neurology that provides Freud with a set of constraints that enable (if not compel) him to think the spatiality and economics of the trace differently; the further Freud moves away from neurology, the more he concedes a fixed and locatable trace. If the conventional cognitive trace is generated via a foreclosure of force and its relation to place, then for Freud, neurology provides the most generative means through which this forceful relation can be explained, maintained, and facilitated.

The transformation of the psychical trace that is implied by Freud, although never fully explored by him, is realized in a number of places in Derrida's work. Drawing on the radical displacement envisaged in Freud's topographical system, Derrida provides a comprehensive critique of the psychical trace that is to be found in conventional accounts of cognition. While both Derrida and cognitive psychology take the trace as the origin of the psyche, the issue at stake here is *what sort of trace* each places at the origin. As already outlined above with respect to the Ebbinghaus tradition, the trace of cognitive psychology is a full and locatable presence. Though it might not be directly observable, this trace is presumed, nonetheless, to be a presence that exists as a discrete, definable, and immobile entity in the cognitive machinery. In a complete and mature cognitive science, the vicissitudes of cognition will be reducible to the effects of such traces within the cognitive apparatus.

The Derridean trace is another matter altogether. While also placed at the origin of the psyche (Derrida 1978a), it is mobilized, explicitly, to contest both the notion of an origin and the idea that any (psychical) entity can be fully present and fully fixed. As Bennington notes, the Derridean trace definitively rejects any interpretation of psychical elements as present atomistic features out of which larger and more complete psychical structures can be built, or to which a system may be reduced. This deconstruction of the empiricist trace is initiated by Derrida's reading of Saussurian pure difference—a reading Bennington cogently summarizes as "every trace is the trace of a trace" (1993, 75). More particularly, however, the Derridean trace exploits the tension between force and place evident in Freudian metapsychology. For Derrida, the dislocation of psychical presence cannot be accomplished simply through a dispersal of locale. Without also invoking an economics of force at the heart of the psyche, we are in danger of presupposing a "[psychical] text which would be already there, immobile: the serene presence of a statue" (Derrida 1978a, 211). Location must always and everywhere be undermined by mobility. A dislocation is never simply a spatial reconfiguration; it is also always already a movement.

Through Derridean deconstruction and Freudian metapsychology a topography of traces that reorients the notions of space and location central to traditional cognitive theory can be formulated. By introducing a psychical trace more in keeping with the radical disruption of space that Freud has already established, Derrida takes us another step closer to understanding the investments and limits of the contemporary cognitive trace. This alliance between Freud and Derrida provides us with valuable tools for rethinking the place and the mobility of the psychical trace. It is, after all, not a matter of discarding the notions of space, locale, and trace, but of transforming their value. If it is through Derrida and Freud that we can formulate a cognitive trace that is not a present, fixed, and locatable psychical entity, then it is in connectionism that we see an instantiation of these principles in a manner that is coherent to scientific psychology. Where traditional cognitive psychology has been articulated through a locatable and self-present trace, connectionism has produced a trace that functions in a manner surprisingly faithful to certain Derridean considerations of inscription and mobility.

~ The Saussurian Machine

McClelland, Rumelhart, and Hinton (1986) open their influential introductory text to parallel distributed processing (PDP) with a few examples of the type of cognitive problem that their PDP models are attempting to solve. For example, bodily movement (e.g., reaching for a small knob on the desk beside the terminal) is constrained by a number of different biological and environmental parameters, specifically the structure and musculature of the body and the position of objects in space. In order for any bodily movement to be successful, the perceptual-cognitive system must be able to take each of these multiple constraints into account. So too it is for language. The successful execution of any linguistic act must take the mutually constraining influences of syntax and semantics into account. McClelland et al. use Selfridge's famous ambiguous letter test as their example of the cognitive constraints within language. Self-ridge's test showed that a letter written ambiguously between *H* and *A* will be read as an *H* when positioned between a *T* and an *E*, but it will be read as an *A* when positioned between a *C* and a *T*. A sentence, word, or letter cannot signify by itself; it is only through the multiple constraints of other sentences, words, and letters that we are able to assign meaning to a linguistic act. However, "the situation here must seem paradoxical: The identity of each letter is constrained by the identities of each of the others. But since in general we cannot know the identities of any of the letters until we have established the identities of the others, how can we get the process started?" (McClelland, Rumelhart, and Hinton 1986, 8–9). This "paradox" restates the question central to Saussure's formulation of a linguistic system: How can identity be attributed in a system that is constituted by the processes of pure difference? More specifically, McClelland et al. are concerned about the origin of such a system—if every word and letter is syntactically and semantically dependent on the other words and letters in the system, how do identity and meaning become established?

The problem of a starting point is resolved with recourse to the presumed ability of the perceptual-cognitive system to explore and resolve "multiple simultaneous constraints." This is the ability, demonstrable in connectionist systems, to juggle a number of different, sometimes contradictory, and often incomplete constraints in the process of reaching an output or solution—put colloquially, to keep a number of different pieces of information in mind at once. Such an ability enables a system to converge on the best-fit solution to a problem that is constrained by a number of different parameters. Thus a connectionist model can recognize a pattern, recall a piece of information, or classify an item based on the type of fragmented yet constraining data common to everyday cognitive tasks. And it can do so with much greater efficiency than a traditional computational model, and in a manner that closely mimics human performance in terms of accuracy and speed. This ability to handle multiple simultaneous constraints successfully is one of the key factors that distinguish connectionist parallel processing from the linear processing of traditional cognitive models.

Of course, this gesture to multiple simultaneous constraints does not reinstantiate the origin or starting point that McClelland et al. note is endlessly deferred in Selfridge's cognitive schema. Instead, when taken as a model for the microstructure of cognition, it generates cognition within a system of pure, nonoriginary cognitive differences. The theoretical implications of such a configuration elicit little explicit comment in McClelland, Rumelhart, and Hinton's introduction. It is these implications that I wish to pursue here. Connectionist networks model cognition in ways that echo Saussure's system of pure linguistic difference. Where Saussure envisaged a system in which "there are only differences *without positive terms*" (Saussure 1959, 120), McClelland et al. demonstrate a model that—having renounced cognition's sequential and linear character—generates neurocognition through a network of multiple, parallel differences. In both these systems identity is given not by the full presence of a (linguistic, cognitive) entity, but through the multiple simultaneous constraints of a systematic play of differences. In the case of a connectionist model, these are spatial and temporal differences between weights, between units, and between networks. Rather than being a set of definable and localized spaces or stores (short-term memory, long-term memory, episodic memory, etc.) within which definable and localized traces are transformed, the connectionist topography is a web of simultaneous and parallel differences (between connections, between units, between layers) that never emerges as a full and present structure.

For example, where in traditional models the cognitive trace is a discrete, self-present entity, in a PDP model the trace is disseminated across a system of changing weights. It is this spatial and temporal scattering of the psychical trace through the connectionist network—so-called "distributed representation"—that marks one of the major disjunctions between PDP and classical cognitive models. Many commentaries on connectionism (e.g., Hinton, McClelland, and Rumelhart 1986; Le Voi 1993; van Gelder 1991) present this distributed trace within the ongoing philosophical debates about global and local representations. That is, the connectionist trace breaks from the dominant, and problematic, tradition of classical cognitivism, which has relied on local representations of knowledge. At first blush, such distributed or global representations appear to provide a valuable opportunity for contesting the domination of locationism in cognitive theory:

> The main difference from a conventional computer memory is that patterns which are not active do not exist anywhere. They can be re-created because the connection strengths between units have been changed appropriately, but each connection strength is involved in storing many patterns, so it is impossible to point to a particular place where the memory for a particular item is stored. (Hinton, McClelland, and Rumelhart 1986, 80)

This has a number of consequences for our understanding of connectionist networks and the nature and locality of a connectionist trace. If the distributed architecture of a connectionist network scatters the presence of a psychical trace through a system of differences, then the identity of the psychical trace can no longer be presumed to exist prior to the psychical system, nor can it be said to exist outside that system or be measured independently of it. The usual separation of cognition from its material context (usually figured through the differences between software and hardware) becomes untenable. Because the locality of the trace is deferred through the operation of spatial and temporal differences between units and connections, this trace cannot become an object to which the cognitive system may be reduced. Having no self-present identity or location, the connectionist trace becomes indigestible within a cognitive machine that demands discrete bundles of information, and unintelligible for a philosophy that would demand a hierarchy of reducible cognitive levels.

However, the distributed trace, as presented in these connectionist texts, goes only part of the way to addressing my concerns about presence and location. It is not enough simply to say that psychical entities (e.g., memories, knowledge) are distributed and thus not localized. As Hinton, McClelland, and Rumelhart point out, distributed models do not necessarily contradict models of localized function in the brain:

Another common source of confusion is the idea that distributed representations are somehow in conflict with the extensive evidence for localization of function in the brain (Luria, 1973). A system that uses distributed representations still requires many different modules for representing completely different kinds of thing at the same time. The distributed representations occur *within* these localized modules. (Hinton, McClelland, and Rumelhart 1986, 79)

Connectionist distribution, in this conventional account, still conforms to a general locationist paradigm. The distributed connectionist trace becomes less a radical displacement of traditional locationist topography than simply the fragmentation and dispersal of such a topography as prototraces or subsymbolic entities. Smolensky (1988), for example, in perhaps one of the most accomplished and influential directives for connectionist research, figures the connectionist trace as operating at the level of the subsymbolic; that is, the connectionist trace lies somewhere between the symbolic level of traditional computational models of cognition, on the one hand, and the neural level of biological models, on the other. While offering a careful and profitable mediation between these two factions in cognitive science, this subsymbolic paradigm nonetheless retains the idea of cognition as locatable, redeploying that presence through a simple dispersal of constituent elements.

The name "subsymbolic paradigm" is intended to suggest cognitive descriptions built up of entities that correspond to *constituents* of the symbols used in the symbolic paradigm; these fine-grained constituents could be called *subsymbols*, and they are the activities of individual processing units in the connectionist networks. Entities that are typically represented in the symbolic paradigm by symbols are typically represented in the subsymbolic paradigm by a large number of subsymbols. (Smolensky 1988, 3)

Connectionism, figured by Rumelhart et al. (1986) as the science of the microstructure of cognition, often tends simply to scatter the vulgar locationism of symbolic models into microsymbolic or subsymbolic localities. There are two problems here. First, the radical dispersal implied in a Saussurian system (and implied likewise by McClelland et al. [1986] with reference to Selfridge) has been curtailed. The production of cognitive identity and effect through differences from other cognitive identities and effects (which themselves have no identity except through their differential relations) has been reduced to a system of empirical, graspable differences between self-present fragments. Even though the Saussurian-like character of a connectionist network effects a displacement of psychical location, a certain self-presence seems to readily return to inhabit this displacement. In the end, the issue that each psychical entity is "represented by a pattern of activity distributed over many computing elements, and each computing element is involved in representing many different entities" (Hinton, McClelland, and Rumelhart 1986, 77) is less important than the realization that the structural elements of such a cognitive system do not exist anywhere as present and locatable entities.

Second, still thinking the trace as a pure locality, these conventionalized connectionist dispersals evacuate the trace of force and mobility. To exploit fully the implications of Saussure's system, pure difference must remain mobile, and must not be recuperated under a single or simple dispersal. That is, a Saussurian displacement of presence must also imply an irreducible dynamism in an otherwise inert dyadic sign. It is this that separates the Saussurian linguistic system, if not definitively then at least strategically, from an orthodox structuralism. Canfield (1993) and Miers (1992; 1993) both argue that connectionist networks exemplify this dual action of force and displacement. For Canfield, it is at the nexus of Derrida, Saussure, and connectionism that the static and brittle notion of the sign in both structuralism and traditional cognitive science is replaced by a more flexible and dynamic model of representation. While both Canfield and Miers are more focused on issues of representation and signification that I have not pursued, they nonetheless bring to the fore the necessity of thinking mobility if one is to rethink cognitive location.

While the so-called connectionist revolution was envisaged as a response to, and a movement against, classical cognitivism, the success of this insurgency has brought a certain rapprochement between connectionist and classical paradigms. Smolensky's (1988) commentary on the possible alliances between these two opposing factions—and his concession to classical morphology that this entailed—exemplifies the direction of this rapprochement. That is, as connectionist approaches become more institutionalized, they more readily concede to the static, self-present parameters of classical cognitivist morphologies. Against such conventionalization, I would argue that the connectionist topography, like a Saussurian topography, is produced in an irreducible negotiation between place and force. Neither a simply located space nor an immaterial force, connectionist processing reorients the traditional notions of space and process embodied in classical cognitive architectures. The psychical trace of classical cognitive models is a discrete and locatable entity, clearly separable from the machine that processes it. In such models, the distinction between information and the information-processing machine remains axiomatic. In the connectionist system, the trace forfeits such a circumscribed identity: Because it is distributed in unlocatable ways across a network, our ability to definitively separate it from the connectionist architecture is frustrated. The trace as a topographical entity becomes indistinguishable from the trace as a movement of activation, and force engages place in an irreducible mediation that refuses both the separation of these operations and their total convergence. If the connectionist trace can no longer be definitively separated from the connectionist architecture, then the trace is no longer a preexisting and inert packet of information to be transformed by a universal cognitive machine. Consequently, the distinction between the connectionist trace and the connectionist architecture becomes incoherent, and the connectionist trace becomes breaching—both structure and trace, both the force that forges a track and the space that such a force discloses.

It is through this coupling of mobility and displacement that the connectionist network comes to exemplify a Saussurian machine more effectively than a von Neumann machine. Rather than a presence-structure, which processes present and locatable traces, the connectionist network is a trace-structure, wherein the familiar and fixed space of cognition is realized through the mediation of location and mobility, place and force. This refiguring of the cognitive trace and architecture inevitably forces a refiguration of cognition itself. Put technically, it is unclear whether cognitive processing in a connectionist system should be construed as a spatial-structural transformation (the propagation of activation through the network, from input to output, and the correlative back-propagation of feedback) or as a change of state in the network as a whole. Put colloquially, cognition is neither reducible to place nor an abstract process floating free from it. If one of the critical concerns about the cognitive sciences has been their reductive tendencies, then connectionist models respond not with a repudiation of place, but with a complex system of spatial and energetic (could we say libidinal?) relations that—if deployed carefully—surpass the imperative for a graspable location.

~ Conclusion

I have argued that the tension between topography and force that is exploited by Bartlett, Freud, and Derrida is indispensable to thinking cognition. However, there is a tendency in traditional cognitive models and theories to strip the trace of mobility and reduce it to an empirically graspable locale. Consequently, cognitive psychology has been inclined to produce models and theories of cognition that are lifeless and inert.

While connectionism produces a cognitive topography that is potentially disruptive of the parameters of these traditional models, it may also progress toward a similar stasis. For this reason, connectionism does not offer a straightforward resolution to the problematics of cognition and location. Indeed, it may perpetuate these problems in much the same way as the models that have preceded it. It seems to me, then, that neural networks present—simultaneously, irreducibly—a more sophisticated notion of the psychical trace and structure than has yet to be devised in psychological theory, and a theory that once again gravitates toward the traditionally reductive doctrines of empirical science. Connectionism, in one and the same gesture, both pushes the limits of contemporary scientific theories of cognition and is tied up all the more carefully in them. More specifically, the accomplishment of the former seems to require the latter. Thus the relation between what could be called the "critical" and "conventional" aspects of connectionist models is not a benign and symmetrical cohabitation, but rather a relation of incommensurate debt. It is for this reason that I contend that what might constitutue the critical and conventional aspects of such models is always generatively unclear.

Likewise, the interventions offered by Freud, Derrida, and Saussure do not seamlessly adjudicate the critical questions of cognition and location. As I have already argued in chapter 4, Derrida's foreclosure of the nature and effects of neurology tends to arrest the utility of his work within scientific contexts. For example, Derrida too easily associates "familiar and constituted space" with the "space of the natural sciences," as if the latter folds readily and without excess into the former. What I have argued in this chapter is that Freud's revisioning of psychical space (on which Derrida is vitally dependent) is drawn, in nontrivial ways, from a negotiation with the natural sciences. Moreover, the cognitive space of a connectionist network is a critique of "familiar and constituted space" that is derived not from certain critical texts, but from an interpretation of biological, cognitive, and mathematical data. Pivotal as the critical interventions from Freud, Derrida, and Saussure have been, they are not instinctively bent toward the critical problems with which connectionism has so effectively engaged.

It has become readily observable in recent years that contemporary critical and contemporary scientific analyses do not operate in a simplistically negative or oppositional relation to one another. I want to demonstrate here that neither do they operate in a simplistically complementary or harmonious relation to one another. Canfield's (1993) figuration of a "parallelism" between connectionism and deconstruction does not sufficiently analyze the complexity of the character of these components and their possible relation. There is a heterogeneous set of affiliations between and among each of these components such that a linear alliance between them is not possible. Moreover, such an alliance is not necessary in order to extract a productive reading of any one of these components. In fact, I maintain that I need the (internal and relational) incommensurability of these various Freudian, Derridean, Saussurian, and connectionist positions as much as I need their points of correspondence. No one of these, on its own, provides the necessary critical tools for the project I have undertaken here. I need both the similarities and the differences, the tensions and the agreements between and within these positions, in order to build this particular perspective on cognition. No one position can be said to master the field under contention here. It is at this asymmetrical, incommensurate nexus of Derrida, Freud, Saussure, and connectionism that the place of cognition can be most productively rethought.

Critical and Cognitive Locations

The enigma of the body . . . is captured in the troubling question of
its location. How are we to identify the fixed transience of this
peculiar substance, that "place" that requires a doubled commentary
to capture the ambiguity of "all constancy and all variation"?
(Kirby 1991, 88)

Both our critical and our scientific formulations are
troubled by the question of location. A doubled commentary is necessary in order to accommodate the resonance of mobility and placement that generates both our political and psychobiological locations. It has been the argument of this book that critical responses to
scientific theories that delineate a biological basis for psychology
and behavior require an orientation that embodies such a doubled
commentary. In particular, as "science studies" become established,
it is important to assess, and perhaps contest, the critical and natural locations that such studies typically enact.

My first concern has been that a sustainable orientation to the
critical studies of the sciences must not be wholly or primarily negative in its approach to scientific theories. That is, such an orientation must be premised on the conviction that the sciences already
(but not always) produce critically and empirically sophisticated
accounts of psychology and behavior. This orientation would not
simply demand that our critical and political orientations be disciplined within the parameters of established scientific knowledge.
But neither would it simply attribute to the sciences the sophistica-

tion that we presume our own critical positions already embody. These gestures enact either an acquiescent or a condescending relation to scientificity. I have attempted to demonstrate in the preceding chapters that the most effective orientation to the sciences is one that positions itself askew to the critical structure governed by such pro- and antiscience sentiment.

I have also argued that the target of any critical engagement with the neurological or cognitive sciences needs to be reconsidered. It has been commonplace to question the social, cultural, and metaphorical entanglements of various scientific claims, but the nature of the biological, material, or natural objects of such claims has remained underexamined. In particular, it has been usual to counter biologically reductionist assertions about the nature of various psychobehavioral phenomena with recourse to the socially or discursively constructed nature of such phenomena. More often than not, biologically oriented theories about the origin or character of verbal ability, sexuality, IQ, aggression, or temperament are countered with a mishmash of environmentalism, social construction, and discursive analysis, all of which leave the nature of neurological, genetic, or biochemical matter to one side.

The analysis pursued in this book has been motivated by a sense that critiques premised on a primarily oppositional relation to the sciences or premised on antibiologism, antiessentialism, or antinaturalism are losing their critical and political purchase—not necessarily because they are wholly mistaken, but because they have relied on, and reauthorized, a separation between the inside and the outside, the static and the changeable, the natural and the political, the chromosomal and the cultural. Too many critiques of the sciences are hopelessly enmeshed in the culture of (scientific) claim and (critical) counterclaim that these divisions manufacture. What unites too many critiques of the sciences, despite the great diversity in their methodological and theoretical affiliations, is the conviction that natural or biological objects require an overlay of social, cultural, or metaphorical analysis in order to become politically viable. It is a restrictive logic of supplementarity that governs these analyses; a biological or natural object *on its own* can only inadequately embody or convey a complex political or critical position. This book has been motivated by the conviction that critical positions that take as their first presumption the belief that biology requires critical supplementation from the "outside" have not only misunderstood the nature of the relation between the inside and the outside, they have also missed the power, subtlety, and productivity of the biological domain in its own right. It has been my argument throughout this book that such critiques are reductive of biological matter—that is, that political critiques of biological reductionism are usually themselves reductions or repudiations of biological politics.

The hypothesis that has guided my readings of the nature of neurocognition has been this: Could we respond to neurocognitive determinism not with a repudiation of the neurocognitive, but with a neurocognitive overdeterminism—that is, with a cognition and a neurology that operate in excess of the limits of presence, location, and stasis? And would this provide not only a more faithful account of the character of neurocognition, but also the means for a more effective critical engagement with it? It has been my ambition not to chastise, restrict, or otherwise marginalize the nature of neurocognition, but to open up "our" critical habits and procedures to the nature of neurocognition's indigenous malleability. This ambition has led me in two different, but related, directions: toward a critique of the authority of a self-present and graspable neurocognitive location, on the one hand, and toward an interrogation of the place from which such a critique may emerge, on the other hand. The idea of breaching governs both these critical maneuvers.

For Derrida, the breach is both the movement of psychical facilitation and the space opened up by that facilitation; it is irreducibly both psychical force and psychical topography. I have juxtaposed the Freudian, Derridean, and connectionist pursuits of psychoneurological breaching in order to show how this dislocating negotiation between force and topography operates at/as the heart of cognition and neurology. I have argued that no cognitive or neurological element is present to itself in such a way that it may house or nurture or dictate a particular kind of psychical or behavioral orientation. I have referred to connectionism under the rubric of "the neurocognitive sciences" in order that the traditional expectations of both psychical place (neuron, neuronal center, brain) and psychical function (cognitive processing) may be reconsidered in a more intimate and constitutive relation to one another. While this relation has been laid out in detail in the final chapters of this book, the political and critical implications of such a relation have not been as thoroughly examined. Moreover, the nature of this relation has been a generic one; no attempt has been made to specify the vicissitudes of this relation in a particular context. A small example here may serve to bring the implications of this analysis to the fore, and to situate neurocognitive breaching in a more specific context.

Simon LeVay's (1991) scientifically and critically contentious claim that homosexual and heterosexual identities have a neurobiological substrate betrays, among other things, a concern with the question of the origin or locale of sexuality. LeVay's hypothesis can be taken as an exemplification of the contemporary scientific proclivity for fixing a complex psycho-cultural-behavioral phenomenon to a contained and rigorously mapped area of the body (cf. genetic theories of schizophrenia and neurochemical theories of depression). Such inclinations have been almost universally received as politically suspicious. Nonetheless, LeVay's attachment of sexuality to biology can be placed beside another set of hypotheses that link sexuality to the body: those that have been raised in certain feminist, queer, and critical contexts. In these contexts, questions of the body—its discipline, its pleasures, its libidinal and constitutive relation to other bodies and objects—have been central to the formulation of politically sophisticated theories of sexuality. The question that first strikes me at this juncture is this: What is the difference between a theory that locates sexuality neurologically and a theory that locates sexuality "corporeally"? Or, to return to a disparity that I opened up in the introduction, what is the difference between a theory that locates sexuality in "this (biological) body" and one that locates sexuality in "the disciplined body," "the cultured body," or "the libidinized body"? Moreover, what is at stake in differentiating these positions: the nature of the body or the nature of location?

At first a differentiation between these two theories appears to be easy. Scientific theories such as LeVay's constitute neurocognitive matter as self-present and originary. Here neurological location has become presence, and sexuality, reduced to a binarized and teleological theory of hetero/homo identities, is readily attached to a locale within a structure of self-present neurocognitive elements. On the other hand, the body of certain feminist, queer, and critical hypotheses has been articulated through a deliberate displacement of biological presence. Here the body is opened up to the vicissitudes of its social and cultural constitution. Sexuality could find no definitive or originary location within this disseminated corporeal field. However, one of my ambitions in this book has been to complicate too easy a division between the political and material stasis of "this neurological body" and the political and material malleability of "the cultural body." LeVay's own work may indeed present neurology within a restricting and reductive framework, but it is critically important not to conflate this particular orientation with a theory of neurology in general. That is, what may be politically and critically contentious in LeVay's hypothesis is not the conjunction neurology-sexuality per se, but the particular manner in which such a conjunction is enacted. To this end, an effective critical response to LeVay's work need not attempt to sequester sexuality from the field of neurology. Indeed, it may decide that such neuroscientific research provides an opportunity to further explore the breach that is enacted by the conjunction of a libidinal force and a bodily location.

The juxtaposition of Freud, Derrida, and connectionist theories of cognition enacted in this book has made it possible to envisage a fundamental mobility as the substance of any neurocognitive location. My own concern, not just with LeVay but also with many of his critics, has been that this neurocognitive mobility has been scientifically and critically foreclosed. Little wonder, then, that on the one hand LeVay's neuroscientific formulations lead to reductive formulations of sexuality and that on the other hand most critical formulations of sexuality instinctively recoil from the neurological domain. As soon as the materiality of neurocognition is presumed to be an inert and originary location, then no theory of sexuality (be it scientific or critical) is able to envisage the relation between the neuron and sexuality as anything other than the relation of originary matter to its secondary derivations. In such scientific and critical contexts, sexuality may be a force visited upon the neuron, but sexuality remains external to the nature of neurocognitive locations. These delibidinized locations become either overly important or overly peripheral considerations, and any subsequent neurocognitive theory of sexuality is rendered hopelessly reductive.

To strip neurocognitive matter of its motility, to place the force of sexuality separate from, or subsequent to, the nature of neurology and cognition, is to generate a reductive, affectless, and sterile ontology. The analytics of breaching pursued here only in their generality hint at a number of more specific hypotheses about how this ontological relation of sexuality and neurocognition could be reconsidered. The first and most fundamental of these hypotheses is this: The facilitating movements and effects of neurocognitive breaching are libidinal. That is, the flow of activation across a neural network is an affective movement that could be described in terms of microintensities, tensions, repetitions, and satisfactions. "Pain," Freud reminds us, "passes along all pathways of discharge" (1895, 307). So rather than considering the vicissitudes of libidinal force (sexuality) to be secondary effects or "constructions" around, after, or upon the materiality of cognition or neurology, they could more acutely be taken to be the very stuff of cognition and neurology. One strategic reversal that would be worth considering in this context is that sexuality is not just one manifestation of cognitive functioning; instead, cognitive functioning is one manifestation of the sexualized breaching of neurocognitive matter. Such hypotheses are not direct responses or rebukes to neuroscientific research on sexuality; however, by refiguring the character of the neurology-sexuality conjunction, they denaturalize and arrest the field in which such research is conducted and critically received.

A breach, then, is also a movement against conventionalization. It is the infraction of immobile boundaries and a displacement of the fixed political-critical spaces they enact. If feminist work in psychology now proceeds through a certain orthodoxy (in terms of its methods and objects), then one of the goals of this book has been to breach the boundaries by which the critical-political spaces of feminist psychology have been rendered coherent and authoritative. As such, my goal is less to broaden the field now known as feminist psychology than it is to refigure the location and logical force of that field.

I have argued in the early chapters of this book that because feminist interventions into psychology are restricted by the question of gender and by a humanism around the centrality of women, they have been unable to intervene into the seemingly more "neutral" or "scientific" spheres of psychology except to target a more or less peripheral sexism. That is, feminist psychology has naturalized a political-critical orientation that excludes an examination of what are, frankly, substantive areas of the discipline: psychopharmacology, neuropsychology, evolutionary psychology, the psychology of perception, the microstructure of cognition, and the psychology of the rat. These exclusions are enforced by, and in turn enforce, a series of epistemological and ontological divisions: human/animal, psychology/biology, nature/environment, fact/politics, normal/drugged, discipline/criticism. The ambition and effect of such divisions is to delineate a set of definable critical, political, and scientific locations (inside/outside) and identities (us/them). Even if such locations and identities have been necessary for establishing an initial critical response to psychology (and it is not clear to me that they have been), they no longer provide the sustenance for an ongoing critical engagement with the discipline. Indeed, what is becoming clear is that the locations and identities of feminist psychology are becoming increasingly restrictive and xenophobic.

In another direction, and curiously apart from feminist psychology, the presumptions and boundaries of certain critical/theoretical procedures are also becoming more conventional. I began this book by discussing Sedgwick and Frank's interest in encouraging the "peculiar double movement" that Silvan Tomkins's scientific theories of affect had invoked. They expressed some concern that the critical purchase of certain theoretical endeavors (those "after Foucault, Greenblatt, Freud, Lacan, Lévi-Strauss, Derrida, and feminism") is becoming less acute. Sedgwick and Frank documented how these theories have become oriented in such a way that the "peculiar double movement" of Tomkins's phenomenological-scientific theories was too readily obscured, or negated, or dissolved. A crucial part of their reading of Tomkins, then, involved a rethinking of these critical habits and procedures. What has been of particular concern for me from the beginning is that these habits and procedures facilitate criticism through antibiologism, and that this has consolidated contemporary critical identity within an antiscientific ideational space. How to think the conjunction criticism-science is thus never simply a matter of adding two discrete and independent domains. It is always an unraveling of the interdependent structure of debts and disavowals that constitutes these domains.

The later chapters present a number of arguments that, I hope, foreshadow a reorientation to the conjunction of criticism and science. What I have aimed to demonstrate is a productive alliance between the domains of the neurocognitive and the critical. It is perhaps worth repeating that by this I do not mean that we can simply generate criticism of the neurocognitive domain, as if it were a passive object of such interrogation. Nor do I mean that the neurocognitive sciences can be mobilized to adjudicate the final word on issues of, say, sexuality, as if this final word is itself not produced by certain political and philosophical inclinations. What I do mean, and I think this is a much more difficult terrain to envisage, is that there can be a kind of interchange (a breach) between the domains of criticism and the neurocognitive sciences that opens each productively and rigorously to the other.

What remains central to everything articulated here is that the rethinking of a neurocognitive locale is also, necessarily, a rethinking of a self-certain and contained critical position. This is the "peculiar double movement" that every location provokes. It is for this reason that the question of location remains pertinent beyond the confines of neurocognitive theories, and beyond scientific psychology in general. That is, the "peculiar double movement" that I have isolated in certain connectionist theories is demonstrable in any location. The critical or political rethinking of *any* location (a historical event, a bodily performance, a representational regime, a legislative inequity) always involves a doubled commentary—that is, an analysis of the mobile character of such locations, and a reformulation of the positions of criticism and politics themselves. The pursuit of secure locations (e.g., regimes of sexuality uncompromised by conventionalization), definitive origins (e.g., unique historical moments), and final explanations or resolutions (e.g., what women really want) forecloses the "peculiar double movement" that is the nature of criticism and its objects. Any critical or political analysis that is not open to this constitutive movement in its location, any analysis that is able to accommodate its objects and methods only when they are sequestered and contained, is an analysis that will inevitably falter and become ossified.

If our critical habits and procedures now risk such ossification, an analytics of breaching is one way to keep these habits and procedures open and generative. The movements of breaching are those that keep the nature of any location, object, or method permanently mobile, and that maintain a dynamic and constitutive relation between such locations, objects, and methods. In this sense, the breach is both the refusal of static boundaries between our locations, objects, and methods, and the space that this refusal opens up. By keeping our critical habits attuned to these facilitations, we may be able to effect critical and political orientations that are open to an iterative productivity. That is, under the logic of breaching, our critical procedures may become more than contained and repetitive analyses of static objects and places. And then in turn each of these objects and places may be opened up to its own mobile disposition.

references

~

Allman, W. F. 1989. *Apprentices of wonder: Inside the neural network revolution*. New York: Bantam.

Armstrong, D. M. 1990 [1981]. The causal theory of the mind. In W. G. Lycan (ed.), *Mind and cognition: A reader*, 37–47. Oxford: Blackwell.

Atkinson, R. C., and R. M. Shiffrin. 1968. Human memory: A proposed system and its control processes. In K. W. Spence and J. T. Spence (eds.), *The psychology of learning and motivation: Advances in research and theory*, vol. 2, 89–195. New York: Academic.

Baddeley, A. 1990. *Human memory: Theory and practice*. Hove: Lawrence Erlbaum.

Baron, R. J. 1987. *The cerebral computer: An introduction to the computational structure of the human brain*. Hillsdale, NJ: Lawrence Erlbaum.

Bartlett, F. C. 1932. *Remembering: A study in experimental and social psychology*. Cambridge, U.K.: Cambridge University Press.

Bechtel, W. 1987. Connectionism and the philosophy of mind: An overview. *The Southern Journal of Philosophy*, 26 (supplement): 17–42.

Bechtel, W., and A. Abrahamsen. 1991. *Connectionism and the mind: An introduction to parallel processing in networks*. Cambridge, MA: Basil Blackwell.

Bem, S. 1987 [1976]. Probing the promise of androgyny. In M. R. Walsh (ed.), *The psychology of women*, 206–25. New Haven: Yale University Press.

———. 1993. *The lenses of gender: Transforming the debate on sexual inequality*. New Haven: Yale University Press.

Bennington, G. 1993 [1991]. Derridabase. In J. Derrida, *Jacques Derrida*. Trans. G. Bennington. Chicago: University of Chicago Press.

Best, J. B. 1992. *Cognitive psychology*. 3rd ed. St. Paul, MN: West.

Bleier, R. 1984. *Science and gender: A critique of biology and its theories on women*. New York: Pergamon.

Bordo, S. 1993. *Unbearable weight: Feminism, Western culture, and the body*. Berkeley and Los Angeles: University of California Press.

Boring, E. G. 1957. *A history of experimental psychology*. 2nd ed. New York: Appleton-Century-Crofts.

Boyarin, D. 1995. Freud's baby, Fliess's maybe: Homophobia, anti-Semitism, and the invention of OEDIPUS. *GLQ: A Journal of Lesbian and Gay Studies*, 2:115–47.

Broadbent, D. E. 1958. *Perception and communication*. London: Pergamon.

Butler, J. 1990. *Gender trouble: Feminism and the subversion of identity*. New York: Routledge.

———. 1993. *Bodies that matter: On the discursive limits of "sex."* New York: Routledge.

Canfield, K. 1993. The microstructure of logocentrism: Sign models in Derrida and Smolensky. *Postmodern Culture* 3, no. 3:1–39.

Canguilhem, G. 1980 [1958]. What is psychology? Trans. H. Davies. *Ideology and Consciousness* 7:37–50.

Cermak, L. S., and F. I. M. Craik. 1979. *Levels of processing in human memory*. Hillsdale, NJ: Lawrence Erlbaum.

Chanter, T. 1995. *Ethics of Eros: Irigaray's rewriting of the philosophers*. New York: Routledge.

Chesler, P. 1972. *Women and madness*. London: Allen Lane.

Churchland, P. M. 1989. *A neurocomputational perspective: The nature of mind and the structure of science*. Cambridge, MA: MIT Press.

———. 1990. Eliminative materialism and the propositional attitudes. In W. G. Lycan (ed.), *Mind and cognition: A reader*, 206–23). Oxford: Basil Blackwell.

———. 1995. *The engine of reason, the seat of the soul: A philosophical journey into the brain*. Cambridge, MA: MIT Press.

Churchland, P. M., and P. S. Churchland. 1990. Could a machine think? *Scientific American*, 262, no. 1:26–31.

Churchland, P. S. 1986. *Neurophilosophy: Toward a unified science of the mind/brain.* Cambridge, MA: MIT Press.

Churchland, P. S., and T. J. Sejnowski. 1992. *The computational brain.* Cambridge, MA: MIT Press.

Cilliers, P. 1990. The brain, the mental apparatus and the text: A post-structural neuropsychology. *South African Journal of Philosophy* 9, no. 1:1–8.

Clarke, E., and L. S. Jacyna. 1987. *Nineteenth-century origins of neuroscientific concepts.* Berkeley and Los Angeles: University of California Press.

Cobb, S. 1960. A salute from neurologists. In F. A. Beach, D. O. Hebb, C. T. Morgan, and H. W. Nissen (eds.), *The neuropsychology of Lashley: Selected papers of K. S. Lashley,* xvii–xx. New York: McGraw-Hill.

Craik, F. I. M., and R. S. Lockhart. 1972. Levels of processing: A framework for memory research. *Journal of Verbal Learning and Verbal Behavior* 11:671–84.

Deaux, K. 1985. Sex and gender. *Annual Review of Psychology* 36:49–81.

Deleuze, G. 1989 [1967]. Coldness and cruelty. Trans. J. McNeil. In G. Deleuze & L. Sacher-Masoch, *Masochism,* 9–138. New York: Zone.

Dennett, D. C. 1991. Mother nature versus the walking encyclopedia: A Western drama. In W. Ramsey, S. P. Stich, and D. E. Rumelhart (eds.), *Philosophy and connectionist theory,* 21–30. Hillsdale, NJ: Lawrence Erlbaum.

Derrida, J. 1974 [1967]. *Of grammatology.* Trans. G. Spivak. London: Johns Hopkins University Press.

———. 1978a [1967]. Freud and the scene of writing. Trans. A. Bass. In J. Derrida, *Writing and difference,* 196–231. Chicago: University of Chicago Press.

———. 1978b [1967]. Structure, sign and play in the discourse of the human sciences. Trans. A. Bass. In J. Derrida, *Writing and difference,* 278–93. Chicago: University of Chicago Press.

———. 1981 [1972]. *Positions.* Trans. A. Bass. Chicago: University of Chicago Press.

————. 1982 [1972]. Différance. Trans. A. Bass. In J. Derrida, *Margins of philosophy*, 3–27. Chicago: University of Chicago Press.

————. 1987. Women in the beehive: A seminar. In A. Jardine and P. Smith (eds.), *Men in feminism*, 189–203. New York: Methuen.

Descartes, R. 1954 [1642]. Meditations on first philosophy. In E. Anscombe and P. T. Geach (eds. and trans.), *Descartes: Philosophical writings*, 59–150. London: Nelson.

Diprose, R. 1991. A 'genethics' that makes sense. In R. Diprose and R. Ferrell (eds.), *Cartographies: Poststructuralism and the mapping of bodies and spaces*, 65–76. Sydney: Allen and Unwin.

Dreyfus, H. 1979. *What computers can't do: The limits of artificial intelligence*. Rev. ed. New York: Harper and Row.

————. 1992. *What computers still can't do: A critique of artificial reason*. Cambridge, MA: MIT Press.

Ebbinghaus, H. 1885. *Memory: A contribution to experimental psychology*. Trans. H. A. Ruger and C. E. Bussenius. New York: Dover.

Eysenck, M., and M. Kean. 1990. *Cognitive psychology: A student's handbook*. Hove: Lawrence Erlbaum.

Fausto-Sterling, A. 1992. *Myths of gender: Biological theories about women and men*. Rev. ed. New York: Basic Books.

Fine, M. 1985. Reflections on a feminist psychology of women: Paradoxes and prospects. *Psychology of Women Quarterly* 9:167–83.

Flanagan, O. 1991. *The science of the mind*. 2nd ed. Cambridge, MA: MIT Press.

Fodor, J. A. 1990. *A theory of content and other essays*. Cambridge, MA: MIT Press.

Freud, S. 1888. Preface to the translation of Bernheim's *Suggestion*. In S. Freud, *Standard edition of the complete psychological works of Sigmund Freud*, vol. 1, 75–87. Ed. and trans. J. Strachey. London: Hogarth.

————. 1891. *On aphasia: A critical study*. Trans. E. Stengel. London: Imago.

————. 1895. Project for a scientific psychology. In S. Freud, *Standard edition of the complete psychological works of Sigmund Freud*, vol. 1, 295–397. Ed. and trans. J. Strachey. London: Hogarth.

———. 1900. The interpretation of dreams. In S. Freud, *Standard edition of the complete psychological works of Sigmund Freud,* vols. 4 and 5, 1–627. Ed. and trans. J. Strachey. London: Hogarth.

———. 1915. The unconscious. In S. Freud, *Standard edition of the complete psychological works of Sigmund Freud,* vol. 14, 166–215. Ed. and trans. J. Strachey. London: Hogarth.

———. 1920. Beyond the pleasure principle. In S. Freud, *Standard edition of the complete psychological works of Sigmund Freud,* vol. 18, 7–64. Ed. and trans. J. Strachey. London: Hogarth.

———. 1923. The ego and the id. In S. Freud, *Standard edition of the complete psychological works of Sigmund Freud,* vol. 19, 12–66. Ed. and trans. J. Strachey. London: Hogarth.

———. 1925a. A note upon the "Mystic Writing-Pad." In S. Freud, *Standard edition of the complete psychological works of Sigmund Freud,* vol. 19, 227–32. Ed. and trans. J. Strachey. London: Hogarth.

———. 1925b. An autobiographical study. In S. Freud, *Standard edition of the complete psychological works of Sigmund Freud,* vol. 20, 7–74. Ed. and trans. J. Strachey. London: Hogarth.

———. 1940a. An outline of psychoanalysis. In S. Freud, *Standard edition of the complete psychological works of Sigmund Freud,* vol. 23, 141–207. Ed. and trans. J. Strachey. London: Hogarth.

———. 1940b. Some elementary lessons in psychoanalysis. In S. Freud, *Standard edition of the complete psychological works of Sigmund Freud,* vol. 23, 281–86. Ed. and trans. J. Strachey. London: Hogarth.

Freud, S., and J. Breuer. 1895. Studies on hysteria. In S. Freud, *Standard edition of the complete psychological works of Sigmund Freud,* vol. 2, 3–309. Ed. and trans. J. Strachey. London: Hogarth.

Gall, F. J. 1835. *Organology,* vol. 4. Trans. W. Lewis. Boston: Marsh, Capen, and Lyon.

Gardner, H. 1987. *The mind's new science: A history of the cognitive revolution.* Rev. ed. New York: Basic Books.

Gatens, M. 1983. A critique of the sex/gender distinction. In J. Allen and P. Patton (eds.), *Beyond Marxism? Interventions after Marx,* 143–60. Sydney: Interventions.

Gergen, M., and S. Davis. 1997. *Toward a new psychology of gender.* New York: Routledge.

Geschwind, N. 1979. Specializations of the human brain. In *The brain,* 108–17. San Francisco: W. H. Freeman.

Gilligan, C. 1982. *In a different voice: Psychological theory and women's development.* Cambridge, MA: Harvard University Press.

Giorgi, A. 1992. Toward the articulation of psychology as a coherent discipline. In S. Koch and D. E. Leary (eds.), *A century of psychology as science* (rev. ed.), 46–59. Washington, D.C.: American Psychological Association.

Globus, G. 1992. Derrida and connectionism: *Différance* in neural nets. *Philosophical Psychology* 5, no. 2:183–97.

———. 1995. *The postmodern brain.* Amsterdam: John Benjamins.

Gluck, M. A., and D. E. Rumelhart (eds.). 1990. *Neuroscience and connectionist theory.* Hillsdale, NJ: Lawrence Erlbaum.

Goldstein, K. 1995 [1934]. *The organism.* New York: Zone.

Grosz, E. 1993. Bodies and knowledges: Feminism and the crisis of reason. In L. Alcoff and E. Potter (eds.), *Feminist epistemologies,* 187–215. New York: Routledge.

———. 1994a. Experimental desire: Rethinking queer subjectivity. In J. Copjec (ed.), *Supposing the subject,* 133–57. London: Verso.

———. 1994b. *Volatile bodies: Toward a corporeal feminism.* Bloomington: Indiana University Press.

Hartsock, N. 1990. Foucault on power: A theory for women? In L. J. Nicholson (ed.), *Feminism/postmodernism,* 157–75. New York: Routledge.

Haugeland, J. 1985. *Artificial intelligence: The very idea.* Cambridge, MA: MIT Press.

Head, H. 1920. *Studies in neurology.* Oxford: Oxford University Press.

Hebb, D. O. 1959. *The organization of behavior.* New York: Wiley.

Henriques, J., W. Hollway, C. Urwin, C. Venn, and V. Walkerdine. 1984. *Changing the subject: Psychology, social regulation and subjectivity.* London: Methuen.

Herrnstein, R. J., and C. Murray. 1994. *The bell curve: Intelligence and class structure in American life.* New York: Free Press.

Hilgard, E. 1964. Introduction. In H. Ebbinghaus, *Memory: A contri-*

bution to experimental psychology, vii–x. New York: Dover.

Hinton, G. E. 1992. How neural networks learn from experience. *Scientific American* 267, no. 3:105–9.

Hinton, G. E., and J. A. Anderson (eds.). 1989. *Parallel models of associative memory.* Updated ed. Hillsdale, NJ: Lawrence Erlbaum.

Hinton, G. E., J. L. McClelland, and D. E. Rumelhart. 1986. Distributed representations. In D. E. Rumelhart, J. L. McClelland, and the PDP Research Group (eds.), *Parallel distributed processing: Explorations in the microstructure of cognition.* Volume 1: *Foundations,* 77–109. Cambridge, MA: MIT Press.

Hinton, G. E., and T. Shallice. 1991. Lesioning an attractor network: Investigations of acquired dyslexia. *Psychological Review* 98, no. 1:74–95.

Holt, R. 1965. A review of some of Freud's biological assumptions and their influence on his theories. In N. S. Greenfield and W. C. Lewis (eds.), *Psychoanalysis and current biological thought,* 93–124. Madison: University of Wisconsin Press.

Hubel, D. H., and T. N. Wiesel. 1979. Brain mechanisms of vision. In *The brain,* 130–44. San Francisco: W. H. Freeman.

Hughlings Jackson, J. 1958. *The selected writings of John Hughlings Jackson.* Ed. J. Taylor. New York: Basic Books.

Irigaray, L. 1977. Women's exile. Trans. C. Venn. *Ideology and Consciousness* 1:62–76.

———. 1985a [1977]. *Speculum of the other woman.* Trans. G. Gill. Ithaca, NY: Cornell University Press.

———. 1985b [1977]. *This sex which is not one.* Trans. C. Porter. Ithaca, NY: Cornell University Press.

Jeffress, L. A. (ed.). 1951. *Cerebral mechanisms in behavior: The Hixon symposium.* New York: John Wiley.

Jensen, A. R. 1972. *Genetics and education.* London: Methuen.

Kantor, J. R. 1969. *The scientific evolution of psychology,* vol. 2. Chicago: Principia.

Kirby, V. 1991. Corpus delicti: The body at the scene of writing. In R. Diprose and R. Ferrell (eds.), *Cartographies: Poststructuralism and the mapping of bodies and spaces,* 88–100. Sydney: Allen and Unwin.

————. 1993. "Feminisms, reading, postmodernisms": Rethinking complicity. In S. Gunew and A. Yeatman (eds.), *Feminism and the politics of difference,* 20–34. Sydney: Allen and Unwin.

Kitcher, P. 1992. *Freud's dream: A complete interdisciplinary science of mind.* Cambridge, MA: MIT Press.

Kitzinger, C. 1993. "Psychology constructs the female": A reappraisal. *Feminism and Psychology* 3, no. 2:189–93.

Klein, D. B. 1971. *A history of scientific psychology: Its origins and philosophical backgrounds.* London: Routledge and Kegan Paul.

Klix, F., and H. Hagendorf. 1986. *Human memory and cognitive capabilities: Mechanisms and performances: Symposium in memoriam Hermann Ebbinghaus, 1885.* 2 vols. Amsterdam: Elsevier.

Koch, S., and D. E. Leary (eds.). 1992. *A century of psychology as a science.* Rev. ed. Washington, D.C.: American Psychological Association.

Kosslyn, S. M., and R. A. Andersen (eds.). 1992. *Frontiers in cognitive neuroscience.* Cambridge, MA: MIT Press.

Kosslyn, S. M., and O. Koenig. 1992. *Wet mind: The new cognitive neuroscience.* New York: Free Press.

Kramer, P. 1994. *Listening to Prozac.* London: Fourth Estate.

Krell, D. 1990. *Of memory, reminiscence, and writing: On the verge.* Bloomington: Indiana.

Kris, E. 1954. Introduction. In M. Bonaparte, A. Freud, and E. Kris (eds.), *The origins of psychoanalysis: Letters to Wilhelm Fliess, drafts and notes 1887–1902,* 3–47. London: Imago.

Kurtzman, H. S. 1987. Deconstruction and psychology: An introduction. *New Ideas in Psychology* 5 no. 1:33–71.

Lacan, J. 1977 [1966]. The mirror stage as formative of the function of the I. In J. Lacan, *Ecrits: A selection,* 1–7. Trans. A. Sheridan. London: Tavistock.

Laplanche, J. 1989 [1987]. *New foundations for psychoanalysis.* Trans. D. Macey. Oxford: Basil Blackwell.

Laplanche, J., and J. B. Pontalis. 1973 [1967]. *The language of psychoanalysis.* Trans. D. Nicholson-Smith. London: Hogarth.

Lashley, K. S. 1960a. *The neuropsychology of Lashley: Selected papers of K. S. Lashley.* Ed. F. A. Beach, D. O. Hebb, C. T. Morgan, and H. W. Nissen. New York: McGraw-Hill.

————. 1960b [1938]. The thalamus and emotion. *The neuropsychology of Lashley: Selected papers of K. S. Lashley,* 345–60. Ed. F. A. Beach, D. O. Hebb, C. T. Morgan, and H. W. Nissen. New York: McGraw-Hill.

————. 1960c [1938]. In search of the engram. *The neuropsychology of Lashley: Selected papers of K. S. Lashley,* 478–505. Ed. F. A. Beach, D. O. Hebb, C. T. Morgan, and H. W. Nissen. New York: McGraw-Hill.

Lawrence, M. 1995. *The anorexic experience.* 3rd ed. London: Women's Press.

Leahey, T. H. 1992. *History of psychology: main currents in psychological thought.* 3rd ed. Englewood Cliffs, NJ: Prentice-Hall.

LeVay, S. 1991. A difference in hypothalamic structure between heterosexual and homosexual men. *Science* 253:1034–7.

————. 1993. *The sexual brain.* Cambridge, MA: MIT Press.

Le Voi, M. 1993. Parallel distributed processing and its application in models of memory. In G. Cohen, G. Kiss, and M. Le Voi (eds.), *Memory: current issues* (2nd ed.), 113–73. Buckingham: Open University Press.

Lewin, M. 1984. *In the shadow of the past: Psychology portrays the sexes: A social and intellectual history.* New York: Columbia University Press.

Lindsay, P. H., and D. A. Norman. 1977. *Human information processing: An introduction to psychology.* 2nd ed. New York: Academic.

Luria, A. 1973. *The working brain: An introduction to neuropsychology.* Trans. B. Haigh. Harmondsworth, U.K.: Penguin.

Maccoby, E. E., and C. N. Jacklin. 1974. *The psychology of sex differences.* Stanford, CA: Stanford University Press.

Marecek, J. 1989. Introduction. *Psychology of Women Quarterly* 13:367–77.

Masson, J. M. (ed.). 1985. *The complete letters of Sigmund Freud to Wilhelm Fliess, 1887–1904.* Trans. J. Masson. Cambridge, MA: Harvard University Press.

McClelland, J. L., D. E. Rumelhart, and G. E. Hinton. 1986. The appeal of parallel distributed processing. In D. E. Rumelhart, J. L. McClelland, and the PDP Research Group (eds.), *Parallel distrib-*

uted processing: Explorations in the microstructure of cognition. Volume 1: *Foundations,* 3–44. Cambridge, MA: MIT Press.

McCulloch, W. S., and W. H. Pitts. 1988 [1943]. A logical calculus of the ideas immanent in nervous activity. In W. S. McCulloch, *Embodiments of mind,* 19–39. Cambridge, MA: MIT Press.

Mednick, M. T. S., and H. J. Weissman. 1975. The psychology of women: Selected topics. *Annual Review of Psychology* 26:1–18.

Miers, P. 1992. The other side of representation: Critical theory and the new cognitivism. *MLN* 107:950–75.

———. 1993. Connectionism and its consequences. *Postmodern Culture* 4, no. 1:1–8.

Miller, J. 1976. *Toward a new psychology of women.* Boston: Beacon.

Minsky, M. L., and S. Papert. 1969. *Perceptrons: An introduction to computational geometry.* Cambridge, MA: MIT Press.

Neisser, U. 1967. *Cognitive psychology.* New York: Appleton-Century-Crofts.

———. 1976. *Cognition and reality: Principles and implications of cognitive psychology.* San Francisco: W. H. Freeman.

Neisser, U., and E. Winograd (eds.). 1988. *Remembering reconsidered: Ecological and traditional approaches to the study of memory.* Cambridge, U.K.: Cambridge University Press.

Newell, A., and H. A. Simon. 1972. *Human problem solving.* Englewood Cliffs, NJ: Prentice-Hall.

Orbach, S. 1986. *Hunger strike: The anorectic's struggle as a metaphor for our age.* London: Faber.

Oudshoorn, N. 1994. *Beyond the natural body: An archeology of sex hormones.* London: Routledge.

Parker, I., and J. Shotter. 1990. *Deconstructing social psychology.* London: Routledge.

Parlee, M. B. 1975. Psychology. *Signs: Journal of Women in Culture and Society* 1, no. 1:119–38.

———. 1979. Psychology and women. *Signs: Journal of Women in Culture and Society* 5, no. 1:121–33.

———. 1991. Happy birth-day to *Feminism and Psychology. Feminism and Psychology* 1, no. 1:39–48.

Penfield, W. 1959. The interpretive cortex. *Science* 129:1719–25.

Plaut, D. C., and T. Shallice. 1994. *Connectionist modeling in cognitive neuropsychology: A case study.* Hove: Lawrence Erlbaum.

Popper, K. 1969. *Conjectures and refutations: The growth of scientific knowledge.* 3rd ed. London: Routledge and Kegan Paul.

———. 1983a [1957]. Propensities, probabilities and the quantum theory. *A Pocket Popper,* 199–206. Ed. D. Miller. London: Fontana.

———. 1983b [1974]. The problem of demarcation. *A Pocket Popper,* 118–30. Ed. D. Miller. London: Fontana.

Pribram, K. H. 1965. Freud's project: An open, biologically based model for psychoanalysis. In N. S. Greenfield and W. C. Lewis (eds.), *Psychoanalysis and current biological thought,* 81–92. Madison: University of Wisconsin Press.

Pribram, K. H., and M. M. Gill. 1976. *Freud's "Project" reassessed.* London: Hutchinson.

Pyke, S., and C. Stark-Adamec. 1981. Canadian feminism and psychology: The first decade. *Canadian Psychology* 22, no. 1:38–54.

Pylyshyn, Z. W. 1984. *Computation and cognition: Toward a foundation for cognitive science.* Cambridge, MA: MIT Press.

Ramsey, W., S. Stich, and D. Rumelhart (eds.). 1991. *Philosophy and connectionist theory.* Hillsdale, NJ: Lawrence Erlbaum.

Robinson, D. 1987. A neuropsychological model of personality and individual differences. In J. Strelau and H. J. Eysenck (eds.), *Personality dimensions and arousal,* 153–70. New York: Plenum.

Robinson, D. N. 1992. Science, psychology, and explanation: Synonyms or antonyms? In S. Koch and D. E. Leary (eds.), *A century of psychology as science* (rev. ed.), 60–74. Washington, D.C.: American Psychological Association.

Rogers, L. 1988. Biology, the popular weapon: Sex differences in cognitive function. In B. Caine, E. A. Grosz, and M. de Lepervanche (eds.), *Crossing boundaries: Feminisms and the critique of knowledges,* 43–51. Sydney: Allen and Unwin.

Rose, H. 1996. Gay brains, gay genes and feminist science theory. In J. Weeks and J. Holland (eds.), *Sexual cultures: Communities, values and intimacy,* 53–72. London: Macmillan.

Rosenau, P. M. 1992. *Post-modernism and the social sciences: Insights, inroads, and intrusions.* Princeton, NJ: Princeton University Press.

Rubin, G. 1975. The traffic in women: Notes on the "political econo-my" of sex. In R. Reiter (ed.) *Toward an anthropology of women,* 157–220. New York: Monthly Review Press.

———. 1994. Sexual traffic. *differences* 6, nos. 2–3:62–99.

Rumelhart, D. E. 1977. *Introduction to human information process-ing.* New York: Wiley.

Rumelhart, D. E., J. L. McClelland, and the PDP Research Group. 1986. *Parallel distributed processing: Explorations in the microstructure of cognition.* 2 vols. Cambridge, MA: MIT Press.

Russo, N. F., and F. L. Denmark. 1987. Contributions of women to psychology. *Annual Review of Psychology* 38:279–98.

Saussure, F. 1959. *Course in general linguistics.* Trans. W. Baskin. New York: McGraw-Hill.

Schilder, P. 1950 [1935]. *The image and appearance of the human body: Studies in the constructive energies of the psyche.* New York: International Universities Press.

Schiller, F. 1979. *Paul Broca: Founder of French anthropology, explorer of the brain.* Berkeley and Los Angeles: University of California Press.

Schlick, M. 1936. Meaning and verification. *Philosophical Review* 45:339–69.

Searle, J. 1980. Minds, brains, and programs. *Behavioral and Brain Sciences* 3:417–24.

Sedgwick, E. K., and A. Frank. 1995. Shame and the cybernetic fold. In E. K. Sedgwick and A. Frank (eds.), *Shame and its sisters: A Silvan Tomkins reader,* 1–28. Durham, NC: Duke University Press.

Selfridge, O. 1959. Pandemonium: A paradigm for learning. In *Mechanization of thought processes (Symposium no. 10),* vol. 1, 513–26. London: Her Majesty's Stationery Office.

Shields, S. 1975. Functionalism, Darwinism and the psychology of women: A study in social myth. *American Psychologist* 30:739–54.

Shiffrin, R. M., and R. C. Atkinson. 1969. Storage and retrieval processes in long-term memory. *Psychological Review* 76, no. 2:179–93.

Smolensky, P. 1988. On the proper treatment of connectionism. *Behavioral and Brain Sciences* 11:1–74.

Snyder, S. 1980. *Biological aspects of mental disorder.* New York: Oxford University Press.

Solanas, V. 1967. *SCUM Manifesto.* New York: Olympia Press.

Solso, R. L. 1995. *Cognitive psychology.* 4th ed. Boston: Allyn and Bacon.

Spivak, G. 1974. Translator's preface. In J. Derrida, *Of grammatology,* ix–lxxxvii. Chicago: University of Chicago Press.

———. 1990. Criticism, feminism, and the institution. In S. Harasym (ed.), *The post-colonial critic: Interviews, strategies, dialogues,* 1–16. New York: Routledge.

———. 1993a. Feminism and deconstruction, again: Negotiations. In *Outside in the teaching machine,* 121–40. New York: Routledge.

———. 1993b. In a word: Interview. In *Outside in the teaching machine,* 1–23. New York: Routledge.

Stengel, E. 1953. Introduction. In S. Freud, *On aphasia: A critical study,* ix–xv. London: Imago.

Stich, S. 1996. *Deconstructing the mind.* New York: Oxford University Press.

Strachey, J. 1966. Editor's introduction to "Project for a scientific psychology." In S. Freud, *Standard edition of the complete works of Sigmund Freud,* vol. 1, 283–93. London: Hogarth.

Sulloway, F. J. 1979. *Freud, biologist of the mind: Beyond the psychoanalytic legend.* London: Basic Books.

Tausk, V. 1992 [1919]. The influencing machine. Trans. D. Feigenbaum. In J. Crary and S. Kwinter (eds.), *Incorporations,* 542–69. New York: Zone.

Tulving, E. 1972. Episodic and semantic memory. In E. Tulving and W. Donaldson (eds.), *Organization of memory,* 381–403. New York: Academic.

———. 1985. How many memory systems are there? *American Psychologist* 40:385–98.

Turing, A. M. 1950. Computing machinery and intelligence. *Mind* 59, no. 236:433–60.

Unger, R. 1993. The personal is paradoxical: Feminists construct psychology. *Feminism and Psychology* 3, no. 2:211–18.

Ussher, J. 1989. *The psychology of the female body.* London: Routledge.

Valentine, E. 1989. Neural nets: From Hartley and Hebb to Hinton. *Journal of Mathematical Psychology* 33:348–57.

———. 1992. *Conceptual issues in psychology.* 2nd ed. London: Routledge.

van Gelder, T. 1991. What is the "D" in "PDP"? A survey of the concept of distribution. In W. Ramsey, S. P. Stich, and D. E. Rumelhart (eds.), *Philosophy and connectionist theory,* 33–59. Hillsdale, NJ: Lawrence Erlbaum.

Vaughter, R. M. 1976. Psychology. *Signs: Journal of Women in Culture and Society* 2, no. 1:120–46.

Watson, J. B. 1913. Psychology as the behaviorist views it. *Psychological Review* 20:158–77.

Weisstein, N. 1970. Neural symbolic activity: A psychophysical measure. *Science* 168:1489–91.

———. 1971. *Psychology constructs the female; or, The fantasy life of the male psychologist (with some attention to the fantasies of his friends, the male biologist and the male anthropologist).* Somerville, MA: New England Free Press.

———. 1993. Power, resistance and science: A call for a revitalized feminist psychology. *Feminism and Psychology* 3, no. 2: 239–45.

Whitford, M. 1991. *Luce Irigaray: Philosophy in the feminine.* London: Routledge.

Wilkinson, S. 1991. *Feminism and Psychology:* From critique to reconstruction. *Feminism and Psychology* 1, no. 1: 5–18.

——— (ed.). 1986. *Feminist social psychology: Developing theory and practice.* Milton Keynes: Open University Press.

Wilson, E. 1995. Knowing women: The limits of feminist psychology. In B. Caine and R. Pringle (eds.), *Transitions: New Australian feminisms,* 29–41. Sydney: Allen and Unwin.

Wong, E., and N. Weisstein. 1982. A new perceptual context-superiority effect: Line segments are more visible against a figure than a ground. *Science* 218:587–89.

Young, R. M. 1970. *Mind, brain and adaptation in the nineteenth century: Cerebral localization and its biological context from Gall to Ferrier.* Oxford: Clarendon.

index

~